THE O DOYNE (*Ó DUINN*) MANUSCRIPT

COIMISIÚN LÁIMHSCRÍBHINNÍ NA hÉIREANN

THE O DOYNE *(Ó DUINN)* MANUSCRIPT

Documents relating to the family of
O Doyne (*Ó Duinn*) from
Archbishop Marsh's Library, Dublin
MS Z.4.2.19

With Appendices.

(SURVEY OF IRISH LORDSHIPS: SPECIAL VOLUME)

EDITED BY

K.W. NICHOLLS

DUBLIN

STATIONERY OFFICE

FOR THE

IRISH MANUSCRIPTS COMMISSION

1983

To be purchased from the
GOVERNMENT PUBLICATIONS SALES OFFICE,
MOLESWORTH ST., DUBLIN
or through any Bookseller

Printed in the Republic of Ireland

CONTENTS

INTRODUCTION

The manuscript in Marsh's Library, Dublin, which bears the shelf-number Z.4.2.19 is for the most part[1] occupied by contemporary copies of documents concerning the lengthy lawsuit between Charles O Doyne (*Cathaoir Ó Duinn*), a Master in the Irish Court of Chancery who died in 1617 and his elder brother Thady or Teig (*Tadhg*) O Doyne. Tadhg and Cathaoir were sons of another Tadhg (*Óg*) Ó Duinn, lord of Iregan (*Uí Riagáin*), the present barony of Tinnahinch in County Laois, from 1558 to 1607, and the dispute between them concerned the succession to their father's lands and chiefries. Charles O Doyne had had, for an Irish chief's son of this period, an unusual career; a student at Christ Church, Oxford, where he took the degree of B.A. on 12 June 1586, and that of M.A. on 9 July 1591[2], he emerged as 'a good scholar and a zealous Protestant'[3], and was appointed to the office of Master in Chancery on 20 September 1602[4]. He subsequently held, besides his Mastership, the office of judge of the prerogative court of Dublin, while he also took the degree of LL.D.[5] He died without issue, having apparently never married, on 17 May 1617,

---

1 Pp. 1-126 of the volume are occupied by *'Acta habita in Ecclesia Cathedrali S. Pat. Dub. loco consistor. coram Rob. Conway L.L.D. Officiali Adami Loftus Archiepiscopi Dub. 1596 etc.',* an entry book of the metropolitan court of the archbishop of Dublin, commencing with entries of Wednesday, 3 November 1596, and breaking off – apparently with the loss of a leaf or leaves – in the middle of those for 28 October 1598. Charles Doyne was the immediate successor of Conway in his Mastership in Chancery and his eventual successor as judge of t' e archbishop's court. The order of the entire volume has been confused by a lat r rebinder; the order of pages now runs 1-28, 159-188, 127-158, 29-126, 189-end.

2 Foster, *Alumni Oxonienses,* I, 433.

3. See Genealogy of the O Doynes by Sir George Carew (Earl of Totnes), in Lambeth MS 635 and the extreme Protestant piety displayed in Charles's will (AppendixV, *infra*).

4 *Liber Munerum Publicorum Hiberniae,* II, 211 = *F.E.,* 6678.

5 Trinity College, Dublin, MS 3.14, f.28. This Ms (which contains Ecclesiastical Visitations of 1591 and 1610) seems to have belonged to Charles Doyne before coming into the hands of Ussher; ff.162-5 contain some memoranda and copies of letters of Doyne's.

leaving as his heir his nephew Brian Óg or Barnaby O Doyne, the ancestor of the later family of Dunne of Brittas[6]. It is interesting to note that in the dispute between the brothers it was Charles, the English-educated lawyer and official, who sought to maintain the validity of the customs of 'tanistry' and 'Irish gavelkind', which his brother Teig the chief denounced as 'barbarous'.

The various documents contained in the volume would appear to have been almost totally ignored by scholars[7], in spite of the great interest which many of them possess. The most important of those copied is the inquisition, taken at Maryborough on 22 September 1607, to establish the exact situation in Iregan preparatory to the proposed surrender by and regrant to Teig O Doyne. The great value of this inquisition lies in that not only does it set out in detail the various rents and exactions of Ó Duinn as lord of the country, but follows this with a recital of all the landowners of Iregan with their lands — many of them very small holdings indeed. This list of landowners — perhaps as a result of omissions by the clerk who transcribed it — would seem to be very slightly defective; in some of the quarters into which the territory was divided there is a small acreage left unaccounted for (while in a few others, on the contrary, there is an excess) while the names of several landowners who appear in the commission issued for the taking of the inquisition (also transcribed in the manuscript) are absent from the inquisition itself. It is nevertheless precious as a complete record of the landownership pattern in a Gaelic Irish territory which had remained practically free from outside inter-ference. Only a single non-native of the territory appears as a landowner in the inquisition, and his holding was an insignificant one[8]. This is in striking contrast with the picture which emerges from the next record of this kind surviving to us, the inquisitions taken for the surrender and regrant of Connacht in 1617[9], where outsiders appear as having taken up a very large proportion of the land. The absence of outsiders among the landowners of Iregan in 1607 may in part be due to the remoteness of

---

6   See Appendix II, Genealogical Table *n*.48, and Appendix V.

7   It is quoted by that great scholar John O'Donovan in footnotes to his edition of The *Annals of the Four Masters* (e.g., IV, 959).

8   Miagh mcCassia (*sic; recte* mc*Cassin) of the Borriesmore 'in the said county' held 8 'acres' in mortgage for four milch cows. Borriesmore was in the barony of Upper Ossory, where the MacCashin family were prominent. I am not, of course, counting either O Doyne's mother, Elizabeth FitzGerald, or Joane neene Carroll, widow of O Doyne's brother Cormac, as 'outsiders' in respect of their jointure lands.

9   These for the four counties of Galway, Mayo, Sligo and Roscommon are preserved both in contemporary transcripts in T.C.D. MS E.3.7 and in the Record Commission's

the area, but may also be ascribed to the success of the Ó Duinn chiefs in monopolising the market for land within their territory. Brian O Connor of Offaly, who seems to have exercised an overlordship over the Ó Duinns, receiving the third part of all fines and like revenue received by Ó Duinn in return for 'protection', had held certain lands within Iregan in 1550[10]. If the O Connors had not fallen the following half-century might well have seen a widespread penetration by them into Iregan; as it was, Brian O Connor's lands in the territory came into the hands of Tadhg Óg Ó Duinn and his brother Toirdhealbhach (Turlough). Tadhg Óg also acquired other lands in the territory from their old possessors — such as most of Reary-more from the O Halagans — and gave them to his sons, of whom he had seven, five legitimate and two bastards. The inquisition gives some interest-ing examples of how an Irish lord could thus acquire the lands of his subjects. Of ten 'acres' in Garroon, 'the proper land and inheritance of Donell mcNeyle' but occupied by Dermott O Doyne, either a natural son or a grandson of Tadhg Óg, it says 'that at thend of the last warres the said Donell beinge verie poore left the said land waste, whereuppon O Doyne entred on the same and bestowed it on the said Dermott O Doyne, who thereuppon yet houldeth the same frome the said Donell'. Four 'acres' in Srahleagh, in the possession of the same Dermott, were claimed by Patrick mcFirr [O Conrahy], who alleged that the land had been taken from his ancestors as a fine for a quarter of a cake of bread left unpaid of Ó Duinn's food-rents. Concerning thirty 'acres' in Bally-kenneen the jury found that one Donoughe mcRorie alleged 'that he or

---

Repertories of Inquisitions in the P.R.O.I. The difference between the versions may be gauged by their renderings of the following entry (inquisition for Kiltartan Barony, County Galway):

E.3.7: 'That John Bourk of Downsandal, Esqr., is seised in his demeasne as of fee and in full possession of the Cartron of Ardneguo, parcell of Killin afforesaid, the Cartron of Gortohowan, parcell of Cappaghbegge aforesaid, and the Cartron of Fowsinbegg, parcell of Cappaghmoore afforesaid, with thappurtenaunts, in the said Baronie'.

Record Commission: 'That John Bourke, Esqr., is seised in 1 is demesne as of fee of Ardnegue (1 cartron), Gortehowan (1 cartron) and Fowsinbeg (1 qr.).'

There are, however, a number of omissions through haplography in the E.3.7 text, while the copyist not infrequently confuses the words 'quarter' and 'cartron'. The corresponding inquisitions for County Clare (where the surrender and regrant never in fact took place) were not taken until 1618 and seem never to have been returned into Chancery. Contemporary copies of three of them (for Clonderalaw and Moyarta, for Corcomroe and for Inchiquin) and of a second series taken in 1621, covering Corcomroe, Inchiquin and Tulla, survive among the Thomond papers in the possession of the Rt. Hon. Lord Egremont, at Petworth, Sussex (Refs. B.16.D.1-2, B.16.E). The great offices for the plantations of James I in Longford, Wexford, King's County, etc., had all vanished before the time of the Irish Record Commission; extracts are to be found among the complaints made to the Commission of 1622 (T.C.D. MS F.3.15 pp. 303ff.).

10 See Appendix IV, *s.v.* Roskeen and Kilcavan.

his ancestors left the same in the hands of O Doyne to be kept for them about 30 years since as the manner of the Countrie is if any freehoulder depart out of the same'. The lands had come into the hands of Tadhg Óg's other natural son, Moriertagh O Doyne[11] who had died in 1601 leaving his only son a child. In May, 1607, Donoughe mcRorie, finding the lands lying waste (as they probably had been since Moriertagh's death), had re-assumed possession. In all, the then chief, his brothers and first cousins and the widows of the family appear in 1607 as holding nearly half of the total area of the territory; the remainder was divided between 132 small landowners, many of whom had mortgaged portions of their land to others. The most important surnames, besides that of O Doyne, were the O Conrahys, O Mellans and O Halagans, although the first and last do not actually appear in the inquisition, the members of these families being denoted by patronymic only.

The inquisition sets out at some length the tributes and exactions levied by Ó Duinn or by his father before him, reciting in this context an order made by the Judges of Assize in the county in August 1606. It may be of interest to quote here for comparison a brief account of the similar exactions which had been levied a little before this date by the lords of the adjacent territories of Fercall and Delvin-McCoghlan[12]. In Fercall, Conall O Molloy (who became chief in 1583),

> did exact divers unjuste customes and duties from thother inhabitants of the said country, out of every principal townland, as one beoffe, two muttons, six Barrens of wheat every Barren containing eight quarts, and one Dishe of Butter with every of the said Barrens as full as O Molloyes servants could fill it, once a year in summer and again once a year in harvest, 32 quarts of milk once a year, 36 Cronocks of Mault every Cronock containing 24 quarts, 18 Cronocks of wheate and 12 Cronocks of oates once a year, 24 horseboyes to gett victualls in every Towne for 24 hours, with Cesse and Couene of horses and boyes as often as it should please O Molloy to send them. And cuttings of money and Beoffs as often as O Molloy had occasion to go to Dublin or elsewhere to defray his charges. And out of every small habitation O Molloy would have and take what his servants and marshals could get ...

And in Delvin,

> About the beginning of the reign of Queen Elizabeth Sir John McCoghlan knight ... was elected Captain of the said Country by the Inhabitants thereof, Who did exact and take of every plowland in the said Country

---

11 Tadhg Óg also had a legitimate son of the same name, Muircheartach. See Appendix II, Genealogical Table.

12 Fercall covered the area of the modern baronies of Ballycowan, Ballyboy and Eglish, in County Offaly. Delvis MacCoghlan corresponded with the barony of Gerrycastle (except the parish of Lusmagh).

in respect of his Captainship 24 hoopes of oat-malte every hoop containing 24 quarts, 13 like hoopes of wheate, nine gallons of butter, 48
quarts of milk, four muttons, 11 groats sterling and two white groats
being 2d ob., one ploughday in wheate season, one workday in harvest
and another in Summer ...[13]

It is probable, however, that in neither of these territories was the level of
exactions so uniform as these accounts suggest. In Iregan, as the inquisition
shows, it varied widely. In the four quarters surrounding Castlebrack,
Ó Duinn received no rents other than a payment of 1d per 'acre' (see
below) of arable land from the freeholders, with a heriot after the death
of any of them[14]. In the division called the *seisreach* of Fasaghely, at
the western extremity of the country, he had nothing but the heriot.[15]
In six quarters — counting the triple quarter of Mointaghmilick as a single
quarter — he received, in addition to other levies, agricultural labour
services — a day's ploughing in winter sowing and a day's in summer
sowing (for the wheat and oat crops respectively) from every plough,
and a day's reaping in harvest from every twenty 'acres'. Such agricultural
labour services rendered to chiefs out of the lands of 'freeholders' are not
uncommon in Ireland at this period. They have been referred to above as
exacted by Sir John MacCoghlan, while in the surrender and regrant of
Murtagh Mac I Brien Arra in 1606 we find similar services out of all the
'freeholders' lands in Arra, and an inquisition of 1624 shows that the
MacBrien lords of Coonagh (County Limerick) claimed them in that
barony.[16] In 1570 the chief of the O Byrnes was entitled to 'a custom
ploughday and a custom reapday of every one that had a plough' in
Shillelagh[17]. The origin of these services is problematical. In England
agricultural labour services were typical of unfree villein tenancies and in

---

13 Lambeth MS 625 (B ff. 20-23, giving extracts from the now lost great offices
taken for the plantations of James I in these areas (see above, n.9).

14 In other quarters, where there was a local *ceannfine* or sept-head, Ó Duinn received
only the heriot of the *ceannfine*, while the latter received that from the freeholders.
See Text, p. 67.

15 In 1569 a dispute between Teig Oge O Doine and Tiralgh mcMoriertagh O Doine
of Garryhiddert, a landowner in Fasaghely, over the former's claim to impose
exactions on the latter was the subject of an award by the Lod Deputy and Council.
The decision would seem to have gone in favour of Tirlagh. See Appendix IV, *s.v.*
Fasaghely.

16 *Calendar of the Irish Patent Rolls of James I*, p. 89; Inquisition *p.m.* on Donogh,
Earl of Thomond (county Limerick, Exch. series, no. 62 of James I).

17 'Acts of the Privy Council, Ireland, 1556-70', ed. John T. Gilbert, in *Historical
Manuscripts Commission, Reports*, XV, App. III (1897), no. 250. The labour services
received by the constable of the castle of Ferns in Elizabethan times and after (*Cal.
of the Irish Pat. Rolls of James I*, 221) were probably a survival from the time of the
Mac Murroughs. Similar services were exacted by the constables of Leighlin and
Carlow (Lambeth MS 606, ff. 84-7).

the mediaeval Irish colony they were likewise characteristic of the tenures of the betaghs and gavellers (tenants-at-will for rent). All over Ireland labour services remained a frequent incident of agricultural tenancies-at-will down to the seventeenth century[18]. What is peculiar about the labour services rendered to the Irish chiefs mentioned is that they were paid out of the lands of so-called 'freeholders'. A number of alternative explanations suggest themselves. That such services were an ancient incident of Gaelic lordship seems unlikely; we have seen that they were confined to particular territories — e.g., O Molloy did not exact them although his neighbours MacCoghlan and Ó Duinn did. A second explanation is that these lands were originally in the hands of agricultural tenants of low status burdened with such services and afterwards passed into the hands of landowners of the ruling stock. This is very possibly the explanation of the labour services received by the Prendergasts of Newcastle, County Tipperary, out of some lands held by members of their own clan[19]. Here the lands might well have been originally betagh lands which were afterwards granted as inheritance to junior members of the lord's family, and this might also apply in the case of the agricultural services received by the earl of Ormond from his freeholders in the manor of Arklow[20]. The fact that the agricultural labour services in Iregan were confined to a section of the territory may also support such an explanation. A third explanation, and that which seems to me the most likely one in most cases, is that these services were imposed by the lords in the fifteenth and early sixteenth centuries in response to a labour shortage due to a low and probably falling population. There seems no doubt that imposed services and exactions of all kinds were being increased during this period, and some sort of belief that the exactions of Ó Duinn had originated in the mid-fifteenth century is implied by the statement of the jury for the great office of Iregan in the Plantation, a few years after the present inquisition, that the exactions were 'at first given voluntarily by the inhabitants unto Teig mcLynagh [Ó Duinn in 1475] greategrandfather to the said Teige O Doyne Esqr. as a helpe to builde

---

18 *Extents of Irish Monastic Possessions, 1540-1541*, ed. Newport B. White (Irish Manuscripts Commission, 1943), *passim;* inquisitions *p.m.* on Sir William Bermingham, Baron of Carbery (1550), in T.C.D. MS F.4.25, ff. 64-5 (giving many details); *Cal. S.P.I., 1647-1660*, Addenda, 277; Strafford Survey of County Sligo (British Library, Harleian MS 2048), *passim.*

19 *Civil Survey*, I, 335, 337-9. The 'poundage hogs' (poundage = pannage) and 'summer sheep' received by Prendergast (*ibid.*, 334) were also incidents of agricultural tenancies [probably the one pig in seven, payable at All Saints', and one sheep in seven, payable at St. John's, of the Bermingham inquisitions (above, *n.* 18)]; for their incidence, see *Calendar of Ormond Deeds*, V, *passim.*

20 *Calendar of Ormond Deeds*, V, p. 212. But I am not disposed to credit the explanation in this instance.

the castle of Castlebrack for the contynue for once, and hath ben exacted by the Cheiffes of the Contrye againste their wills'[21]. No trace of such a belief appears in the 1607 inquisition. It would seem more rational if the statement referred only to the customs of 'building, repayring and keepinge stanche of the Castles, Halls and Bawnes belonginge to O Doyne from tyme to tyme' which the 1607 jurors declared 'was don by Compulsion and not of Righte'. This was the custom of Musteroon, which seems to have been almost universal in late mediaeval Ireland[22]. The 'meate and drinke to O Donn's tayliors and carpenders everie Sondaie and Holydaie throughout the year' which the inquisition recorded as an exaction imposed on the freeholders of Iregan is also recorded in the Ormond territories in the first half of the sixteenth century[23].

Many of the other documents transcribed in the volume are of considerable interest and value. Even the long series of recriminatory arguments between the brothers Thady and Charles (from which neither emerges with credit) throws a considerable light on the principles behind the practice of 'surrender and regrant', into which modern historians have perhaps read much that is justified neither by legal theory or by practical effects. (In this context one should especially note the statement of Thady, completely valid in law, that 'he canot surender anythinge but what himself hath rightfully, for if he should surrender other men's lands and the Kinge regraunte other men's lands by Patent the same would be meerelie voyde'.) A document of some interest also is the schedule of lands, divided into shares, prepared for the intended partition between the brothers; this includes information on the out-offices and subsidiary buildings attached to the castles of Castlebrack and Tinnahinch and affords some clue to the appearance of the countryside, in its acreages of arable, pasture and woodland and its references to roadways as boundaries. It is particularly to be remarked that this schedule gives no support whatever to the belief, now widely held, in the general existence of a system of infield and outfield in Gaelic Ireland, although if such a system had been practised in the area one would expect to find it in operation in connection with such established centres of settlement as Castlebrack an . Tinnahinch.

The territory of Iregan was divided into divisions called quarters (with one triple quarter, Mointaghmilick, and a division called the shisseragh [seisreach] of Fasaghely). Each of these contained a round but varying

---

21 Lambeth MS 625, (B), f. 30.

22 Kenneth Nicholls, *Gaelic and Gaelicised Ireland in the Middle Ages* (Dublin, 1972), 33; *Desmond Surveys,* ed. John A. Murphy, *passim.*

23 Hore and Graves, *Annuary of the Royal Historical and Archaeological Association of Ireland* (Dublin, 1870), pp. 200, 244-5; *Cal. of Ormond Deeds,* IV, no. 296.

number of nominal 'acres' — 80, 120, 180 or 240 — and a table at the end of the manuscript — forming part of some slightly later additions to the original[24] dealing with the plantation of Iregan — sets out the nominal acreage of the various quarters along with their actual profitable acreage as surveyed for the plantation. This shows that the 2780[25] nominal 'acres' of the territory were surveyed as containing 12,105 acres of profitable land, besides woods, bogs, mountains and other waste lands[26]. Another contemporary source gives the acreage as 12,301 acres profitable and 15,011 acres of waste[27]. (The actual area of the barony of Tinnahinch, according to the Ordnance Survey, is 54,187 statute acres.)

In editing the text of the inquisition, I have omitted a certain amount of common form where this is repeated, and have converted the Roman numerals, except in recited documents, into Arabic. I have done the same with those written out in full in the Fiant. Otherwise I have reproduced the contents of the volume as they stand. Although the long and recriminatory arguments between the brothers, with their subsidiary documents, are repetitive and often tedious, any attempt at condensation which would preserve the sense would have resulted in only a trivial saving of space. Of the Appendices, I, II and III deal respectively with the history of the territory of Iregan, the genealogy of the Ó Duinns and the ecclesiastical history of the old parish of Oregan, coterminous with the territory. Appendix IV contains a break-down by quarters of the information on landownership contained in the inquisition, with some additional information and genealogical notes on the landowning families. Appendix V contains subsidiary documents from other sources, in a few instances reproduced in full but in general in calendared form. I have deliberately omitted from this collection documents bearing on the history of the territory during the plantation and between then and 1641, although these are often of interest; the grants made under the plantation, for instance, not only contain a large number of otherwise unknown and obsolete place-names but give — like the schedule of division — valuable information on the then proportions of arable, pasture, bog and woodland in the various denominations. While those of the grants which were

---

24 They are in a different handwriting from the rest of the collections.

25 2704 acres 'of the measure of the country' in Lambeth MS 625 (B) f. 30 is an error

26 12,103 acres, given at the commencement of the added notes is an error, as the addition of the areas for the quarters shows. From the grants made under the plantation (see Appendix VI) it appears that woodlands were not reckoned among the profitable acreage.

27 British Library Add. MS 4756, p. 131.

issued under King James I can be found in the printed *Calendar of Irish Patent Rolls* of that monarch, those (the greater number) issued under his son are not available in any printed source and I have therefore included a brief abstract (extending only to the description of the lands in each grant) as Appendix VI.

The present volume, as is indicated on its title-page, is intended as a special volume of the series *Survey of Irish Lordships,* which is in general arranged on a different pattern, the surviving and accessible material on the topography and the structure of landownership in the various regions of Gaelic and Gaelicised Ireland during the fifteenth, sixteenth and early seventeenth centuries being broken up and arranged under the headings of the various lordships, districts and individual townlands. In the case of Iregan, the fact that by far the greatest part of this material was contained, along with other interesting documents, in a single source, the MS Z.4.2.19, suggested a different approach, that followed in this volume. Volume I of the *Survey of Irish Lordships,* covering the lordships of Uí Maine (O Kelly's Country) and Sil Anmchadha (O Madden's Country) in Counties Galway and Roscommon, has been now in completed form for several years, but technical difficulties have hitherto prevented its publication. A large portion of Volume II, Clan Riocaird, has also been completed.

The present text is published by the kind permission of the Governors and Guardians of Archbishop Marsh's Library, Dublin.

                                                    K.W. Nicholls
                                                    1983

TEXT

PETITION OF TEIG O DOYNE FOR SURRENDER AND REGRANT

To the Right honor*able* the L*ord* Deputie
and the rest of the honorable Com*m*issioners
for takinge of surrenders.

Humbly sheweth to your honors your supliant Teig O Doyne. Where he is justly seised of a smale Cantred or Territorie of land called Iregaine contayninge some demeane land, Rents and other services extendinge within the Queenes County which he is desirous to surrender unto his Ma*jestie's* hands, and to have the same backe from his highnes to be houlden of him by some certaine service. That it may please your honor to vouchsafe to direct Commission to some discreete gent*lemen* there-aboutes to take an Inquisition of the quantitie and qualitie of the said poore, wylde and wooddy Cantred returnable by the next Easter terme and to accept a surrender thereof of your suppliant and the same to regraunte unto him and his heyres to be houlden of his Majestie by knight service. And in respect that the land is barren and litle worth, and that he is alredie bounde to paie a greate[r] composition then the land is well able to beare, that it may please your honnors to reserve none other rent upon the same. And he shall alwayes pray, etc.

Ex. per me Jo: Cottell.

1

INQUISITION TAKEN AT MARYBOROUGH, 22 SEPTEMBER 1607

An inquisition indented taken at Marriborogh in the Queen's County the 22nd day of September 1607 and in the year of the Reign of our sovereign lord King James of England, France and Ireland the fifth and of Scotland the one and fortieth before Sir Henry Power, knight, William Parsons, Esq., surveyor general of all his Majesty's possessions within this realm, Robarte Piggott, Esq., Alexander Barringtonn, Esq., Piers Owingtonn, Esq., being amongst others assigned in this case Commissioners by virtue of his Majesty's Letters Patent under the great Seal of this his Highness's realm of Ireland bearing date at Dublin the third day of July in the fifth year of his Majesty's reign of England, Fraunce and Ireland and of Scotland the fortieth which is to these presents annexed. And also after public proclamation in, and by the sheriff of, the said Queen's County in the next market towns where the lands underwritten are situate, lying and being, in manner as in the said Commission is required, by the oaths of good and lawful men of the aforesaid County whose names are here underwritten:

> Robert Whitney of Shiane
> Marten Shelton of Slety
> Thomas Fitz Gerald of Emoe
> William O Dwigin of Balliduffe
> George Hetherington of Tully
> Arthur Keatinge of Ballickemoyler
> Geffrey mcFene of Tentuor
> Donell mcDermotte of Clone
> William mcMahowne of Ballinraly
> Donell FitzPatricke of Grangebegge
> Shane mcDonell of Formoyle
> William O Fullaine of Knockvaline
> Thomas Hardinge of Marriboroghe
> Lawrence Allen of the same
> John Devevete of the same
> Shane mcCassyn of Culkyry

Who being duly sworn do upon their oaths find and present that:

Teig Oage O Doyne now chief of his name is now seised in his demesne as of fee of and in the several castles, towns, villages and lands hereunder particularly recited, that is to say: A castle and 60 acres of land of that country measure in the town and fields of Bollinumer *alias* Tinehinche in the territory or country of Iregan, 7 a. of the said measure in the town and fields[1] of Moynequid in the said territory, 20 a. in Achmore in the quarter of Kiltegrallagh in the said territory, a castle and 215 a. of the aforesaid measure in Castlebracke, 60 a. in Ballinmunnin in the quarter of Clancoumey, 20 a. in Achuane in the said quarter, 30 a. in Balligarvan in the quarter of Clancaroll[2], 24 a. in AchneCrosse [and] Coolicknoule in the quarter of Derrie[3], 20 a. in Farrenclankein in the quarter of Mointaghmilick, which said last 20 a. Patrick Malone claims as his inheritance, 5 a. in Ardarraghmoyle in the said quarter, 6 a. in Garricough in the said quarter, 51 a. in Cappabrogan, 5 a. in KnockchoneCloghaine in the quarter of Mointaghmylicke, which said 5 a. is claimed by Brien O Doyne brother to the said Teige as his land by conveyance from his father, 30 a. in Lackaghmore in the quarter of Moniquid.[4]

And they find and present that the predecessors of the said Teige holding the name and place of O Doyne have from time to time taken and received of and from the inhabitants of Iregane these several rents, duties, customs and services underwritten:

Of and from the inhabitants of the quarter of Rerrymore in the said territory yearly; two beeves, 24 Cronocks of oats, 40 cakes of bread, 13 dishes of butter, 18 barnes of malt, 8s in money, a heriot upon the death of every Canfinny, one hook in harvest out of every 20 a., custom ploughs one day in winter and summer sowing, meat and drink for 24 horseboys or 4s for their diet.

Of and from the inhabitants of the quarter of Ballikeneine; two beeves, 24 cronocks of oats, 12 cakes of bread, 4 dishes of butter, a heriot after the death of every Canfinny[5], and custom plough, reaping hooks and diet

---

1 These words, which occur throughout the inquisition, are henceforth omitted.

2 Clancarroll *alias* Kilkevan in Teig O Doyne's surrender, recited in the Fiant for Letters Patent (below).

3 Dery *alias* Dromenbehy, *surrender.*

4 The surrender inserts here 'the parcel of pasture land, wood and underwood called O Doyne's Forest', which may possibly have been omitted in error from this transcript of the inquisition.

5 Every free tenant, *surrender.* See no. 24 of 'Exceptions exhibited by Charles Duinn' (p. 67, below).

of horseboys as in Rerrimore aforesaid, besides 20d in money claimed but not proved by the said Teige.

Of the inhabitants of the quarter of Cappabrogan yearly; two beeves, 24 cronocks of oats, 24 cakes of bread, 8 dishes of butter, heriots after the death of every Canfinny[6], and custom ploughs, reaping hooks, and diet of horseboys as aforesaid.

Of the inhabitants of the quarter of Garrough yearly; two beeves, 24 cronocks of oats, 24 cakes of bread, 8 dishes of butter, heriots after the death of every Canfinny[7], and custom ploughs, reaping hooks and diet of horseboys as aforesaid.

And of the inhabitants of the three quarters of Mointaghmilicke yearly; six beeves, 72 cronocks of oats, 72 cakes of bread, 24 dishes of butter, heriots after the death of every CanFinny, and custom ploughs, reaping hooks and diet of horseboys as aforesaid.

Of the inhabitants of the quarter of Sraghleighe[8] in the said territory yearly; two beeves, 24 cronocks of oats, 12 cakes of bread, 4 dishes of butter, heriots after the death of any of the CanFinnies,[9] and custom ploughs, reaping hooks, and diet of horseboys as aforesaid.

[*Of the inhabitants of the quarter of Kiltegrallagh; two beeves, 24 cronocks of oats, a heriot after the death of every *Canfinny, and diet of horseboys as aforesaid[10].]

Of the inhabitants of the quarter of Boell[11] yearly; two beeves, 24 cronocks of oats, 4s in money, four quarters of a beef, four horseloads of drink or in lieu thereof 52 barrines of malt, whereof 4 barrins in bear malt and 12 barrins in wheat, heriots after the death of every Canfinnie, and diet of horseboys as aforesaid.

---

6   Every free tenant, *surrender.*

7   Every free tenant, *surrender.*

8   Sraghleighe *alias* Glanruishe, *surrender.*

9   Every free tenant, *surrender.*

10 This item for Kiltegrallagh Quarter, which is not present in the text of the inquisition, has probably been omitted by the copyist. It has been restored here from the surrender, which, however, reads 'a heriot after the death of every free tenant'. As in every other instance the inquisition gives the heriot as being after the death of a Canfinny, I have restored the Kiltegrallagh entry to read likewise.

11 Boell *alias* Boeman, *surrender.*

Of the inhabitants of the quarter of Rirribegge yearly; two beeves, 24 cronocks of oats, 12 cakes of bread, [4 dishes of butter[12]], 6 Carnes of malt, heriots after the death of every Canfinny[13], diet of horseboys, and 10s in money.

Of the inhabitants of the quarter of Derrie[14]; two beeves, 24 cronocks of oats, heriots after the death of anie CanFinny, and diet of horseboys in manner aforesaid.

And of the inhabitants of the quarter of Corbolly[15] yearsly; two beeves, 24 cronocks of oats and 8 cakes of bread, 6 dishes of butter, heriots after the death of every CanFinny and diet of horseboys as aforesaid.

And of the inhabitants of the quarter of Tenyll yearly; two beeves, 24 cronocks of oats, 12 cakes of bread, 4 dishes of butter, heriots after the death of every CanFinny, and diet of horseboys in manner aforesaid.

And of the inhabitants of the quarter of Clonmachow, otherwise called Ballintegart, yearly; two beeves, 24 cronocks of oats, 12 cakes of bread, 4 dishes of butter, heriots after the death of every CanFinny[16], and diet of horseboys as aforesaid, besides 20d in money.

And of the inhabitants of the quarter of Clanmorchowe[17] yearly; two beeves, 24 cronocks of oats, heriots after the death of every Can-Finny[18], and diet of horseboys as aforesaid.

Of the inhabitants of the quarter of Lackagh yearly; two beeves, 24 cronocks of oats, 12 cakes of bread, 8 dishes of butter, heriots after the death of every Canfinny[19], and diet of horseboys as aforesaid.

And of the inhabitants of the quarter of Moniquid yearly; one penny

---

12 Omitted from inquisition transcript. It is restored here from the surrender.

13 Every free tenant, *surrender.*

14 Dyrry *alias* Dromnebehy, *surrender.*

15 Corbolly *alias* Glanmylle, *surrender.*

16 Every free tenant, *surrender.*

17 Clanmorchowe *alias* Cowlevoghlan, *surrender.*

18 Every free tenant, *surrender.*

19 Every free tenant, *surrender.*

an acre of arable land[20], and heriots after the death of every CanFinny[21] (excepting only 60 a. in the said quarter belonging to Brian mcRorie which is free from this charge).

And of the inhabitants of the quarter of Clancarroll yearly: one penny an acre as aforesaid and heriots after the death of every CanFinny[22].

And of the inhabitants of the quarter of Clancowmey yearly; one penny an acre and a heriot after the death of every CanFinny[23].

And of the inhabitants of the quarter of Castlebracke[24] yearly; one penny an acre and a heriot after the death of every CanFinny[25].

And of the inhabitants of the Sisseragh of Fassaghelly only an heriot after the death of every CanFinny[26].

All which rents, duties and customs the said Teig O Doyne still claims as due and payable to himself as now holding the Captainship of the country and the name of O Doyne, but the said jurors do find that by consent as well of the said Teige as of the freeholders and inhabitants of Iregane all the said rents, customs and duties have been of late reduced to a further certainty by Sir Anthony St. Leger, knt, and Nicholas Kerdiff, Esq., Justices of Assize in the said county, as by an order particularly expressing and limiting the same signed by the said Justices more at large may and doth appear; the terms of which follow in these words:

By the Lords Justices of Assize, 20th August, 1606.

Patrick mcFirre and others the freeholders of Iregane, *plaintiffs.*

Teige Oge O Doyne in the behalf of himself and Teige O Doine, chiefe of his name, Chiefe Lord of Iregan aforesaid, *defendants.*

---

20 *Surrender* adds 'belonging to every free tenant', and places the clause relating to Brian mcRory as qualifying this item only.

21 Every free tenant, *surrender.*

22 Every free tenant, *surrender.*

23 Every free tenant, *surrender.*

24 Castlebrack *alias* Ballycaslanbracke, *surrender.*

25 Every free tenant, *surrender.*

26 Every free tenant, *surrender.*

By virtue of a reference made unto us as Justices of Assize from the right hon. the Lord Deputie dated the fourthe of June in the yeare 1606, we have hard and examined the contents of the petition so referred unto us in the open assize in the presence of the parties, and find that those only of the quarter commonly called Clonehein in Iregane doe find themselves most grieved and did complaine before us. Uppon hearing of the complaints we find that there hath bine auciently due and payed as services out of the said quarter, *viz.* twoe beoves at Christmastyde, six dishes of butter, everie dishe contayninge eight wine quarters and noe more, and xviii Cakes of Breade, the one half thereof to be payed in sommere, thother half in harvest, and xxiiii Cronockes of oats at easter for all services due for the said quarter, which were payed as auncient services by the said Freeholders of that quarter to O Doine their cheife lord. And where there have bine of longe tyme further payed by the Freeholders of that quarter to the Cheife lord O Doine four quarters of a beef and the tallowe, one Fatte hogge of a yeare and an half ould, Twelve cronocks of wheate, xxxii cronocks of malte and a marke in money, which by the depositions taken before us appeared to be for a quiddie and not a rent service, we therefor order by consent of all parties that from hencefoorth the freeholders of the said quarter shall be freed of all the same, save only the marke, and noe more but one marke shalbe demanded and payed yearely for the same, which marke with consent of the said parties we thinke fitte shall be paid yearly from henceforth, for that it appeared to us that the whole had long bine paide allthough uppon examination it was manifest to bee for a quiddy. Allso wher the freeholders of the said quarter in the name of all the freeholders of O Doynes country commonly called Iregane did complaine of divers extortions exacted upon them by compulsion and cohercions of distresse by O Doine their Cheife lord and his predecessors, as namely, upon every quarter in the said country he and they would exact two melsh cowes or if they liked not of them, then one pound of Englishe money for everie of the said cowes. Item, two peckes of somer oates for his horses, meate and drinke for four and twentie horseboyes in som\u00a0\u00a0er, and soe in winter. Item, twentie two measures of wheate which\u00a0mounts to a pecke to O Donnes stoodkeeper. Item, meate and drinke to O Donn's tayliors and carpenders everie Sondaie and Holydaie throughout the yeare. Item, seaven payer of brogis everie yeare to O Donne's marshalls and officers to be payed by everie shoomaker inhabitinge upon the said freeholders' lands. Item, sixteene horsshoes unto O Donn yearly and eighte horsshoes to everie of his horsmen of everie smith dwellinge uppon the said freeholders' lands. Item, that O Doyne everie yeare laied upon everie of the said freeholders all his horses twice a yeare, at which tymes they were to give to everie Cheife horse xxiiii sheaves of oates and to everie hackney xvi sheaves. Item, that O Doine accumtomably used at his going to Dublin or the Sessions to cutt, impose and leavie upon the freeholders' lands as might beare his chardges. Item, uppon everie leavie of Beaves for his Majestie's armie upon that Country that O Doine leavyed the same only upon the freeholders, and the mony receaved from the state for the same he used to keepe for his owne use, not payeng the freeholders anie part thereof. Item, that he used to lay his kerne and bonnaughts upon the said freeholders for meate and drinke. All which greavances wee find to be meere Irishe extortions, and although the same or many of them have somtymes long since bene layde on them, yett uppon examination we finde that the same have not beene demanded of them for many yeares past, But by Teige Oage O Doyne now Cheife of that Country of his own disposition have bene abolished and lefte off and noe such extraordinary Irish exactions layed uppon them since his taking uppon him the name of the Cheife of the Country. And yet leaste the same should be hereafter exacted of them we doe order and set downe by consent of the said freeholders and of the said Teige Oage that the said freeholders should be ever hereafter freede of the said extortions or exactions, only for beoves to be levied for the state or army at all tymes excepted, the same to be taken upp of the said freeholders and the money paid for them to be aunswered and truly payed unto them from whom the same are taken. And that all such other dueties and services as have bene payed and awnswered out of everie the quarters in the said country to the Cheife lord thereof shalbe hereafter duely payed as accustomeablie they have byn. And for anie other attendance of all and anie the said freeholders towching roades, hostinges and other publique accounts we doe order that the same shalbe only uppon the Kinge's Majestie's, his heyres' and successors', Kinges of England and Ireland, as all the freeholders of England are and as the freeholders of this kingdome ought to be.

Anthony St. Leger. Nicholas Kardiffe.

And the said jurors do further say that all the several quarters of land in Iregane aforesaid have been heretofore by the predecessors of the said O Doine chardged with cuttings, Coiney of horse and man, bonnoghtes, Cosheries, works and Customs of cutting and drawing wood and Timber, all which the jurors do say are and were but extortions. And also with building, repairing and keeping staunch the Castles, Halls and Bawnes belonging to O Doyne from time to time, which the said jurors do also say was done by compulsion and not of right.

And the said jurors further find and present that controversy being between the said Teige O Doyne and his brother Charles O Doyne for the said Charles's challenge to certain lands and chiefries in Iregan, the said Teige and Charles of their own accord submitted themselves to the award and arbitration of certain persons, who made the award as followeth in these words:

Where controversie and difference hath bene betwixte Teige Oage O Doine of the one partie and Charles *alias* Cahir O Doine brother to the said Teige of the other partie, for and concerning the Countrie and Cantred of Iregan and the seinor thereof with other the hereditaments and appurtenances pertayning to the said seignory, Countrie and Cantred of Iregane; the said Teige and Cahire *alias* Charles afforsaid having of ther owne mutuall consentes both yielded and submitted themselves in all and everie parte of there said variances and differences for, touchinge and concerning all the said controversies, to the adward, determination and ordere of us, Sir James FitzGerrald of Ballisonan, knighte, James Terrell of Castlloste, gent., Gerald FitzGerald of Allone, gent., and Sir Edward FitzGeralde of Ticrohan, knight, arbitrators indifferent chosen by theafforsaid Teige and Cahire *alias* Charles to examine, discusse and determine of all the premisses, and therin and of everie parte of the said differences and variances betwixt the said Teige and Cahire to take, conclude and determine a Full and Finall ende of all their said variaunces betwyxte them for and touching the premisses before recited: We therefor the aforesaid arbitrators uppon the said parties submission, having accordingly taken uppon us the decidinge of the said Cause have therein determined and doe pronounce our order touchinge all to be and remayne in manner and soarte hereafter followinge, *viz.* First, we the said arbitrators do enioyne the said Teige and Cahire by virtue of both ther said submissions to us that from hence Forward ther shalbe and remayne betwixt them booth a brotherly love and kind regarde to be observed betwene them in such amitie as never to cross, vex or molest onanother in noe matter, but to remayne in their advise and loves asistant to each other in all honest Causes, truly and faithfully licke brothers without frawde or geile, and there to be sworne each to other so to continew and remaine for ever. Secondlie, we doe order and adward that all the lands, tenements and hereditaments, in the said country of Iregan with all the Seignories thereunto pertayning and all other the appurtenances that is now in variance and difference betweene them (allowinge nor yielding to the said Teige nor Cahir noe propertie in aniethinge within the aid country to be excepted to them beyond this our order, but such lands or tenements allwayes reserved and excepted to them or either of them in especiall to be without the scoope of this our order that apparantly hath bine allreade six daies at anie tyme befor the date hereof acquired, purchased or gotten by them or anie of them meerely by acquisition of ther owne privat industrie, to be and remaine to themselves as excepted). And the two Castells of Castlebracke and *Tenehinse[27], all the rest of the aforesaid countrie and cantred of Iregan with the seignories and all other the lands, tenements and hereditaments with their appurtenances

---

27 Terehinse, MS.

within the circuit and perambulation of the meares of the said countrie
and cantred to be devided and shared equally into four quarters or
Partes, with all the lands, tenements and hereditaments, mores,
meadowes and pastures, woods, underwoodds, watercourses, milles
and all other the Commodities and Seignories arisinge or growinge in
profitt within the said countrie. And after such division equally made
of all as afforesaid by thafforesaid Cahir *alias* Charles or otherwise at
the election of the said Teige yf he please to make the division as before
recited, with this condition, that if the said Teige shall take uppon him
the said division that then the said Cahir to have the first choyse of
the said partes or portions, to be and remaine to the said Cahir and
the heyers male of his body lawfully begotten, free and exonerated
from anie seignories, taxation of rent, duetie or anie other chardge
by the said Teige demaundable, and thother three partes to the said
Teige and heyers males, or to such as by the state acquired from the
kinge in all the premisses before shalbe given and limited. And for
default of the heyers male to be continued of the body of the said
Cahir lawfully begotten, the remainder over [to] the said Teige
his brother, and the remainder further to be as the limitation of the
kinge's graunt and estate to be passed out of the said Country and
Cantred of Iregan maie or shall importe. Yf (otherwise by Teige's
allowance or choice) that Cahir shall make the division of the said
country in manner afforesaid, then Teige to have the first choice of
the said four the quarters or portions and Cahir to second him to have
the second choice, to be continued and remaine to him or his heyers
males as befor is expressed. Further, touchinge such portions as the
other brothers of the said Teige and Cahir hath or ther mother the
widdow of O Doine, which hapely is freed from the Scoope of theise
divisions and not liable therunto, the right being in themselves, our
meaninge is not to discuss or order theise portions in those divisions to
be don as afforesaid (excepte that Teige may iustilie claime to have
them, and theruppon a fourth parte therof still meante to be continued
in Cahir). Touchinge that parte allso (yf anie such be) and the said
fourth parte and portion so to be given the said Cahir of the said
Country and Cantred in manner aforesaid, that the said Teige within
tenn dayes after the date of these presents shall enter into a bond of a
thousand pounds sterling to Cahir and assigns with conditions that yf
at anie tyme and whensoever and as often as that shalbe reasonably
required by the said Cahir or his assignes at the said Teige's hands, his
heyers and assignes, to passe from them and everie of them a perfect,
sure and indefeasible estate in law to the said Cahir and his heyers
males lawfully begotten of the said fourth parte and portion that so as
beforesaid of the said Country and Cantred of Iregan shalbe chosen and
elected by the said Cahir, and the said estate to be fortyfyed still by
the said Teige and his heyers from tyme to tyme uppon anie defects in
the said title so had such as the learned Counsell of the forsaid Cahir

and his heyers shall devise or advise. Further, touchinge anie chardge that shalbe in procuring the settled estate of the said Country or Cantred of Iregan from the king uppon anie surrender to be made by the said Teige, the said Charles to be comporsioner in the fourth parte of anie such Chardge, excepte the Countrye all would contribute there-unto, whereuppon to have or to be allowed the fourth parte of there contribution to the asistance of his owne Chardge in that Busines, which is meante to be the fourth parte of Teige's graund Chardge of labouringe and procuringe the same in effecte. Lastelie, it is ment and so ordered by us the said arbitrators afforesaid that whate Rent uppon gettinge forthe of the Pattents shalbe reserved to the kinge uppon the said Country or Cantred of Iregan, that yf the fourthe parte of the said Rent doe not exceede the some of fortie shillings sterling then the said Cahir his fourthe parte and portion as afforesaid to be freed and dischardged therof and onlie to be due and in demand uppon Teige's three partes. And if yt exceed in the fourthe parte to be in proportion above fortie shillings sterling as before recited, then Cahir's parte and proportion to beare only a fourthe parte of the overplus that exceedes that limitation. And such other Countrie Chardge of Beoves, Risinges out or Cariadges for the king's armie, uppon lick occasions Cahir's parte to contribute his just proportion in that still withe the rest of his Countrie. Allwayes provided that the surrender be done (yf soe yt be expedient) with meeteste speede and conveniency that may be. In Wittnes of all the recitalls and layinges downe as afforesaid to be our order and adward touchinge all the premisses we have herunto subscribed our handes the xith of Aprill, 1607.
James FitzGerald: James Tyrrell: Gerrott FitzGerald: Edward fitzGerald.

And the said Teige by his deed obligatory became bound for the perform-ance of the award above written, as by the tenor thereof may appear:

Noverint universis per presentes me Thadeum alias Teige O Doine de Tenehenchie in Comitatu de le Queenes Countie, armigerum, teneri et firmiter obligari Carolo alias Cahir O Doine Armigero, ino magis-trorum Cancellarie Hibernie in mille libris bone et legalis monete Anglie solvendis eidem Carolo alias Cahir, heredibus, executoribus et assignatis suis ad voluntatem suam ad quam quidem solucionem bene et fideliter faciendum obligo me, heredes et assignatos meos firmiter per presentes. In cuius rei testimonium presentibus sigillum meum apposui. Datum bono die Aprilis Anno Domini 1607.

Where controversie hath bine and is dependinge betwene the above bounden Tady *alias* Teige O Doine on thone partie and thabove named Charles *alias* Cahir O Doine of thother partie, both sonnes to the late O Doine deceasede, for and concerninge the right, title, intereste and claime of the Chiefery, Seigniory and lordship of the Countrie, Cantred or Territorie of Iregan, and allso for and concearning the manners, townes and castles of Castlebracke, Tenehenchie and Rierymore with their appurtenances, together with all the other landes, tenementes, woodes, bogges, lackes, rentes, services and Dueties which doe meerely belonge or appertaine to the Chiefry, Seignory and Iregan or to the name or callinge of O Doine, Captaine or Chieftaine of the said Iregan, and all other the landes tenements and hereditaments with the appurtenances in the said Cantred of Iregan and in the seisin or possession of either the said Tadie *alias* Teige or Charles *alias* Cahir or in the seisin or possession of others to their uses or uses. And that the said parties have willingly of their actuall consents and agreement submitted themselves to the adward, order and arbitration of Sir Edward FitzGerald of Tecrohan, knight, Sir James fitzPiers fitzGerald of Ballysonan, knight, Gerald FitzGerald of Kilmawke and James Tyrrell of Castleost, Esquiers, arbitrators indifferentlie nominated and chosen by the said parties to order, arbiter, adwarde and conclude a Final end betweene them for and concearning all variances, Controversies, douptes, questions, challenges and demaundes whatsoever for and concearning the premisses. The condition therfor of this obligation is such that the above bounden Tady *alias* Teige O Doine his heyers and assignes, feoffees of trust to his use, or anie other person or persons clayminge by or under pretence or collor of any right derived from or by the said Tady *alias* Teige, his heyers and assignes, shall from tyme to tyme well and truly performe, fullfill, keepe, observe, obey and accomplish on his and their partes and the parte of everie of them the order, arbitrament and adward of the said arbitrators for and concerning all and singular the said Controversies for the premisses and everie parte and parcell hereof in all pointes, articles and conditions such as on his parte by the said order he shalbe enyoyned and adwarded to doe. And shall not procure, sett on or willingly suffer or permit anie person or persons to goe about to transgresse or violat the said order or any parte therof, but truly to performe his and their parte therof accordinge as the same shalbe layed downe by the said Arbitrators under their handes' writing according their true meaning therin without anie Fraude, Covine or deceipte, that then this obligation to be voyde and of none effecte, otherwise to stand and Remaine in Full force and vertue in lawe. Provided that this order shalbe published in writing under thandes and seales of the said Arbitrators at or befor the xiiiith daie of this presente moneth of Apriell nexte ensuinge the date abovewritten.

Tadie Doine

Presente at thensealinge and delivery herof those whose names ensueth: Edward fitz Gerald: James fitz Gerald: James Tyrell: Gerald fitz Gerald: Johne Doine.

The said jurors also find that Brian O Doine brother to the said Teige O Doine makes challenge to Brittas and other lands in the quarters of

Lackagh and Garrogh now found for the said Teige, the said Brian entitling himself by force of a writing in paper purporting a gift thereof to the said Brian from his father Teige Chief of his name, which writing the jurors find was signed and delivered by the said Teige the father to Brian aforesaid in his lifetime in manner as it is now, the tenor of which writing is in these words:

Be it known unto all men by these presentes that I O Doine, Chiefe of my name, have given and graunted unto my sonn Briam O Doine, his heyers or assignes, the whole land that belongeth to myself in the quarters of the Lackagh, in the quarter of the Garrough, that is to say the Brittas [   ] [28] and the Beachane and Ballidullen with the rest that belongeth unto me in both quarters with their pastures, wooddes, underwoddes, etc. Also I have given in like manner all that belogeth unto myself in the land of Milicke in the parishe of Rossanoliss. And allsoe I have given and graunteth all that belogethe unto me or I shall have in the Leakamore in the Parishe of Casteltone in [   ] [29] by these presents. I have putt my hand and seale to the hole graunte and gift.

O Doine D is marke (T)

Which writing is endorsed in these words:

Being presente at the givinge and sealinge of theise [those] whose names ensuethe: Dermott O Cahassa is marke: Edmond Eustace is marke: Edmond Keatinge: Morogh O Doine of Ballickiny is marke: Meache mcCassin: Cahir mcFirr is marke: Hillarius [   ] [30].

And the said jurors do find and present that Charles Duinn, Esq., brother to the said Teige is now seised in his demesne as of fee of and in: 30 acres in the town and fields of Aculagha in the quarter of Clancarroll, 5 acres in Laackagh begge, 5 acres in Farren Carroll reogh in the quarter of Mointagh Milicke, 24 acres in Garrygallaraide and Ferren hucristinne in the said quarter, 5 acres in Garruoragh in the said quarter and 5 acres in Garrikenanie in the said quarter.

Brian O Donne, another brother to the said Teige: 40 acres in Brittas in the quarter of Lackagh (whereof Rorie Oage O Doine [claims] 7 acres), 40 acres in Milicke, 3 acres in Garrimore in the quarter of Clancarroll, 20 acres in Beachane in the quarter of Garrough, 5 acres in Garrough and

---

28 Blank in MS.

29 Blank in MS.

30 Blank in MS.

20 acres in Ballydowline in the said quarter (which 20 acres in Ballidowline is claimed by Patrick mcDavie).

Johne O Donne of Killkevan, gent.: 24 acres in Capparogan, 60 acres in Kilkevan in the quarter of Clancarroll (whereof 30 acres are now claimed by Owny O Donne), 30 acres in Coolemoran in the said quarter (which is now claimed by Dermott mcJames), 17 acres in Garrimore[31] (whereof Edmond mcDermott claims one half, and Brian O Donne above mentioned claims the other acre[32] of the same in mortgage).

Rorie Ooge O Donne of Glauckrim, gent.: 5 acres in Gurtin in the quarter of Capparogan.

Brian mcRorie O Donne[33] of Coolenpiesie, gent.: 60 acres in Coolenpisie (except only 3 acres thereof which Morough mcCahir holds in mortgage).

Brian mcRorie mcDavie of Ballintegarte, gent.: 40 acres in Ballintegart and 15 acres called Coolebeg, lying and being in Fassaghely.

The abovenamed Charles O Doyne, Esq.: 60 acres which was formerly belonging to Teige Galogan and Clandonill Donn lying and being in the quarter of Rerrymore, 14 acres called Mecowill in the said quarter, and also 20 acres called Racowgh in the said quarter of Rirrymore.

Patrick mcFyrr and William mcFyrr of Clonhine, gent.: 36 acres in Clonhein aforesaid.

Teige mcDermott and Donell mcDermott of the same, gent.: 4 acres in the said Clonheine.
Murtagh mcQuinn makes claim to the one half of all the lands in Clonhein aforesaid.

Hugh mcDermott makes claim to 20 acres there called Ballimoyle.

Morgh mcWilliam makes claim to the other 4 acres of the lands in Clonhein aforesaid.

Cahir mcOwny of Clongaghe, gent.: 2½ acres in Cloinga, in the quarter of Clancarroll.

---

31 *Corrected from* Ballidowline, *MS.*

32 *Sic,* MS.

33 In the Index of freeholders at the end of the MS (f. 404) he appears as Brian mcRorie McChahir.

William mcRosse of the same: 2 other acres in the said Cloinga.

Edmonde mcJames and Donnel mcMorish of Cappaghloghan, gent.: 25 acres in Cappoughlouchane in the quarter of Castlebracke. And there is issuing out of the same land as a chief rent unto Teige mcEdmonde and Neile mcDermott and his kinsmen yearly, 4d current money of England, 7 barrnes of oat malt and a quarter of a hog. And the said Teige mcEdmonde, Neale mcDermott and the rest claim the said chief rent to be 18 barrins of oat malt, 12 d of the money aforesaid, a whole hog, and a heriot.

The said Edmond mcJames and Donell mcMorish: 20 acres in Achvoan in the quarter of Clancoony (which said 20 acres is claimed by Teige mcMorogh and his brother as their inheritance).

Mortogh O Doine of Coolevoghan, gent.: 50 acres in Coulvoghlan (which same is claimed by Tyrrelagh O Dunne as in mortgage, and also Dermott O Doine claims 20 acres of the said land as his inheritance).

Rosse mcNeale and Edmond Oge of Corballie, gent.: 12½ acres in Corbally.

Patricke mcMortagh of the same, gent.: 1½ acre in Corballie aforesaid.

Brian mcNeile and Mortagh mcBrien of the same, gent. 16 acres in Corballies aforesaid.

Patricke O Melane, in right of Lisaghe mcQuinn a child: 1½ acres in Corballies aforesaid.

Donogh Moyle of the same gent.: 3½ acres in Corbally aforesaid. (Patrick O Melane makes claim to one of the said three acres as in mortgage.)

Shan mcDarie of the same, gent. and his two brethren: 7½ acres in Corbally aforesaid.

Mulmore mcCarroll: 12 acres in Cappaghroe aforesaid[34] in the quarter of Dirry.

Donell mcNeile of Carhowne, gent.: the town and lands, or village, of Carehowne in the quarter of Shraghliegh.

Finola neene Morroghe of Derrin, gent.: 5 acres in Dirrin in the quarter

---

34 *Sic*, MS.

of Shraghliegh. And there is a chief rent of 5 white groats yearly issuing out of the said 5 acres to Teige mcEdmond and his sept. (And Dermott Oage O Doine claims the said land as his inheritance.)

William mcRorie of Ballinloigge, gent.: 14 acres of Ballinloige in the quarter of Killingrallagh, (which land is claimed by Teige O Doine as his inheritance).

Laghlein mcShane of Tenyll, gent.: 17 acres in Tenill aforesaid in the quarter of Tenill.

Carroll mcMurtagh of the same, gent.: 8 acres in Tenill aforesaid. And the said Carroll mcMurtagh has mortgaged 2 other acres of land to Edmond mcOwen who now holds the same in mortgage. And there is a chief rent of 12d in money and 20 barrins of oat malt issuing out of the said 10 acres yearly, viz. to Brian O Doine 10 barrins of the malt and to William mcLawrence the other 10 barrins, and the said 12d to be divided between the said Brien and William. Provided that the said mortgaged land is free from the said charge during the time it is in mortgage.

Donogh mcDonogh of Skarkehoune, gent.: 8 acres in Skarhowne in the quarter of Garrough (which land is claimed by Teige mcDonell as his inheritance).

Rory mcMelaghlin and Connor mcTeige of Kilmanvan, gent.: 10 acres in Shanclone in the quarter of Ballinteggarte, 20 acres in Ballinteggart in the said quarter, and 5 acres in Achmonre in the said quarter. There is issuing and payable out of the 20 acres aforesaid in Ballitegart to Mortagh mcOwen a chief rent of 18 cronockes of oat malt, 6 barrins of bread, 4 quarters of butter and 18d in money yearly. (But this chief rent is claimed by Owen mcShane and Teig mcEdmond, alleging that it is but in mortgage from their ancestors, and Patricke O Doogan claims all the lands last above written as his inheritance.)

Neale mcDermott of Clonaghaduffe, gent.: 20 acres in Roskene in the quarter of Clanconny.

Morrogh mcCahir[35] and Shane mcEdmond of Ballikenein, gent.: 23 acres in Ballikeinin in the said quarter.

Edmond mcDonogh and Owen mcShane of Ballikeneinn, gent. and Sibell[36] neene Edmond: 22 acres in Ballikenin aforesaid. (Teige mcMorish

---

35 He is called Murtagh mcCahir in the Index (MS, p. 408).

36 The Index calls her Sylie nyne Edmond (MS, p. 405).

claims 4 acres of the said 23 acres last above written as in mortgage.)

Edmond O Melone and Dermott O Melone of Cappaghbegge, gent.:
10 acres in Cappaghbegge and Reynn in the quarter of Mointaghmilicke.

Rory O Melane of the same, gent.: 7 acres in Cappaghbegge aforesaid.

Owen O Melone of Newry, gent.: 7 acres in Rinn in the said quarter.

Morish O Melane of the same, gent.: 4 acres in Rynn.

James O Melane of the same, gent.: 7 acres in Rynn aforesaid.

Brian O Melane of the same, gent.: 8 acres in Rinne aforesaid.

Patricke O Melane of the same, gent.: one acre in Rinn aforesaid.

The said Patrick O Meloan claims 5 other acres in Rinn aforesaid
(parcel of the said town) in mortgage.

Hugh O Melane of the same, gent.: 7 acres in Cappaghbegge and Rinn
aforesaid in the said quarter of Mointagh Meelicke (which 7 acres is
claimed by William O Melane as his inheritance).

Dermott mcTeige of Tiraghcullen, gent.: 1½ acre in Tragh Callen in
the quarter of Boell.

Art mcDonogh of Gurtinn, gent.: 40 acres in Gurtin in the quarter of
Mointagh Meelicke.

Neale mcRory of Clonekylly, now a child: 10 acres in Clonkilly in the
quarter of Corbolly. There is a chief rent of 10 barrins of oat malt issuing
out of this land to Brian mcRory.

Dermott mcEdmond of the same, gent.: 5 acres in Clonkill in the
quarter of Corbolly.

Rory mcTeige, gent.: 5 acres in Clonekill aforesaid. And Brian mcNeale
claims a chief rent of 10 barrins of oat malt issuing out of this last 5 acres.

Donogh mcMorish of Coolemonyne, gent.: 6 acres in Coolmonnin in
the quarter of Killnegrallagh.

Dermott mcMorish of the same, gent.: 19 acres in Coolemonyne
aforesaid.

William O Davie,[37] gent.: 5½ acres in Coolemonin aforesaid.

Mortagh mcMorgh of the same, gent.: one acre in Coolemonyne afore-said.

James Oge Carpenter of the same, gent.: 3 acres in Coolemonyne aforesaid, as his inheritance.

It was alleged before the jurors that all the lands last above written in the town of Coolemonnine have been but mortgaged to some of the ancestors of the now possessors by some of the ancestors of O Doine.

Dermott mcMorish of [   ][38], gent.: 5 acres in Coolincossan in the quarter of Boellie.

Miagh mcCassin of the Borriesmore, gent.: 8 acres in Roishnoyer in the quarter of Dyrry (which 8 acres is claimed by Arte O Doine as in mortgage for 4 melch cows).

Morogh mcEdmond of [   ][39], gent.: 2 acres in Boell in the said quarter.

Donogh mcRory of the same, gent.: one acre in Boell aforesaid.

Ferrduffe[40] of the same, gent.: 2 acres in Boell aforesaid.

Davie mcTeige of the same, gent.: one acre in Boell aforesaid.

Shane Oge mcShane claims all the said lands in Boell as his inheritance.

Patrick mcMorish of Shraduffe, gent.: 5 acres in Shraghduffe in the quarter of Lackagh.

Mortagh mcMorgh of the same, gent.: 5 acres in Shraghduffe afore-said. And Rorie mcShane claims these last 5 acres as his inheritance.

Shane mcJames and James mcDavie of [   ][41], gent.: 7 acres in Roishinoylish in the quarter of Tenill. And the said Shane and James do

---

37 William O Divoy, Index (MS, p. 405).

38 Blank in MS.

39 Blank in MS.

40 *Sic*, MS. The patronymic was perhaps omitted by the copyist, but the Index also has only simple name.

41 Blank in MS.

now likewise hold 2½ acres in the town aforesaid from William mcLawrence in mortgage for 2 melch cows.

William mcLawrence of Tenyll, gent.: 30 acres in Tenyll in the said quarter. And also there is an acre of land in Tenyll in the hands of Mortagh mcMorish by way of mortgage from the said William mcLawrence for a heifer. And also one other acre in the said town in the hands of Rory Duffe in mortgage from the said William for 20s in money. And also one other acre there in the hands of More Reoghe in mortgage from the said William for 15s in money. (And also More neene Knawdan claims 4 acres of the lands of Tenill aforesaid as her inheritance. And Melaghlin mcShane and his brother claim their shares of other 4 acres of the lands in Tenill aforesaid.)

Shane mcDavie of Cappard, gent.: 5 acres in Ballinteggart in the quarter of Corbolly.

Tirleagh mcMulmory of Ballicowlin, gent.: 4 acres in Dirrellemoige in the quarter of Clonhein.

Brian O Doine of Ballicowlin, gent.: 4 acres in Dirrelemoige aforesaid.

More neene Morogh of the same, gent.: 4 acres in Dirrlemoige aforesaid.

Davy mcMurtagh of the same, gent.: 4 acres in Dirlemoige aforesaid.

Teige mcWilliam of the same, gent.: 4 acres in Dirrelemoige aforesaid.

Melaghlin mcOwen holds one stang out of every of the aforesaid acres of land[42] except only Davie mcMurtaghe's portion. And the said Melaghlin mcOwen claims likewise one acre out of the aforesaid portion of land.

Dermott Oge O Doine of Sraghliagh, gent.: 10 acres in Garrhowny in the quarter of Sraghliagh (which 10 acres is claimed by Morish mcConnor as his inheritance).

Rory mcFirr and Murtagh mcFyrr of Clonagh, gent.: 4 acres in Clony in the quarter of Tenyll.

Teige mcOwen of Cappanagraige, gent.: 42 acres in Cappanagraige, 15 acres in Boell, 10[43] acres in Coolecossan, and 14 acres in Ballinteian, all lying in the quarter of Boill. (All which lands in the said quarter is claimed by Tirleogh mcCooleima, Shane mcShane and their kinsmen as their inheritance.)

---

42 Those in Derrylemoige.

43 Corrected from either *5* or *15.*

Cooleymy mcTeige of Rerrybegg, gent.: 7 acres in Rirribegge. And the said Culemy hath now in his hands in the said town 5 acres by way of mortgage from Donogh Reogh for three cows, one heifer, one garran, two bull calves and 50 groats in money.

Teige mcArt and his brethren[44] of Dirry, gent.: 36 acres in Dirry. (And Murtagh O Doine claims 20 acres of the said lands as his inheritance, alleging that he himself mortgaged them to the said Teige's father about 20 years since for five cows or five garrans.)

Morish mcDonell of [   ][45],' gent.: 5 acres in Shraghduffe in the quarter of Lackagh.

James mcCarroll of the same, gent.: 5 acres in Sraghduffe aforesaid.

Patrick mcRory of the same, gent.: 5 acres in Shraghduffe aforesaid.

William Duffe mcDonell makes claim to 10 acres of the said 15 acres as his inheritance.

Moriertagh mcMorogh of Clarchill, gent.: 30 acres in Carchill[46] aforesaid, and 5 acres in Coolemonyne, all lying in the quarter of Boell.

Dermott mcRory of Garrough, gent.: 15 acres in Garrough aforesaid.

William mcTeige of the same, gent.: 10 acres in Garrough aforesaid.

Brian O Donne of the same, gent.: 5 acres in Garrough aforesaid.

Rory mcMelaghlin of the same, gent.: 7 acres in Garrough aforesaid.

Donogh mcDonogh of the same, gent.: 7½ acres in Garrough aforesaid.

Owny nene Donne, in right of her son Derby mcMorough who is heir, has in her hands 7½ acres in Garrough aforesaid.

Sheelie neene Doine and her husband have in their hands, until such time as her marriage goods be paid, 7½ acres in Garrough aforesaid.

Donogh mcGilpatricke claims the 5 acres abovewritten in the possession

---

44 The Index names them as Tirlagh mcArte and Owney mcArte (MS, p. 406).

45 Blank in MS.

46 *Sic*, MS.

of Brien O Doine as his inheritance, alleging that it was but mortgaged by his ancestors to Patricke Kregan.

Mortagh mcOwen of Moniquid, gent.: 10 acres in Parke and 10 acres in Moniquid, all lying in the quarter of Moniquid.

Dermott mcOwen of the same, gent.: 10 acres in Parke aforesaid.

Teige mcBrian of the same, gent.: 20 acres in Parke aforesaid.

Cahir mcLeynagh of the same, gent.: 20 acres in Parke aforesaid.

James Oage[47] O Donne of the same, gent.: 20 acres in Parke aforesaid.

William O Boolie of the same, gent.: 7 acres in Moniquid aforesaid.

Morough mcCahir of the same, gent.: 16 acres in Monyiquid aforesaid, whereof the said Morogh mcCahir holds 2 acres in mortgage from Neale mcDermott for 12 barrins of wheat. (And that William mcRory claims 2 acres of these lands in Moniquid last abovewritten as his inheritance.)

Owny mcDonogh of Killeine, gent.: 8 acres in Killackandrony in the Sisheragh of Fasaghely, (which Owen mcCahir O Doine claims as his inheritance).

Joane neene Carroll late wife to Cormocke O Donne holds for term of her life as her jointure: 10 acres in Garryhider, 12 acres in Killackandrony and 40 acres in Cargin, all lying in Fasaghely aforesaid, (which said 40 acres is claimed by Edmond mcDonogh and his kinsmen).

The said Owen mcCahir: 20 acres in Killackandronny aforesaid and 10 acres in Garryhidermore.

Teige Reogh of Lismerood, gent., by way of mortgage: 10 acres in Garrihidermore, (which is also claimed by Owen mcCahir aforesaid).

Donogh mcWilliam of [   ][48], gent.: 4 acres in Garricanochoe in the quarter of Mointagh meelicke.

---

47 Could this name be an error for *Shane* Oage? Shane Oge mcShane O Doyne of Park appears as a remainderman in Teige O Doyne's settlement in 1616 (App. V), after Cahir mcLeynagh and before Teige mcBryen O Doyne of Park.

48 Blank in MS.

Patrick mcShane of Cappard, gent.: 5 acres in Ballinecilly in the quarter of Corbolly. And Rosse mcNeale and his brother claim this as their inheritance.

Donell mcCormocke O Donne of the same, gent.: 7 acres in Ballinekilly aforesaid.

Melaghlen mcOwen of the same, gent.: 2 acres in Ballinekilly aforesaid.

Melaghlen mcOwen of Cappollane, gent.: 24 acres in Cappullan and Kinnaghan in the quarter of Clonheine.

Donell mcShane of the same, gent., by way of mortgage: 4 acres in Cappullane and Kinaghan aforesaid.

Murtagh mcHughe of Killmacrygare, gent.: 20 acres in Killmacrygarre in the quarter of Clancarroll.

Donogh mcMorish of Sraghculleen, gent.: 8 acres in Stragcullen in the quarter of Boell, (whereof William mcMurtagh claims 2 acres as his inheritance).

Owen mcMelaghlin of the same, gent.: 3½ acres in Stracullen aforesaid.

John Fiane of the same, gent.: 3½ acres in Stracullen aforesaid.

William mcRorie of Gragafollagh, gent.: 22½ acres in Graguefollagh in the quarter of Boell.

Hugh mcShane of the same, gent.: 21 acres in Gragnefolagh aforesaid.

Murtagh mcMorish of Shianbege, gent.: 4 acres in Tenyll in the said quarter. And also of one acre in Tenyll aforesaid which he holds by way of mortgage from William mcLawrence.

Patrick mcDavie of the Brockagh, gent.: 4½ acres in Brockagh in the quarter of Clonemorchoe.

Dermott Oge O Donne of Straghleigh, gent.: 5 acres in Dyrren in the quarter of Straghleighe, and also 50 acres in Straghleigh aforesaid. (Donell mcFarrin claims the first 5 acres in Dyrren as his inheritance and Neyle mcDermott claims likewise a chief rent of 5 white groats yearly issuing out of the same. And also Shane mcDavie claims 25 acres of the 50 in Straghleighe abovewritten as in mortgage. And Dermott Leaghe claims other 4 acres there as his inheritance. And Patricke mcFirr claims other 4 acres there called Larraghbane as his inheritance alleging that they were taken from his ancestors for a quarter of a cake of bread as a fine.)

Teige mcOwen of Cappanagraige, gent.: 7 acres in Ballimickrory in the quarter of Killtegrallagh.

Donogh mcMorish of Coolemonyne, gent.: 7 acres in Ballimickmullore in the said quarter.

Edmond mcMurtagh of Killart, gent.: 12 acres in Brockagh in the quarter of Clanmorogh.[49]

Brian mcDonogh of [   ][50] gent.: 4 acres in the said town of Brockagh.

Moriertagh mcOwen O Donne of [   ][51], gent.: 3 acres in Cappan-skibboll in the quarter of Rirrybegg.

Brian mcRory and Leynaghe O Doine[52] of Killowrine, gent.: 4 acres in Moniquid in the said quarter.

Shane mcMorogh of Rirrybegge gent.: 7 acres in Rirrybegge.

Tirrelagh mcOwen, Shane mcOwen, Edmond mcOwen, Murtagh mcOwen and Brien mcOwen of [   ][53], gent.: 35 acres in Garrifoolane in the quarter of Mointagh meelicke.

Mulmory mcDonogh of Dirrygall, gent.: 34 acres in Ballikill kein roe in the quarter of Rirrybegge.

Teige mcEdmond of Clonoghadow, gent.: 10 acres called Coshbegge, 20 acres in Fertane, 20 acres[54], and 6 acres in Clone Gooddow, all lying in the quarter of Clancomy.

Neale mcDermott of Clonaghadow, gent.: 20 acres in Roskene and 4

---

49 There is an X in the margin of the MS, as if to indicate an error or omission, but it is not caught up.

50 Blank in MS.

51 Blank in MS.

52 He is called Leynagh mcRorie in the Index (MS, p. 407).

53 Blank in MS.

54 *Sic,* MS.

acres in Cloncoddow. And Daniell mcCormocke claims 7 acres of the 20 acres in Roskene aforesaid as in mortgage for 28s 8d sterling.

William mcMorish of Rerrimore, gent.: 7 acres in Rerrymore in the said quarter. And Rory Oge O Sten[55] now holds 15 acres more in the town and fields aforesaid parcell of the said William mcMorishe's lands by way of mortgage for 18 cows of his[56] marriage goods.

Charles O Doine of Dublin, Esq.: 8 other acres in the town aforesaid, concerning which 8 acres the jurors find that the abovenamed William mcMorishe was formerly seised thereof and mortgaged them to Teige O Doine father to the said Charles, who thereupon entered and was seised thereof by way of mortgage and being so seised conveyed his whole estate therein to the said Charles, who has enjoyed the same ever since. And afterwards during the life of the said Teige the said William mcMorish repaid the mortgage of the said lands to the said Teige in redemption of the said land.

The said Charles O Doine, by force of conveyance from his father: 16 acres which did anciently belong unto the heirs of Teige O Halogan and Clandonelldonn in the quarter of Rirrie More, 14 acres in the said quarter called Mecowlle, and 20 acres in the said quarter called Rathcowaghe.

Moriertaghe O Doyne, late of Ballykinen, gent. was in his lifetime seised of 35 acres in Ballykenin and died so seised 20 September 1601. And Keadoghe mcMoriertaghe is his son and heir and now of the age of 13 years. And the said Moriertaghe and those by whom he claimed was in quiet possession of the said lands 30 years before his death. And concerning the said lands the jurors find that one Donoughe mcRorie is now possessed of the said lands, who finding the same waste about May last entered thereupon, alleging that he or his ancestors left the same in the hands of O Doyne to be kept for them about 30 years since, as the manner of the country is if any freeholder depart out of the same. And James Duffe mcCarroll makes claim to 10 acres of this as in mortgage for 10 cows.

Donoughe mcRorie of [   ][57], gent.: 5 acres in Ballykenine aforesaid.

---

55 The Index calls him Rory Oge O Steene (MS, p. 407).

56 Has the word *wife's* been omitted after *his*?

57 Blank in MS.

Dermott O Doyne of Sraghleigh gent. is possessed of 10 acres in Garhowne in the quarter of Dyrry, but the jurors say that the said 10 acres is the proper land and inheritance of Donell mcNeyle. And it was alleged on behalf of the said Donell mcNeyle that at the end of the last wars the said Donell being very poor left the said land waste, whereupon O Doyne entered on the same and bestowed it on the said Dermott O Doyne, who thereupon yet holds the same from the said Donell. And Rossa [mc] Neyle claims a chief rent of 14 barens of oat malt yearly issuing out of this land.

Shane mcDonoughe O Doyne of Cappaloughran, gent.: is seased as his freehold for term of his life of 30 acres in Couilmoran in the quarter of ClannCaroll, the reversion thereof expectant to Art O Doyne of Gurtin gent. and his heirs in fee simple. And there is a chief rent of 5s sterling in money yearly during the said Shane's life issuing out of his land to the abovenamed Art O Doyne. (And Dermott mcJames and his brethren claim these lands as his and their inheritance.)

Teige O Doyne the elder, father unto the now Teige O Doyne, was in his lifetime seised of the castle and 60 acres in Roskyne, 43 acres in Reriebegg, 20 acres in Agheny in Reriebegg, [and] 20 acres in Lawagh. And the said Teige, being so seised, by his deed dated 20 October 1583 enfeoffed thereof Piers FitzGerald of Ballysonan esq. and Christoffer Flatesburie of Osberstowne Gent. to certain uses and intents in the said deed more at large expressed, the tenor whereof ensues:

Sciant presentes et futuri quod ego Tadeus alias dictus Tady Oge O Doine de Tinehinse in Comitatu Regine generosus dedi concessi et hac presenti carta mea confirmaui Petro FitzGerald de Ballisonan in Comitatu Killdar' Armigero et Christoforo Flatsbury de Oberston in eodem comitatu generoso omnia castra, messuadgia, terras, tenementa, redditus, reversiones et servicia, moras, pratos, pascua et pasturas, boscos et subboscos et omnia alia hereditamenta mea quecunque cum omnibus suis membris et pertinentiis que habeo in Rosceine, Loughduy, Reriebegge, [et] viginti acras de Leavaghe. Habenda et tenenda omnia predicta messuadgia, castra, terras, tenementa, redditus, reversiones et cetera premissa prefatis Petro et Christoforo, heredibus et assignatis suis imperpetuum, de capitalis dominis feodi illius per servicia inde debita et de iure consueta. Et Ego vero prefatus Thadeus et heredes mei omnia et singula castra, messuadgia, terras, tenementa et cetera premissa de praerecitatis prefatis Petro et Christoforo, heredibus et assignatis suis, contra omnes gentes warrantizabimus, acquietabimus et imperpetuum per presentes defendemus. In cuius rei testimonium presentibus sigillum meum apposui. Datum vicesimo die Octobris Anno Domini 1583.

Thentente, purpose, full meaning and consideration of the above-written feoffment is and at the making therof was that the said feoffees, their heyers and the heyers of the survivor of them shall presently and forthwith stand and be seised of the premisses to the use of the said Teige for tearme of my liffe. And after my decease to the use of Elizabeth my wife and her heyers for ever in consideration of such somes of money as I have receaved of my said wiffe's Father and other her friends. Provided allwaies and the further intent allso therof is that my said wife Elizabeth shall convey or otherwise devise the said lands to one or more of my sonnes begotten uppon her boddie as she shall think good. To have and to hold to him or them to whom yt shalbe so conveyed or devised in fee or in fee Tyle after her decease, otherwise my said feoffees and the survivor of them and his heyers to stand seised of the premisses to my wiff's said use for Tearme of her liffe for and in consideration of her third parte and jointur of all my landes, and after her decease to the use of me the said Teige and myne heyers. Present at the sealing and delivery herof and at making of livery and seisin to the within named Piers in name of the rest of the feoffees according the purport of this deed those whose names ensueth: Tady O Duie: Teige Heury: John Doine: Mortagh Doine: Richard Oliver.

By force whereof the said Elizabeth FitzGerald wife to the said Teige hath now the use and possession of all the premises in Roskene, Rerrybege, Loughduffe and Lawagh. And Teige mcEdmond claims 12 of the acres in Roskene abovementioned as his inheritance, and also all other the land in Roskene aforesaid in general. And Edmond mcMelaghle[n] claims 8 a. of the abovewritten 43 a. in Rirrybegge as his inheritance and that they are held in mortgage from him.

And the said jurors further find and present that controversy being between the said Teige Oge O Doine Chief of his name and Brian O Doin his brother, an order was made between them by the consent of both parties the tenor whereof is:

Articles of agreement betwixt Teige O Doine of Castlebrake of the one parte and his bretheren Cormocke, Brien and Mortagh O Doine of the other parte by us whose names are subscribed. Item, *in primis* that the said Teige for his parte and the said Cormocke, Brien and Mortagh O Doine of their parte and their heyers forever shall live and deale brotherly and kindly one with another, in all Cases asisting and helping one another against all people, the Queene's Majestie, her heyers and successors allwaies excepted. Item, that at a daie to be appointed by us or any three of us the said parties shall deliver unto our hands all writtings and conveyaunces made unto them by their Father, and shall after make such releasses and guarantie[?] one to another as their

Councell shall devyse accordinge to the intent which we shall then
publish. Item, that after the death of Teige O Doyne Cheiffe of his
name and Father to the said Teige, Cormocke, Brien and Mortaghe the
said Teig O Doyne of Castlebracke shall have all the lands, seignories
and duties belonging the Cheiffery of Iregan to him and his heyres of
his bodie lawfullie begotten, the remaynder to the said Cormocke and
his heyres males, the remainder over to the said brothers and their
heyres males legitimat, and that none of the said brothers shall seeke to
alter or change in any parte this course of inheritinge. And in so much
as the said brothers are cutt of from any hope to have the said cheifferies
while the said Teig or annie heyre male lawfully begotten or to be
gotten of his bodie shall live, that the siad Teig shall by deede in writing
chardg his lands or som parcell thereof well able to beare that chardge
with three beoves yearlie to the said Cormocke and his heyres, two
beoves to the said Brian and his heyres and two beoves to the said
Mortaghe and his heyres, which deede is agreed shall after perfection
remayne in the custodie of one of us the said arbitrators unless it
*chance[58] the said Teig or his heyres to denie to paie the same, at which
tyme ther the said deed to be delivered to the said Cormocke and his
brothers or their heyres, which beoves to be paid and delivered by the
said Teig or his heyres to his said brothers. And that the said Teig
and his lands shalbe dischardged for ever of the said beoves if the said
brothers do eyther seeke or endevor to putt back or extinguishe annie
of the duties which hath beene usually taken upp by the O Doynes,
Cheiffe lords of Iregaine, or doe faile to help and assist to the uttermost of their power the said Teig and his heyres against all such as will
seeke or endevor to extinguish or put of the same or any parte therof.
Item, that the learned Councell of eche of the said parties shall devise
what assurance and securitie they shall thinke good for performance
of theise articles, and also devise conveighances from Teig O Doyne
father to the said Teig, Cormocke and the rest of such lands as they
have by gift from their said father to everie of them during their lives,
the remainder to his heyres males lawefullie begotten or to be begotten,
with clause of non-alienation and reintrie to the said Tei   and his
heyres if he or his heyres shall commit or perpetrat felonie or treason
against her Majestie, her heyres and successors, and therof be convicted
by course of the lawes of this realme, unles the said crime shalbe
followed, proved or informed by the said Teig or his heyres. Also,
it is agreed that after the decease of Teig O Doyne now living father
to the said brothers the said iiii beoves to be given to the said Brian
and Mortagh shall beare their due part, according the rate of the
Cheifferie and lands belonginge to the same, of the third part of Elizabeth FitzGerald their mother for soe longe time as she shall chaunce to

---

58 change, MS.

overlive the said Father, and that the said brothers shalbe faithful and
serviceable unto their said brother Teig and his heyres mayle lawfully
begotten. Also it is agreed that the said Teig uppon the conditions
aforesaid shall not seeke nor demaund any Cony, worke plowes or
[corkesur] [59] of any of the said brothers out of the lands which themselves may manure, but may lawfully take the same of their tenaunts.
Piers FitzGerald: James Terrell: Jhon FitzPatrick: Neyle Mageoghagan.

And the said jurors further find and present that all the castles, lands
tenements and hereditaments abovewritten have been hitherto held and
have descended according the Irish Custom of Tanistrie, notwithstanding it
appears unto the said jurors by examination that the lands and lawful
seignories of O Doyne are lineally come to Teig O Doyne aforesaid now
living from father to eldest son for certain descents and hathe been so
enjoyed from time to time accordingly. And that all and singular the
lands, etc., abovewritten are held of the king, by what services the jurors
know not other than by the service of 24 footmen victualled and furnished
for forty days at every general hosting within this kingdom. And there is
paid to his Majesty yearly by way of composition out of all the lands in
Iregan aforesaid the sum of £3: 10s sterling. And all the lands abovewritten of which the said Teig Oge O Doyne, Charles O Doyne and
Elyzabeth FitzGerald are seised are valued by the year at 2s 6d each
quarter, and all the other lands abovewritten of which the inferior freeholders are seised are valued yearly above all reprises at 12d a quarter.

And the said jurors present that Teig O Doyn of Tenahinsy aforesaid
showed before them a writing signed by James FitzGerald, Edward Fitz-
Gerald and James Terrell tending somewhat to the explanation of some
points contained in the general order and award made by them and others
abovementioned between the said Teig and his brother Charles, the tenor
of which writing is:

Whereas, uppon the order past by Sir James FitzPiers, James Terrell,
Gerald fitzPhillip and Edward fitzGerald, arbitrators chosen indifferentlie by Teig Oge O Doyne and Charles O Doyne his brother for and
concerninge the question and difference betwixt them for the Countrie
and Cantred of Iregaine, and where in the layinge downe of som particulers incerted by them touchinge the said order, some question and
doubt is made of their meaning and layinge downe in the said matter
which as then was ordered and concluded by the said aribtrators; the
point wherof doubtfullie as is thought resting uppon the surrender
made before the devision, whether of them should have done it. The

---

59 A blank in MS here. The word *corkesur* (*coirce samhraidh?* : 'summer oats') is
restored from a second transcript of these articles, found at pp. 387-9 of the MS.

full truth and meaninge by the said arbitrators was and is that first the surrender should be made by Teige whoe had precedence in yeares to doe the same, before which surrender he should enter into bond of a thousand pounds to his brother Charles Doyne that within tenn daies after the patent had been Foorth to make an sure and indefeasible estate such as the learned Councell of the said Cahir should advise to the said Cahir and his heyres male of the fourth part of all the lands, tenements and hereditaments and all other the profitts, seniories and comodities of the said countrie of Iregaine unto the said Cahir and his heyres males as aforesaid, the remainder over for want of Charles is heyres males backe againe to Teige and his heyres. Note that all the Castles in the said Countrie was reserved to be in speciall to Teig withoute division and nothing els. But Cahir was to have a fourth part of all the rest, accordinge as further the same appeareth in the said order more at lardge, which was the meaninge of the said arbitrators and of myself in speciall and hereunto for the more explaininge hereof have for that part hereunto subscribed my hand. Xth of Septembre, 1607. James fitzGerrald: Edward fitzGerrald: James Terrell.

In witness whereof as well the jurors above mentioned as also the Commissioners above mentioned have to theise presents interchangeablie put to their seales the day and year first above written.

    Henrie Power.   William Parsons
                                          Supervisor generalis
    Robert Piggott.

COMMISSION, 3 JULY 1607, FOR TAKING OF INQUISITION

James by the grace of god kinge of England Scotland Fraunce and Ireland defender of the faith, etc. To Our Right trustie and welbeloved Sir Richard Wingfield, knight marshall of our Armie and kingdome of Ireland. Sir Henrie Power, knight, Sir Thomas Coche, knight, William Parsons, Esquier, surveyor generall of our possessions in our said kingdome of Ireland, Nicholas Kennye, Esquier, Escheator of our province of Lenster, Robert Pigott, Esquier, Alexander Barrington, Esquier and Piers Ovington, Esquier, and to everie of them Greetinge. Knowe yee that wee, reposinge speciall trust in your Care, dilligence and Circumspections, have nominated, constituted and appoynted you to any three or more of you, whereof we will that you the said Sir Richard Wingfeild, our Surveyor or Escheator to be alwaies one, to be our Commissioners. And doe hereby give unto

yow or any three or more of yow as aforesaid full power and authoritie
to enquier as well by the oathes of good and lawfull men as by all other
good waies and meanes whatsoever what Castles, Mannors, lands, tenements
and hereditaments Teig O Doyne of Tenahinsye in the Queenes Countye,
Charles O Doyne of Dublin, Esquier, Elizabeth fitz Gerrald alias Doyne,
widowe, Barnaby alias Brian O Doyne of the Brittas, Donell mcCormocke
O Doyne, Jhon mcTerlaghe O Doyne of Kilkevan, Brien mcRorie O Doyne
of Cowlenapisse, Brian mcRorie mcDavid of Ballintagart, Pa[trick] mcFirr
of Clownhine, Mortagh mcOwen of the Parke, Dermott mcOwen of the
same, Cahir mcLeynaghe of the same, Jhon mcDonoughe O Doyne of
Cowillmoran, Mortaghe mcHughe of Killmaccragdare, Cahir mcOwhnie
of Cloyniga, Neile mcDermott of Clownagheduffe, Edmond mcJames of
Capullcauaghe, Morish mcCarroll of the same, William Reoghe of Castel-
bracke, Donoughe Duffe mcDermott of the same, Moroughe mcCahir of
Monyquid, William mcRossa of Cloinga, William mcEdmond of Monyquid,
Donoughe mcMorishe of Srathecullen, Melaghlen mcOwen of Cappillane,
Lauras mcDermott of Tenyll, William mcLaurence of the same, Art
mcDonoughe O Doyne of the Gurtine, William mcDavid of the Carrally,
Rossa mcNeyle of the same, Patricke mcMortaghe of the same, David
mcMortaghe of Dyrilymeoge, Teige mcWilliam of the same, Brian O
Moloyne of the Rine, Owen, mcDavid of the Carrawlly, Patricke mcShane
of the same, Neyle mcRorie of the same, David mcNeile of the same,
Jhon mcDavid of the same, Edmond Oge mcEdmond Oge mcEdmond
of the same, Mortaghe mcBrian of the same, James O Moloyne of the Rine,
Edmond mcMulmorie of the Cappaghe Roe, Malaghlen mcShane of the
Graigge, Mortaghe McMoroughe of the Clareghell, Teige mcOwen of
Cappanagraigge, William Glass mcRorie of Graiggeafolla, Hugh mcShane
of the same, Owen mcMelaghlen of Sratheullen, Mortaghe mcWilliam of
the same, Donoughe mcMorishe of Cawillvonine, William O Divoye of
the same, Dermott mcMorishe of the same, William mcMorishe of Rerimore, Mortaghe O Doine of Cuilivoholan, Dermott Reoghe mcFinn of
the same, David mcDonoughe of the Brockaghe, Edmond mcMortaghe
of the same, Rorie mcMelaghlen of the Skarrowne, Rorie mcMoroughe
of the same, James mcCarroll of Sraduffe, Patricke mcRorie of the same,
Patricke mcMorishe of the same, Rorie mcShane of Lackaghbegge, Morishe
mcDonnell of Sraduffe, Donell mcMortaghe of Lackaghbegge, Edmond
mcDonoughe of Ballekenine, Owen mcShane of the same, Moroughe
mcCahir of the same, Jhon mcEdmond of the same, David mcRorie of
Ballintagart, Knoghor mcMorishe of Sharrechowne, Piers mcCarroll of
Killmanvane, Knoghor Duffe mcHughe of the Skarrowne, Donnoughe
mcDonnoughe of the same, Pat: mcDavid of the Brockaghe, Dermott
mcTeige of Srathcullen, Melaghlen mcRorie of Killmanvane, Dermott
mcCulemie of Killmanvan, Rorie mcOwen of Dromnebehie, Owney
mcDonoughe of Killockandronyc, Rorie mcTeg of Clowinkilly, Dermott
mcRorie of Garroughe, William mcTeig of the same, Tyrelaghe mcMulmora
of Dyrylemoge, Rorie mcFirr of Clownaghe, Cowlema mcTeig of Rery-

begg, David mcEdmond of Balykinine, Dermott mcEdmond of Carrile, Owen O Moloyne of the Nerye, Dermott O Moloyne of the Cappaghebegge, Edmond O Moloyne of the same, Teig mcArt of the Dyrry, Tirrelaghe mcArt O Doyne of the same, Rorie Oge mcRorie mcSkayne[1], Dermott Oge mcDermott, Donnoughe mcEdmond O Doyne, Shane mcDonoughe mcEdmond, Patricke Duffe O Moleyne, Morishe Duffe O Moloyne, Rorie mcConnor O Moloyne, Owen mcCahir O Doyne, Shane mcTeig O Doyne and Shane Revaghe mcCuratha of Syanebegge, and everie or any of them are lawefullie seised of in demeasne and possession or in cheiffry and service or wherein the said Teig O Doyne, Charles O Doyne and the rest of the personnes abovenamed or any of them joyntelie or severallie can make any other good and lawfull Claime or tytle eyther by course of discent from any of his or their Ancestors or according to the Irish Custome of Tanistrie or by his or their owne good and lawfull purchase or otherwise. And what estate, right or tytle the said Teige O Doyne, Charles O Doyne and other the personnes abovenamed have or any of them had in or to the premisses or any part thereof. And of what quantitie the said Castles, mannors, lands, tenements, hereditaments and premisses with the appurtenaunces are accordinge to the number of plowghe lands, quarters or acres or any other measure used in the Queenes Countie aforesaid. And what are the certaine limitts, meares and bounds of all and singuler the premisses and howe much thereof the personnes above- named and everie of them have in demeasne and how much in services, and of what yearlie value the same premisses and everie of them are. And of what lord or lords the same and everie of them are holden and by what tenures, rents, duties, Customes or services. And what other Freehoulders, tenaunts or occupiers have or ought to have any estate, tytle or interest in them or any of them. And what estate or estates such other Free- houlders, tenaunts or occupiers have or ought to have in them or any of them. And what Customes, services, rents or duties the said Free- houlders, tenaunts or occupiers doe or ought to yealde to us for the same. And what rents, Customes, duties or services they or any of them have or ought to have yealded and paid to the said Teige O Doyne, Charles O Doyne and the rest before named and to everie of them sythence the establishment of our Composicion in that Countie. And what parcell and howe much of the premisses are in the severall possessions or occupacions of everie of the personnes above named. And further to enquiere howe longe the said Castles, mannors, lands, tenements and hereditaments and other the premisses have continued to the possession of the said Teige O Doyne, Charles O Doyne and other personnes before named or any of their aunccestors or of others whose estate they nowe have. And further to enquier of all such other points and circumstances concerninge the premisses as yow or any three or more of yow as aforesaid shall thinke meete and Convenient. And of your doinges herein to certefie us in

---

1. Sic.

our highe Courte of Chauncery *in Quindena Michaelis* next ensuinge the date hereof or before. Provided allwaies that yow our said Commissioners or any three or more of yow as aforesaid doe within the space of fourteene daies at the least before the executinge of this Comission give direction unto the Shiriffe of the Countie in which the land lyeth that he make or cause to be made proclamation inopen markett in the next markett towne adjoyning to the lands mencioned in this Comission of the tyme and place of the execution thereof. And to this end wee Comaund all mayors, sheriffes, bailiffes, constables and all other our lovinge subjects that to yow and everie of yow in the execution of the premisses they be obedient and assistant as becometh. In Wittnes wee have caused these our letters to be made Patents. Wittnes our Right trustie and welbeloved Councellor Sir Arthure Chichester, knight, our deputie generall of our Realme of Ireland, at Dublin, the third daie of July in the fifth yeare of our Raigne of England, France and Ireland and of Scotland the fortieth kinge.

DEED OF THADEUS OR TEIG O DOYNE TO HIS SON CAHIR OR CHARLES (1595?)

In Dei nomine Amen. Omnibus ad quos presentes littere pervenerint Thadeus O Doine alias O Doine alias O Doyn, Capitaneus de Oregan, salutem in Christo sempiternam. Sciatis me prefatum Tadeum dedisse, concessisse et hac presenti charta mea dare et concedere meo dilecto filio Carolo alias Cahir O Doyn in artibus magistro prehabit*a* sufficient*e* et matura deliberacione totum tenementum seu villam Nachulacha in parochia de Tuaghe Smertha in predicta Oregan ac triginta accras terre arabilis ad predictum tenementum seu villam pertinentes. Habenda et gaudenda et annuatim percipienda a me omnibusque meis heredibus et assignatis predictum tenementum cum triginta predictis accris prefato Carolo alias Cahir suisque heredibus et assignatis inperpetuum cum omnibus et singulis suis pratis et meduis, pascuis, aquis, aquarum cursibus, boscis, suboscis, silvis, grunnis, nemoribus, atriis, aliisque *quibuscunque comoditatibus et pertinentiis, libere, quiete et pacifice sine aliquo onere ordinario sive extraordinario, homagio, servicio, exactione, demanda *quibuscunque, in tam ampliis modo et forma prout melius potest concedi aut tribui. Ac ulterius ego predictus Tadeus dedi, concessi, confirmavi, ac presenti Charta mea do, concedo et confirmo predicto meo filio Carolo alias Cahire tenementa in Riremore in predicta Oregan in parte templi orientalis sita et collocata, cum quadraginta accris in predicta Riramore. Habenda, gaudenda et annuatim percipienda a mei omnibus [que] meis heredibus et assignatis predicta tenementa in Riramore ac predictas xl

accras cum Coill Chrubin ...^{2} videlicet, xvi acras *filiorum^3 successorum et heredum Thadei Y Alaguin pariter et Donaldi Brondi alias Domhnaill Guinn hi Alagain, silicet accras ix illas liberas sine aliquo onere ordinario vel extraordinario, et xiiii accras mic Comaill de eadem cognacione, et alias octo accras de feudis propriis Wllielmi Mic Moiris, cum quatuor accris in Correile, ac cum suis integris particulis et portionibus universis liberisque consuetudinibus in Coyllchrubin, Iosgarta Failghe et Pollach Rire Moir Ite et Conmaithe [?] aliisque silvis, meduis, pascuis, nemoribus, grunnis, cum omnibus suis commoditatibus et pertinentiis quibuscunque. Ac etiam do, concedo et warrantizo quinque accras terre arabilis in Garrdha Cnaigin in Mointeach, parte aquilonali et orientali feudi na Sgethi Cuirrthe cum omnibus suis pasturis, silvis, nemoribus et pertinentiis prefato Carolo alias Caher O Doyne suisque heredibus et assignatis imperpetuum unacum omnibus aliis predictis tenementis et feudis sine aliqua seu omni revocatione. Ac etiam ego predictus Thadeus O Doine predictas omnes et singulas donaciones et concessiones, videlicet, na gCulach, Rira Mor, Garrdha Cnaighin [   ]^4 warrantizabo ac defendam prefato meo filio Carolo alias Caher suisque heredibus assignatis imperpetuum. Provisse semper quod si contigerit predictum Carolum alias Cahir predictas Naculcha, Riramore, Baile mic Cnaighin, alias Garrdha Cnaighin in toto vel eorum particula jure aut facto privare, tunc presentis Charte tenore do et concedo prefato Carolo alias Cahir equivalentem porcionem illius partis private seu ammesse ex feudis per me concessis in Cuilic an Abhall *et* Baile Garbain meo filio Mauricio alias Muircertach O Doyn. In cuius Rei fidem et testimonium presenti Charte sigillum meum cum manuale subscriptione datum
Anno Domini 1559.^{5} T
                                         D

Sealed and delivered in presence of those whose names doe ensue:

Tady Doine.	Cormocke Doyne
By me Barnaby O Doine	
Edmondus Brien Curatus	Shane m^{c}Moroughe is marke.
de Rossenolisse testis	Carolus m^{c}Morishe vicarius
ad hoc rogatus et	de Oregan testis ad hoc
requisitus.	rogatus et requisitus.

---

2 Two indecipherable signs, probably representing the clerk's attempt at reproducing Gaelic contractions which he did not understand. I can make nothing of them.

3 *filorum* MS.

4 Blank in MS.

5 *Sic. Recte* 1595?

SETTLEMENT BY TEIG O DOYNE IN FAVOUR OF HIS SONS, 20 JULY 1593

To all Christian people to whom theise presente writing shall come, I, Teige O Doyne, *alias* O Doine, Captaine of Oregan send greetinge in the Lord everlastinge. Whereas heretofor often variances have risen amongst my predecessors of the O Doines as competitours for the Captainry or Cheifery of the said Countrie commonly called Oregain, whereabie eftsomes it came to passe that he obtained the name of O Doine which could wynn the same by the stronger hand and force of armes. Wherefor I the said Teig for avoyding the occasions that might hereafter nourish anie such controversie amongst myne owne issue and posteritie, and seinge that accordinge the auncient custome of the said Countrie I could not make an estate of inheritance of the said Captainry to any of my sonnes and his heirs by lineall descente without great inconvenience and danger of him to whom such an estate should be made when the rest of my sonnes should perceive themselves to be putt beside the name of O Doine contrary to the custom of the said Oregane. And consideringe allso that ther is none remanent of my nation that would seek the said captainry after me, Thought good for the said considerations to make assurance of the said Captainry and the manners, Castles and lands belonging unto it unto my sonnes Teige, Cormocke, Brian, Cahir and Mortogh successively by course of the eldershipp and senioritie to succeed to the said Captainry and name of O Doine during the life of everie of them, excepting such portion of my landes and rentes which I intende to assure to everie of my said sonnes in severaltie to live by, which my intent I communicate to my said sonnes before the perfection of this writing: Know ye therefor that I the said Teig O Doine *alias* O Doine as well for the said considerations as for the naturall love which I beare unto my said sonnes, and being desirous *that all my land and chiefery should remaine for and hereafter in them and their heyres after such a manner as doth resemble the custome of the said Oregane, have given and graunted and by these presents doo give and graunt unto my said sonnes Cormocke, Brian, Cahir and Mortagh, all the Captainry, Chiefry or Lordship of the said Oregaine, the townes, mannors and Lordships of Castlebrak and Tenahinshe and the quarters, landes, tenements, segniories, rents and customes belonging to the said Castlebrak and Tenahins, the wooddes of Mucluain and the Forraies, All and singular the Castells, edifices, rents, reversions, moores, medowes, parkes, pastures, stones, quarries, Iron mynes, woods, underwoods, milles, rivers, waters, locks, bogges, mountaines, comodities, jurisdictions, liberties and customes, which I have enyoide or held or belonge the name of O Doine and Cheiftaine of the said Oregain, excepting such lands and tenements as I intend to assure to everie one of my said sonnes and ther heyers in particular as portions to live by. To have and to hold all and singular the premises to the said

Cormocke, Brian, Cahir and Mourtagh and their heyers and assignes for ever to the purpose in this writinge hereafter expressed. And I the said Teige *alias* O Doine, my heyers and assignes shall warrant and defend all and singular the premises unto the said Cormocke, Brian, Cahir and Mortaugh, their heyers and the heyers of everie of them against all person and persons forever. And I the said Teige *alias* O Doine have made and perfected this feoffment to the use and intente that the said feoffees and the survivor and survivors of them during his and ther lief or lives, and after the decease of the survivor of them their heyers and assignes, shall stand seised of all and singular the premises (except before excepted) to the use of me the said Teige *alias* O Doine for tearme of my lieff and after my death to the use of my son Teige O Doine during his lief and after him to the use of the said Cormocke and after to the use of the said Brian during his lif and after him to the use of the said Cahir during his life and after him to the use of the said Mortaugh during his liefe. And after him to the use of the son and heyer of the said Teige during his life, and after him to the use of the son and heyer of the said Cormocke[6] and after him to the use of the son and heyer of the said Cahir, and after him to the use of the son and heyer of the said Murtough. And so successively by course of their eldershipp to the issue male of my said five sonnes onne after an other during their lives. And after them to the use of my heyers in generall. Provided allwaies and it [is] my intent that the said feoffees shalbe seised of all and singular the premises uppon this condition, that if any of my said sonnes Teige, Cormocke, Brian, Cahir or Mortaugh, their heyers or the heyers of any of them shall either doe, procure or suffer to be done anie arte or thinge for defeating, altering or taking away anie of the premises contrary to the said deede of feoffment and the said uses, that then such of my sonnes and his heyers shall immediately after such an acte don loose and forfait the said two townes of Castlebreake and Tinehinsie with all and singular the lands belonging unto them to the rest of my sonnes and their heyers in manner in the said deede and uses specified. And I the said Teige *alias* O Doine by these presents have made and constituted the said Cormock, Brian, Cahir and Murtaugh or him whom they will agree upon and authorish or the survivor or survivors of them my lawfull attorney or attornies to surrender all and singular the premises unto the Queene's Majestie, her heyers and successors, and the same to be againe by Letters Pattente to me and myne heyers accordinge the intent and purposes in the said feoffment expressed. In witness whereof I the said Teige *alias* O Doyn have hereunto putt my hand and selae the xxth of July 1590.[7] Dated in the quarter of the Monteaghe within the parishe of Rossanolaies.

O Doines $\begin{smallmatrix} T \\ D \end{smallmatrix}$ marke

---

6 The name of the third son, Brian, seems to have been omitted by the copyist.
7 *Sic. Recte* 1593.

Present when the said Teige *alias* O Doine sealed and delivered this writing and delivered livery and seisin accordinge the contents unto the said feoffees the said daie and yeare: Bernaby mcRorie O Doine: Daui mcEoghaine's marke: Conchur Moylle O Molloine's marke.

LETTERS OF TADY DOYNE TO HIS BROTHER CHARLES, 1606

Brother, for endinge our variance by friendly course if it stand with your likinge I will this afternone at ii of the Clocke meate yow when yow please and will bringe thether two or three loving gent*lemen* and a layer that shalbe nothing partiall but very lovinge to us both. And I pray doe yow the licke and then lett us make choise of four of them. And so to god I leave yow and doe expecte your awnswer by the bearer. At my lodging the iiiith of February 1606.

    Your very loving Brother   Tady Doine.

To my very lovinge brother mr. Charles Doine theise.

Brother, I have written to Sir James and my Cossen Terell to repaire accordinge the forme of your letter and Sir Edwards and then wilbe at Kildare if I may possible and in the meane tyme I wish to yow as to myself. Castlebrak. the xvii of March 1616.[8]

    Your very loving Brother
                Tadie Doyne.

To my worshipfull good brother mr. Charles Doine theise.

Brother, I have not only conferred with myne owne Counsell but allso with others. And the resolucion that he gave me is that the obligacion drawen do differ much from the order, first, for the yt is not in me before the surrender to make an assured estate in all and yf I would, that the remainder by the order lefte to me is Cleare gon and yf it please yow which is not so meant by the order and that lickwise yow maie putt me from the beneffytt of the advantadge of the first obligacion and

---

8 *Sic. Recte* 1606.

withall that the date of the last drawen obligacion is not limitted within the compasse of the time formerlie limitted and that still yow maie if yow list take halt if any forfeyture therbe as yow alledge alredie. I make no doubt that yow intend any such hard Course by cause they are unnaturall and unconscionable, therefore I praie let us joyne to surrender, and the estate beinge setled in me I will take it uppon my salvacion that as my meaninge is nowe to make good unto yow in full som all that is imported in the order, that after the surrender I will accomplishe the same and ame now content to inter unto bond to fullfill the same. Also as light is given me, if I should passe the last obligacion drawen by yow in form as it is, it were unpossible for me but to forfeit it, and as I have setled my mynde in all sinceritie and love toward yow so I praie let it goe forward and hould an even course in the like measure unto me. I would have gone to yow myself this morninge but that my shooe was cutt over my Toe and therefore could not goe drie. And so wishinge to yow as to myself I end. St. Patricks this present sundaie.

Your assured loving brother
Tady Doyne.

For my verie lovinge brother Mr. Charles Duinn theise. D.D.

ORDER OF LORD DEPUTY AND COUNCIL, 15 FEBRUARY 1607/8

Decimo quinto die February Anno regni domini nostri Jacobi die gratia Anglie etc. quinto et Scotie xlẗ^o coram Arthuro Chichester milite domino deputato Hibernie et aliis Commissionariis.

Uppon longe debating of the matter in controversie touchinge the surrender of Teige O Doine Esqr. and Charles O Doine Esqr. of the Chiefries and of the Territories and Countrie of Iregan it is ordered that the said Charles O Doine shall befor the feast daie of Easter now next Comming make an instrument in writing purpartinge a division in four partes to be devided of the said Cheiferies, lands, Tenements, medowes, pastures, woods, underwoods, moores, bogges and moyntaines of the Countrie of Iregan. And the said Teige thereuppon shall make and have his election first of two partes of the said four and the said Charles shall secondly have and make his election of the third parte for his porcion and the said Teige to have the said fourth parte. And it is further ordered that the surrender of the said Teige and Charles shalbe accepted of their severall partes and his highnes letters uppon their surrenders shalbe graunted to the said Teige. And further the said Teige shall enter into a statute stapple of the som of Two Thousand pounds Irish to make a good and perfecte estate unto the said Charles and the heyres males of his body lawfully begotten or to be begotten dischardged of all incumberances of the third parte that shall be chosen by the said Charles as by the Councell learned in the lawes of the said Charles shalbe devised or advised. And it is further ordered that the statute stapple that shalbe entred into as afforesaid shalbe delivered to the right honnourable the lord deputie to remaine with his Lordship to the intent that advantadge maie not be taken uppon nice exceptions but uppon the substanciall breache of this order. And uppon the making of a good and perfecte estate by the said Teige to the said Charles and the heyers males of his body as afforesaid the said Statute shalbe forth Cancelled, made voyde and dischardged.

Johannes Cottell. Cler. surrender.
Copia Vera.

NOTE BY TADIE DOYNE OF HIS LANDS, AND COVERING LETTER, 20 MARCH 1607/8

Brother, I have sent yow here underwritten the not of my landes and therefor would have yow to make the division forth yf it may be to thend I might dispatch home now in sowinge tyme. And so to God I leave you this present Twesdaie.

Your lovinge Brother yf you will
Tadie Doyne.

In Castlebrak 120 a. Thother 120 are thus: — 80 a. in Parkemore gotten by myself, 30 a. in Cappacloughan and thother 30 that is in the Srade and that belongeth to Dermott mcJames and the rest that my father when he gave me the lands befor good wittnesses did exempt from his gifte.
In Ballimonyn 60 a.
In Achauam 20 a.
In Balligarvan 240 a.[9]
In Lackaghemore 30 a.
In Moniquid 7 a.
In Tennehinsie and Achamore 94 a.

---

9 xii^{xx}, certainly an error of the copyist.

In Cappabrogan 50 a.
In Farran Claufyn 20 a.
and in Cnock korecloghan 5 a.
Coillvickanowall and Achauacrossie 24 a.

Brother, I repaired purposely from Dublin in hope that som end may be taken concearning our affayres. Therefor I thought good to pray you that if greater occasions doe not lett you, to meet me uppon Twesdaie next aboute none at the Moate of Balligarvan that we may consulte together what is best to be done. From Ballicowline this present Sondaie, the 20th of Marth, 1607.
Lett me understand with speed your resolucion herin.

> Your lovinge brother
> Charles Duinn.

I am occasioned that daie uppon a matter as I can not then mete and when after the hollidayes yow will I will mete yow and untill then I rest your lovinge Brother

> Tady Doyne.

To my loving Brother Mr. Tady Doyn.

VALUATION OF THE 'DUTIES' IN KIND

Note concearning the partition following:

I have reduced the severall Dueties found by office belonging to the Chiefry of the territorie of Iregan in the Queene's Countie to a supposed value in money as they were usually rated, *vizt.*

A Beoffe	30s	ster.
A Cake of bread	1s	ster.
A Cronock of oates	4d	
A Dish of Butter, *alias*		
12 quartes, and 3 pints to a quarte	6s	
A kearne of malte, *alias*		
a pecke of malte	4s	
A plough worke *per diem*	2s	
A ripping hoocke *per diem*	6d	

A horse load of drink   10s
One quarter of a beoffe   5s

The cause whie I allowe more acres of arrable land to the 3rd parte
than to anie of the rest of the partes in the division following is by reason
that the first & 2nd partes hath a castle, a hall, orchardes, etc, added unto
them which the 3rd parte wanteth and the 4th parte hath more pasture
and wood than the 3rd parte by 256 a.

SCHEDULE OF THE DIVISION OF THE LANDS AND CHIEFRIES

A Division into 4 partes of the landes and
Chiefries in suite between Tadie Doyne
and Charles Doyne.

The First Parte.

The Castle at the towne of Castle brake, the hall, the parlour at thend
of the hall, the kitchen, the brewehouse, the Backhouse and the rest
of the houses within the Bawn, the haggart and Barnes on the south
syde of the castle, the garden, the orchard, the parke, the stable and the
houses for Cattell on the west syde; and also the houses and tenements
for tenants and other uses situated on the north and west partes of the
said towne of Castle bracke in the territorie of Iregan.

And 60 a. of arrable land in the lande and fieldes of Parkemore northward of the said Castle. And 10 a. counted for erable land in the one
moytie of the wood of Mucluain lying next to Belaclone. And 70 a. of
erable land in these following parcells of landes, *viz.* in the land betweene
the west syde of Ballinnovin and the east syde of the Parkemore and the
Bater which leadeth from the said Castle to the town of the Parke; the
south end of which land reached to the towne greene; certaine fields
thereof are called Fiaghebegge, Fiaghemore, Crossinagha. And the fields
and lands called Achatry   caoynain, otherwise lying northward of the
Batir and highway leading from the said Castle to Killiffy and southwest of the said Parkemore. And the land lying betweene the said Achachaynaine and the fountain called Tobar differnan, called Kapahinellin.
And the landes which ly westward of the said Castle and do yoine to
the west end of the said Park and to the south syde of the said Kapahinellin
and are extended in length hard by the west syde of the great Batir that
goeth to Mucluain and lyeth southwest of the said Castle, and which

meareth at their south end with Iskirre granisie, which land also is called Feran an muarreduiffe, westward of the said Bater leading to Mucluain. And the land called the Grainsagh land *alias* Feraine ne gransie, lying southward of the said Iskirry gransea and reaching to the bogge which is on the south syde of the said Castle. Which several parcells of land and the lands of the said Parkemore and Mucluain hath 43 a. of pasture and bogge lying in the quarter of Castle brak, etc. (140a).

And [   ] [10] a. of arable called the Lauaghmore[11], westward of the said Castle about a caliver's shott, and 10 a. of pasture and bogge in the quarter of Moincuid, etc. (30 a.)

And 10 a. of arable land and 3⅓ a. in the village of Cloncaddow and in the quarter of Clancomey, etc.

And the rents, customes and dueties issuing from these severall quarters in the said territory, *vizt.* The quarter of Boell *per annum;* 4s Irish, 2 beoves, 24 Cronockes of oats, 4 quarters of a beoff, 3 horseloads of drinke or in lieu thereof 52 barrins of wheate, 4s for meat for horseboys.

One quarter in Mointagh melicke; 2 beoves, 24 Cronockes of oates, 24 Cakes of bread, 8 dishes of butter, one hoocke in harvest, one plough-daie in winter sowing uppon everie 20 a. and one daie in summer sowing, and 4s for diett of horseboys.

The quarter of Ballikenine *per annum;* 2 beoves, 24 Cronockes of oates, 12 Cakes of bread, 4 dishes of butter, one hook in harvest out of everie 20 a., one ploughdaie in winter sowing, 4s for meate of horseboys.

The quarter of Clannmachow *per annum;* 20d Irish, 2 beoves, 24 Cronockes of oates, 12 Cakes of bread, 4 dishes of butter and for diett of horseboyes 4s.

The quarter of the Dyrry; 2 beoves, 24 Cronockes of oats, and for diett of horseboys 4s.

The quarter of Castlebrak; a penny for every acre of arrable land *per annum* of the said acres, and 11½d upon 11½ a. in the quarter of Moynecuid.

And the fourth part of all such heriotts as doe belonge to O Doine as

---

10 Blank in MS.

11 *Recte* *Laccaghmore.

do appertaine to the chiefry of the said territorie of Iregan.

The summ of the acres inserted to this first parte:
of arable land 130 a.
of pasture and bogge 56⅓ a.

The summe of the chiefry allotted to this first parte according as it is reduced to a supposed value in silver ...   £31: 7s: 9½

The second Parte

The Castle of Tenahinsie, the hall, the chamber in thend of the hall, the stone wall of an hall which yoyneth to the Castle, the kitchin, the brewhouse, the backhouse, the stable, the porter's lodging and all the houses within the bawn, the two gardens, the 3 orchards, the parke and the meddow at the south side of the Castle, the myll and all the houses on theaste syde of the river of the Barrow in the towne and fields of Tenahinsie, etc.

And 20 a. of arable land hard by the said Castle northwest of it in the fields of Achawore and 60 a. in pasture and 20 a. of wood in the quarter of Killnegrallagha, etc. (20 a.).

And 20 a. of arrable land, 30 a. of pasture and 30 a. of woodd in the village and fields of Achanacrossie and Cowlickanawall and in the quarter of Dyrrie, etc. (20 a.).

And 43 a. of arrable land and 59 a. of pasture and bogge and 27 a. of wood in the town and fields of Rirybegge and in the quarter of Rirybegge. (43 a.)

And 6 a. of arable land, 2 a. of pasture and bogge in the towne and fields of Moynecuid and in the quarter of the said Moynecuid. (6 a.)

And 20 a. of arrable land and 6⅓ a. of pasture and bogg in the towne and fields of Lawagh and in the quarter of Monicuid. (20 a.)

And 60 a. of arable land and 12 a. of pasture and 3 a. of meddow in the towne and fields of Ballimonine and in the quarter of Clancoevy. (60 a.)

And 6 a. of arable land, 12 a. of bogg and pasture and 6 a. of wood in the towne and fields of Gary Camagh [?] in the Mointeach Milicke. (6 a.)

And 5 a. of arable land and 5 a. of pasture and woodd in the towne and fields of Lackagh in the quarter of the said Lackagh. (5 a.)

And the rentes, customes and dueties issuing out of theise quarters followinge, *viz.*

The quarter of Rirymore *per annum;* 8s Irish, 2 beeves, 24 Cronockes of oates, 40 Cakes of breade, 13 dishes of butter, 18 Carnes of malt, one hooke in harvest out of every 20 a., one ploughdaie in winter sowinge and one day in sommer sowing, 4s for meat of horseboys.

The quarter of Rirribegge *per annum;* 10s Irish, 2 beeves, 24 Cronockes of oats, 12 Cakes of bread, 6 Carnes of malte and 4s for diett of horseboyes.

The quarter of Killnegrallagh *per annum;* 2 beoves, 24 Cronocks of oats and for diett of horseboyes 4s.

The quarter of Clonhine; a marke in mony, 2 beoves, 6 dishes of butter, 18 Cakes of breade, 24 Cronockes of oates.

And 18s 4½d upon 219½ a. in the quarter of Clanconwey, from which charge the 20 a. of Achauayne to be freed.

And the fourth part of all the heriotts, etc.

The summe of the acres of this second parte (besydes the said Castle of Tenahinsie, etc.):
> of arable land 180 a.
> of pasture and bogge 189⅓ a.
> of woodd 83 a.

The summe of the Chiefry allotted to the second part, etc. ...
> £31: 7s: 9½d ster.

The third Parte.

60 a. of arable land, 120 a. of mountaine and pasture and 60 a. of wood in the fields and towne of Bualyanumarre *alias* Tinehinsie and the houses which are seated in the east syde of the river called the Barrow in the said Tinnehensie *alias* Bualianuamair and in the quarter of Bualyanuamare. (60a.)

And 20 a. of arable land, 26 a. of Bogge and 14 a. of woodd in the towne and fields of Achauey and in the quarter of Rirribegge. (20 a.)

And a certaine parcell of land called the Iland of Loghduffe in the quarter of Rirribegge, valued at 4 a. of arable land. (4 a.)

And 30 a. of arable land and 20 a. of pasture and bogge and 5 a. of wodd in the fields of Naculacha and in the quarter of Clancurrall. (30 a.)

And 20 a. of arable land and 5 a. of pasture in the hamletts and fields of Achauaine and in the quarter of Clancowey. (20 a.)

And all the houses and tenements lying in the east and southeast sydes of the Castle, bawn and hall of the towne of Castlebrake, and 15 a. of arable land in the fields lying betweene the said towne of Castlebrake and the said Achavane. And 5 a. joyning to the east syde of the said Achanahaha in the fields and lands called the Grangcorr. (20a.)

And 15 a. in the towne and fields of Kappanliug lying between the said Castletowne and the Cappaulcannagh, which 15 a. of Fohananhaha and the 5 a. in Graige and theise 15 a. of Kappanluig hath of Commons, pasture and bogge 13 a. in the quarter of Castlebrake. (15 a.)

And 20 a. of arrable land lying in Lenith[?] hard by the east syde of the said bater which goeth southward from the said Castlebracke to Iskyrne Gransy, which land on his east syde yoineth to a bater lyding westward of the towne and fields of the said Capanliuge in the quarter of Castlebrake. (20 a.)

And a certaine parcell of land or woodd commonlie called the Forest woodd *alias* Kayllnifarase worth by estimation 21 a. of arable land. (21 a.)

And 30 a. of arable land, 30 a. of pasture and bogge and 5 a. of woodd belonging to the towne and fields of Balligarvaine and in the quarter of Clancorrall. (30 a.)

And 10 a. counted for arrable land in the one moytie of the woodd of Mucluaine lying next Bellana nachaine.

And the rentes, customes and dueties arrising out of these quarters in the said Oregaine, *viz:*

Out of one quarter of Mointeagh Milicke which is next to the west syde of the river called the Barrow and where the Malones doe dwell; 2 beoves, 24 Cronocks of oates, 24 Cakes of breade, 8 dishes of Butter, one plowedaie in winter sowing and one daie in sommer sowing, and one hooke in harvest out of every 20 a., 4s for meate of horseboys *per annum.*

And the quarter of Sraliagh *per annum;* 2 beoves, 24 Cronocks of oates, 12 Cakes of breade, 4 dishes of butter, one hooke in harvest out of everie 20 a., one ploughdaie in winter sowing and one daie in sommer sowing, 4s for meate of horseboyes.

And the quarter of Corbolie *per annum;* 2 beoves, 24 Cronockes of oates, 12 Cakes of breade, 4s for diett of horseboyes, 18 Cakes of breade and 6 dishes of butter.

And the quarter of Tenyll *per annum;* 2 beoves, 24 [Cronocks] of oats, 12 Cakes of breade, 4 dishes of butter and for diett of horseboys 4s.

And the quarter of Clanworchow *per annum;* 10s Irish, 2 beoves, 24 Cronocks of oates and for diett of horseboyes 4s.

And 18s 3½d uppon 180 a. in the quarter of Clancarroll and uppon 29½ a. in the quarter of Monyquid.

And the fourth part of the heriotts due to O Doine or which doe appertaine to the Chiefry of the said Oregan.

The somme of the acres of this third quarter:
        of arable land 240 a.
        of pasture and bogge 189 a.
        of woodd 76 a.

The somme of the Chiefry of this 3rd part, etc. ...   £31: 7s: 9½d.

The fourth Parte.

79 a. of arable land and 158 a. of pasture and bogge and 40 a. and 19 a. of woodd belonging to the said arable land in Moentagh Melicke, *viz.* 20 a. of arable land in Faranclankeine. And 5 a. of arable land in Ardaragh meyly. And 6 a. of arable land in Garriconoughe. And 5 a. of arable land in Cnockachorecloghain. And 5 a. of arable land in Farenkarrellreogh. And 24 a. of arable land in Farengallarard and FerranehiChristine. And 15 a. of arable land in Garri[ ] nayne in the said Monteagh. (79 a.)

And 50 a. of arable land in Rirrimore and 100 a. of pasture and bogge and 50 a. of wood belonging to the said 50 a. of arable land [*viz.* 16a called] Ferandoynny Taighielugaine[12] and Cloynnydonyllduine. And 14 a. called Mecomylly. And 20 a. of arable land called Racomagh and in the quarter of Rirymore. (50 a.)

And 51 a. of arable land, 136 a. of pasture and 58 a. of woode in Cappabrogan and in the quarter of Cappabrogan. (51 a.)

And the rents, customes and dueties issuing out of these quarters following in the said territorie and Countrie, *viz.*

---

12 *Read* *Ferancloynny Taig I Alagaine?   I have restored the words in brackets, omitted in the text.

Out of one quarter of Monteach Melicke; 2 beoves, 24 Cronocks of oates, 24 cakes of breade, 8 dishes of butter, one hoock in harvest out of everie 20 a. and one plowday in winter and one day in sommer sowing, and 4s for meat of horseboyes.

And the quarter of Cappabrogan *per annum;* 2 beoves, 24 Cronocks of oates, 24 Cakes of breade, 8 dishes of butter, one hoocke in harvest out of everie 20 [a.], one plowday in winter sowing and one day in sommer sowing, and for diett of horseboys 4s.

And the quarter of Garough *per annum;* 2 beoves, 24 Cronocks of oats, 24 Cakes of Breade, 8 dishes of butter, one hoocke in harvest out of everie 20 a., one ploweday in winter and one daie in sommer sowing and 4s for diett of horseboys.

And the quarter of Lakcaghe *per annum;* 2 beoves, 24 Cronocks of oates, 12 Cakes of breade 4 dishes of butter and 4s for diett of horseboyes.

And 10s 9½d sterling uppon 129 a. in the quarter of Moynecuid and uppon half an acre in the quarter of Clancowey in the said territorie.

And the fourth parte of everie heriott due to O Doine or which doe appertain to the chiefry of the said territory.

The sum of the acres of this fourth parte:
>   of Arrable land 180 a.
>   of Pasture 394 a.
>   of Woodd 129 a.

The sum of the chiefry of this fourth part according to the reduction, etc. ...   £31: 7s: 9½d

This booke was delivered by the Lord Deputie to Mr. Teige O Doine to be considered of that so he might make his choise this 9th of May 1608.

                         Will. Usher

ORDER OF THE LORD DEPUTY AND COUNCIL, 9 MAY 1608

Novo die maii anno Regni domini Jacob Die gratia Anglie etc. sexto et Scotie xli. Coram Arthuro Chichester milite domino Deputato Hibernie, Thoma Dublinense Cancellario, Jacobo Ley milite capitali justicio Capitalis Placeae dicti domini Regis Hibernie, Nicolao Walshe milite capitali Justicio Communis Banci, Humfrido Monch milite capitali Barone Scaccarii, Olivero St. John milite et Galfrido Fenton milite principalibus secretis Commissariis.

Wheras by a former order made the fiftenth daie of February last past yt was ordered that Charles O Doine should make a booke purporting a division in four partes to be devided of the countrie and cheiferies of Irregan in the Queenes Countie: And forasmuch as the said Charles hath made a booke of the same accordingly, It is therfor now ordered that the said booke of the division afforesaid shalbe delivered unto Teig O Doine Esqr. and he the said Teig is to Consyder of the same and to redeliver the said booke within three dayes then next following, and yf he shall refuse to performe the said former order that then the said Charles shalbe allowed to Choose one parte of three worst partes of the said four and the fourth and best parte shalbe reserved to the said Teige and uppon such Choise to be made by the said Charles he the said Charles shalbe permitted to surrender and to have new letters Pattentes graunted upon the same.

Copia Vera. Jho: Cottell Cler: Surrender:

DEED BY TEIGE O DOINE TO HIS SONS, 18 MAY 1593, AND BOND BY THE SONS, 8 OCTOBER 1593.

Be it knowen unto all men by theise presents to whom this present writing shall com to be reade that I Teige O Doine Cheife of my name did give and hath given my full consents to my sonnes to make and sewe to gett a Pattent or Conveyance uppon this Condition followinge; that my son Teig Oge should have the benefitt of the lordshipp of my countrie during his life and after his decease to my sonn Cormocke and so the three sonnes one after another, and from the laste sonne of my owne Bodie to the eldest son of Teig, to the eldest son of Cormocke, and so to the eldest son of the rest of my other three sonnes which is Brien, Cahir and Mortaghe and so turne in degrees to the second son of each of them, and in default of heyers after them, that the next of my Blood to inyoie their rome, and if in anie meanes that my son Teige hath brought anie other writtinges in my presence and did enforme that the writting was according the contents of this thabove writting and deceaved me in confessing was soe, if it be otherwise then theffecte of this thabove writing I doe protest that it was not my meaning and in proffe wherof I did wish this my entent befor iii or iiii wittnesses iii yeares befor my son Teige brought the writing befor me and all so don putt my hand to theise in presence of those whose names are under written this eightenth of May 1593.

> Teige O Doine + his mark.
> Teige mcMorishe is marke +
> Mortagh mcMorish is marke.
> Arte O Doine is marke.
> Rori duff mcDermott is marke.
> Murtaghe O Doyne's marke.
> Danyell mcShane's marke
> Bernaby mcRorie.
> Connor Moyle O Mullane.
> Davie m^{c}Owen's marke.

Memorandum that whereas the state mad unto us unto the Captainry or Cheifry of Oregan, *viz.* Teige, Cormocke, Brien, Cahir and Murtaghe by our father O Doyne Captaine of the said Oregan is contrie should the lesse take anie effecte or be dayly brought to passe accordinge to our purposes. And in truthe if we had not while tyme servethe be voluntary sticked together and combined against all our adversaries that now are or herafter shall happen to be any way endevoring to crosse us in our lawfull entents to obteine the said Captainry accordinge the manner and order sett downe by the said O Doine our Father as it appeareth more at lardge in his graunt unto us, thought therfor good for the better bringing to passe of this our lawfull purpose severalie and distinctlie to be deposed uppon the Holi Evangelist one to another, that all other several [?] contro-versies settinge aparte and by vertue of theise presentes doe testifie ourselves to be deposed as afforesaid to yoine and combyne together in all lawfull meanes against any adversaries or competitors whatsoever for the obteyning of the said Capteinry according the manner sett downe by our father as above specified, and allsoe by reason the same cannot be impetrated without Chardges, Wee lickwise by vertue of our oaths bind ourselves to contribute to him or to them will sue or obteine the said Capteinry in the maner above specified, *viz.* as followethe, I Cormock iii lib. currant money of England mor then Brian, etc. I, Brian, iii li. lickwise more then Cahir. And Cahir finally in three poundes exceedinge Mortaghe. And howesomever of us the four next specified should happen to disburse his owne mony for the gettinge out of a Pattent of the said Captainry, that if yt should be lawfull for him to distraine upon the rest of us four by the partie distrained upon without any contradiction, suffringe the same accordinge the next progressionable division, and the rest of som in the Suite savinge that to be equallie devided uppon us, and thus to stand in full effecte so that our brother Brian doe consent unto it. In Wittnes wherof we have herunto putt our handes the eight of October 1590.[13]

Murtahe Doyne   Cormocke Doyne

Bernabe Doyne   Charles Doinny

CHANCERY BILL OF TEIGE O DOINE AGAINST HIS SON TEIGE
(1593)

To the Right Honorable the Lord Chaunceellor.

Humblie makethe petition to your hoonorable lordship Teige O Doine of Tenahinsie. Wher your suppliant was seised in his demeane as of fee of the lordshipp, manner, towne and landes of Dowhie o Regaine and beinge so seised hath therof continued for many yeares past seised. And of late yt pleased the aeternall god to bereave your suppliant of his eye sight wherby your suppliant beinge visited by the hand is woorke of god did resolve with himself for the staie and reliefe of his sonnes, beinge in number five, to make som assurance of his little livinge, the cheefe portion and interest wherof he was determined to assigne unto Teige O Duinn the eldest of his sonnes, to whom he purposed the rest of his children to succeede in remaynder and therwithall he pretended to allott unto the rest of his sonnes som competent portions wherby they might have som staie for ther necessarie sustentation and relife. With this his advised and resolute purpose he often did accquaint the said Teige his eldest sonn, who seemed discontented that any allotment or assignment shold be made to either of his brothers of any part of the premisses or that any assurance should be made of the whole unto him otherwise then in course of absolute inheritance. Your suppliant notwithstandinge beinge by naturall instincte as carful of the rest as of the said Teige did persist in his former resolution and for that he would not be removed from that his intention the said Teige his eldest son laboured with one or other of skill to draw an absolute estate and conveyance of all and singular the premisses unto himself and to his heyers from your suppliant, which conveyance being ingroced ready

---

13 *Recte* 1593?

to be perfected was brought about a fortnight past by the said Teige unto your suppliant in the absence of others your suppliant's children, and your suppliant being in his chamber removed from Companye was in thes manner spoken unto by the saod Teige: 'Sir, you desired of a longe tyme to assure your inheritance unto me and that my bretheren should successively after me be interested therin and that som parcell shold be yelded to eache of them in severaltie for their maintenance to live uppon. And howebeit I have byn against this course of assurance and against the dismembringe of your litle livinge, notwithstandinge for that it pleaseth yow to have it soe I have gott out theise conveiances drawn accordinge your meaninge to be by you perfected.' Wherunto your auppliant aunswered that if the conveyances weir mad to that effect he *willingly would perfecte them. And the said Teig most confidently affirminge that the said conveyances were drawen accordinge your suppliant's former intent, and noe other declaration being made unto your suppliant of the trew contents of the said writtings, your suppliant theruppon being to credulus and voyed of all suspicion of the false measure towards him did perfect the said writinges. And theruppon the said Teige desired som few that were in place to keepe the same secrete and your suppliant said: 'It is not hurtefull how few know therof, but lett the rest of your bretheren who are interest with you be mad privie therunto.' Within few dayes after others of your suppliant's children came acquainted with the secrete of this practise and theruppon they repaired unto your suppliant to know of him in what sorte he was induced into perfection of the said conveyances, wherunto your suppliant did awnswer that he did perfecte conveyances accordinge his former resolution, and that if that the conveyances did import any other maner of assurance he would disalow them and manifest his unduetifull practise used towards him, wheruppon your suppliant's said sonnes did assueyr your suppliant that he was deceived and deluded, and they putt beside all staie and hope of livelyhoode. Forasmuche therfor as this practise is verie intollerably and ungodly, and that the said conveyances were otherwise expounded unto your suppliant, beinge a man not lettred and destitute of his eye sight as is afforesaid, and therfor voyde in law, and notwithstandinge might breede iarres and contention in tyme betweene your suppliant's children and their posteritie to the daungerof their subvercion and absolute overthrow, May it therfor please your lordship to lett call the said Teige eldest son to the said Complainant to awnswer the said premisses in this honnorable Courte the last daie of this easter tearme and to bringe with him the said conveyances. And uppon proofe of the former faleitie and deceipte to cancell the conveyances, wherby your suppliant may dispose of his said inheritances to the quiet and benefitt of his said children and their posteritie. And he shall praie, etc.

DEED OF TEIGE O DOINE IN FAVOUR OF HIS SON CHARLES,
12 JULY 1593

To all Christian people to whom these presents shall come greeting in
our lord God everlasting. Wheras I, Teig O Doine of Tenahinsie *alias*
O Doyne have by former conveyance made some assurance unto Teige
O Doine my son and heyer of my manners, landes and tenements and
other hereditaments in Oregaine, Know ye to whome theise presents shall
com that I the said Teig O Duinn *alias* O Doine do hereby testifie, protest
and declare that long tyme befor the perfection of any such conveyance
and at the time of the making and perfecting therof my Full and resolute
intent and purpose was to assure all my landes, tenements and other hereditaments, excepting certaine parcells which I intended to assigne unto the
rest of my sonnes, unto my said sonn and heyer during his lief, after whose
decease the same to remaine to other of my sonnes successively, each as
they proceed in adge so to succeed in the seissin and possession therof
during their lives, and soe the heyers males of each of my said sonnes to
succeed each after other, accordinge the antiquitie and Course of my
succession of my said sonnes, so as my meaninge was that my Cheifery, lordship and possession should forever continue in my line and house in som
degree licke the aunncient usadge and custom of the said Countrie with
which resolution and purpose of myne I often tymes did make my said
son and heyer Teige O Doyne accquainted, whoe was not well pleased
theruppon and neverthelesse he found himself in Shew therunto and by
advise of som of his Councell he gott a conveyance drawne in my name
importing as now I doe understand an absolute estate of Feoffment in
Fee simple from me unto him [and] his heyers of my said lordship, landes,
tenements and other hereditaments, which conveyance being brought by
my said sonn unto me I was by him borne in hand (the rest of my sonnes
being absent) that the said conveyance was made for assurance of my
land and living to continue in course of succession according my former
purpose as before is specifyed. And therfor I was required by my said son
Teige to perfecte the same, wherunto I awnswered *if the conveyance was
made to that effect I would perfecte the same, and my said sonn confidently aunswered that yt was made to noe other effecte, I then did
perfecte the said conveyance with ceremonies and circumstances as I was
required. And understanding soone after that the forsaid conveyance did
import an absolute estate of inheritance contrary to my meaning and
contrary to the assurance made unto me by my said son, I theruppon did
preferr suit in the Chauncery against my said sonn, which as yett dependeth
and discloseth the secresie of the former practise, intendinge therby
to gett the said fraudulent conveyance cancelled leste by cullor therof
the rest of my sonnes should be brought in question or Trouble for the
portions which I meane to assure unto them to live uppon. And being
enformed by my Councell that the said assurance procured fraudulently

and rede and expounded unto me being blind and unlettered otherwise
then in truth yt purportede is voyde in Lawe. And that therby I am not
disabled to make further disposition or assurance of my land for the
benefitt of my other sonnes, I therfor the saied Teige O Doine *alias* O
Doyne, for fatherly affection which I carry unto Cahir O Duinn my
fourth sonn and for other good causes and good considerations moving
me, have given, graunted and confirmed unto Cahir mcFyrr O Mulloy of
Balliboy in the King's Countie, gent., Brian mcRory O Doine of Ballintaggart in the Queene's Countie, gent., and Edmond Keating of Cappa-
brogain in the said Countie, gent., the manners, Townes, villadges and
hamletts of Rirrimore, Ballivickena, Rachohie, Corilie, Kappaghbegge,
Sraghaduffe, Gurtin, Ballikowell, Fearon kearoll Riagh, Garrigallared,
Fearay hi Christin, five acres in Garriconnoghe, Garriknaighery, Cowlagh
and the quarter of Cloincaroill, and the rents, segniories and Chieftenry
issuing out of the Brittas and Rathlacka in Oregain afforesaid with all the
landes, tenements, services, rents, reversions, reservations and seigniories
in the quarters commonly called the quarter of Rirrimore, the quarter
of Lackagh, in one quarter of Mointagh milicke in the said Oregaine with
all the pastures, meddowes, woods, waters, Commons and other appurtenances unto the premisses or to anie parte or parcell therof belonging
or appertayning. To have and to hold all and singuler the premisses with
ther appurtenances unto the said Cahir mcFyrr, Brien mcRorie and Edmond
Keating, their heyers and assignes for ever from the cheife lords of the Fee
by due and anie accustomed services to the uses and interests herafter
specified. And further I the said Teig O Doine *alias* O Doine, my heyers
and assignes, shall warrant, accquite and defend all and singuler the
premisses with their appurtenances unto the said Cahir, Brien and Edmond
and their heyers, and to everie of them and the heyers of everie of them
against all maner of person and persons for ever. And lastly I the said
Teige have made, consented, and appointed my welbeloved in Christ David
mcRorie of Ballintaggart afforesaid, gent., my true and lawful attorney to
enter for me and for my name into all and singuler the premisses, and after
such entree made to deliver therof or of anie parte therof in name of the
rest actuall possession and liverie of seisin unto Cahir mcFyrr, Brian
mcRorie and Edmond Keating afforesaid to entre unto them, their heyers
and assignes according the true intent and purpose of this presente deede.
And whatesoever my said Attorney shall doe or cause to be don as concearning deliverie of seisin of all and singuler the premisses I ratifie,
establishe and allow. In Wittnes wherof the parties afforesaid have to theis
indentures interchangeablie sett their hands and seales the twelth daie of
July in the five and thirtieth yeare of our Sovereigne Ladie Queene Elizabethe and in the yeare of our lord God 1593.

The intente and true meaninge of this presente deed of feoffment is
and was at the making and perfection therof that thabove named Feoffes,
their heyers and assignes and the heyers and assignes of the survivor of

them shall stand and be seised of all and singuler the premisses to the use, benefitt and behooffe of the said Cahir O Duinn fourth son unto the Teig O Doine afforesaid and to the use of the heyers and assignes of the said Cahir for ever. And the said Cahir O Doine shall satisfie and paie the said Teige the Feoffor during his naturall liefe for his reliefe the som of four pounds currant money of England by the year, to be paied by equall portions at Michaellmas and Easter. Provided that if Elizabeth fitzGerald wiffe to the said Teige shall happen to overlive the said Teig that then the said Feoffees shall stand seised of all and singuler the landes, Tenements and hereditaments befor specifyed to the use of the said Elizabethe duringe her naturall liefe. And after the decease of her to the use of the said Cahir O Doine, his heyers and assignes in forme afforesaid.

Cahir O Mulloye: Barnaby Doine: Edmond Keating.

Being presente when the within named Feoffees sealed and delivered this as their deed to the within specified Feoffees[14] the persons under-written:

> Tirrelaughe mc + Kowlemis marke.
> Murtaghe mc + Daui is marke.
> Murtaughe mc + Brien is marke.
> Donell mc + Shane is marke.
> Fite[15] mc + Donnoghe is marke
> Rorie mcDermott is marke.[16]

---

14 *Sic.*

15 *Sic.*

16 At p. 366 of the manuscript there is a note referring to this deed, which states that 'My L. Chauncellor indorsed these words uppon the feoffment whose coppie beginneth folio 272, which was signed by the Lord Deputie sittinge at the Concell Table the second of March 1608: It is agreed that all the contents of this deede shall stand firme to Charles and his heyres. Arthure Chichester.'

KING'S LETTER FOR A SURRENDER AND REGRANT
BY AND TO CAPTAIN TADY DOYNE, 29 JUNE 1608

James Rex.

Right trustie and welbeloved wee greete yow well. At the humble suite of our welbeloved subiect Captayne Tady Doyne Esqr. cheife of his name and in consideracion of his dutifull carriadge and good service done to our Crowne and state here in the late warres in that oure Realme of Ireland to the danger of his lif and loss of his goods, as is grediblie[17] informed, wee are gratiouslie pleased and doe hereby requier and authorise yow to accept of the said Tady Doyne a surrender of the Countrie of Iregan and of all the lands tenements and hereditaments in the said Contrie, scituat in the Queenes Countie in that oure Realme, Wherof he and his ancestor[s] have been possessed. And thereuppon to make a graunt or graunts from us oure heyres and successors in due forme of lawe by letters patents under the great seale of that oure Realme of the said Countrie of Iregan and of all the lands, tenements, Tyethes and hereditaments therin and therto belonging and of all felons goods and deodands therein hapeninge unto the said Tadye Doyne, his heyres and assignes for ever in fee simple, to held[18] of us oure heyres and successors in fre and Common socage as of oure Castle of Dublin. And our further pleasure is and soe wee hereby will authorise and requier yow that in and by the same letters patent soe to be made frome us of the premises unto the said Tady Doyne and his heyres as aforesaid yow doe give and graunte full power and aucthoritie from us oure heyres and successors unto the said Tady Doyne his heyres and assignes at his and their will and pleasure be hould and keepe within the said Countrie of Iregane in such fitt places and at suche Convenient times weekelie or yerlie Court leets and Courte barrons, marketts and fayres as to yow shalbe thought fitt. And whereas wee are informed that there is and hath beene a controversie depending in oure Courte of Chauncery there betweene the said Tady Doyne and som of his brothers, our will and pleasure is and soe wee doe hereby will and requier yow, to take such order that the said Controversie maie eyther receave a full and Judiciall hearinge and sentence in our said Courte of Chauncery or in som other of our Courts of Justice of Record there and not otherwise. And that yow doe affoord unto the said Tady Doyne your lawfull favour in all his just causes. And these our letters shalbe your sufficient warrant and dischardg in this behalf.

Given under our signet at the Pallace of Westminster the 29th daye of

---

17 *Sic.*

18 *Sic.*

June in the sixt yeare of our Raigne of greate Brittaine Fraunce and Ireland.

To our Right trustie and welbeloved Sir Arthure Chichester knight deputie of our Realme of Ireland and to the Chancellor there now beinge and to the deputie or other Cheiffe governor or governors of that Realme, and to the Chauncellor or keepers of the great seale there that hereafter for the tyme shalbe and to any other to whome it doth or shall appertaine and to everye of them.

Concordatum Cum originale. Extractum per me Jacobum Newman clericum in officio magistri Rotulorum.

That which Teig oge O Doyne is content to afford to his brother Charles.

He agreeth to 85 acres *vitz.* 41 in Reriemore, 30 in the Culaghes and the 15 in Moyntaghe milicke by his father's graunte to him and no more lawfully he hath not that waye by his father's conveighance.

To that he is content in Cheifferie to yeald the Cheiferies issuinge out of one quarter that Charles is foster brethren[19] houldeth and the Cheifferie of the half quarter of Milicke in the said Moyntaghe Milicke, the cheifferie of the quarter of Dyrrye, and the cheifferie of half a quarter in the quarter of Lackaghe, which mounts to be neere the fourth parte of all the cheifferie due uppon the freehoulders of that countrie and that cheifferie to be to him for tearme of his life, or ells in demeasne lands to him foure score acres *vitz.* thirtie acres in Ballygarvan, twentie six in the one moytie of Ballinvonyne next adjoininge to Ballygarvane and foure and Twentie acres in Cully kinawhall, the said demeasne lands to be to him and the heyres males of his body lawfully begotten in tayle, the remainder for want of such issues to Teig and his heyres. And this much to satisfie your Lordship I ame contente and to no more I will not agree and that uppon the conditions formerelie and doe humbly beseeche your Lordship not to wrest me farther for to more I will not consent. And soe prayinge your Lordship to dispatche me I end. 18th of December 1608.

Your honnors most humble in all service to command.
Tady Doyne.

Copia Vera drawen out of a kind of a letter pined by the said Teige according our Certaine knowledge of his hand sent to Sir Arthur Chichester

---

19 Were these foster-brethren of Charles the O Melanes (or O Meloynes) of Mointaghmilick, four of whom appear as beneficiaries in his will?

knight Lord Deputie of Ireland. Bar: Doyne. Donnell Doyne. Bar: Doyne.

To the Right Honnorable the Lord Deputie.

Objections by Charles Duinn against the
Particular made by his Majesty's Surveyor
for Teig O Doyne.

In primis, that 50 acres founde by the Inquisition for the said Charles
in the quarter of Ririmore are chardged proportionably with the Cheifferies
imposed in the said particular uppon the said quarter, which are freed
from the said Cheifferie by his father's Conveiance.

Item, that 49 acres founde by the said Inquisition for the said Charles
in the quarters of Moyntaghe milicke likewise proportionately freed from
the Cheifferies due uppon the said quarters in the said Particular.

Item, that fiv acres founde in the said Inquisition for the said Charles
in the quarter of Lackaghe are freed from the Cheifferies of the said
quarter.

Item, that 30 acres called Naculagha in the quarter of Clanncarroll
are by the said Inquisition found to be the inheritance of the said Charles
and freed from the Cheifferies of the said quarter.

Item, that the said Inquisition findeth that there was an Adward
Betweene the said Teig and the said Charles whereby the said Charles
is to have the 4th part of the lands and Cheifferies mentioned in the
said Particular.

Item, that the said Charles is in Remaynder of the Castle and three
score acres of Bualyanumer *alias* Tenehensye mentioned in the said particular by Conveiance from his father. And in Remaynder of the Castle
and 215 acres in Castle bracke incerted in the said Particular. And in
Remaynder of the land called O Doyne's Forest and in Remaynder of
all the Cheifferies in the particular for the said Teig.

Item, that the said Charles by conveyaunce from his father hath to him,
his heyres and assignes, the Cheifferies issuinge out of Rerimore mentioned
in the said particular. And the duties and Cheifferies out of the quarter of
Lackaghe mentioned in the said particular. Which conveyaunces the said
Charles by the intreatie and persuasiones of the said Teig did forgoe to
cause to be founde by the said Inquisition, fearinge that any controversie fallinge then between them the freehoulders of the Countrie should
be encouradged thereby to diminishe the said Cheifferies, wherunto he did
then the more willinglie yeald. By reason that the said Teig did undertake

uppon his salvation to make good unto the said Charles the 4th part of the lands and Cheifferies in the said Particular by force of an order taken by there friendes. The like proffer he hath formerlie made as may appeare by his letters redie to be shewed.

Item, in case no such evidences were extant the said Charles could prove by the Contrie of Iregan assembled at the tyme of the said Inquisition that he was to succeede as Cheiftaine to the Cheifferies and all the lands in the said particular by the auncient Custome of the said Iregaine.

Item, that the said Charles might give in evidence to the Jury of the said inquisition sworne that he was to have to his portion as Coheyre to the said Teig as much as should be allotted unto the said Teig in quantitie of the lands in the said particular by the auncient of the said Iregan, if he had not then relied uppon the said Teig is earnest protestations to assure unto him the 4th part of the lands and Cheifferies in the said particular accordinge unto the said order.

Item, that your lordship cannot dulie signe the warrant written after the said particular and directed to his Majesty's Counsayle learned in the lawes, without overthrowing the estate of more than an hundrethe Freehoulders whose inheritance is found by the said inquisition, notwithstanding any Provisoes for savinge their right, by reason of their ignorance and Dishabilitie to wage lawe with so skillfull a competitor as the said Teig is, of whome there remaineth as yet great hope that your lordship will have a speciall Care accordinge your usuall manner to your singuler Comendations ever.

Item, that your lordship canot pass the tythes of Iregan in fee simple to the said Teig, the same being alredie past in Fee farme to another, without inconvenience to his Majesty's tenaunt and the diminishinge of his highnes' Rent.

Item, that unless the said Charles your [suppliant] and the said Brien his brother and their Nephewes and tenants be excepted from the Court leets and Baron graunted to the said Teig by his Majesties letters, It may drawe their whole dependancye continually uppon the said Teige and his assignes to the disadvancement of his Majesties service hereafter, and this no smale hindraunce in so Remote and as yet unsetled a Contrie, full of montaynes, Glines, Bogges and woods and but newelie shyred, beinge an unfitt Receptacle for the like Courts.

Item, that by your lordship's order the xvth of February 1607 the said Charles is to have the 4th part of all the lands and Cheifferies in the said Particular. By which order in that respect the said Teig is concluded not to seeke any benefitt of his Majesties letter.

In Tender Consideration of the premisses your suppliant most humbly beseecheth your lordship to stoppe the grauntinge of letters to the said Teige in a matter wherin his Majestie hath beene missinformed before your lordship drawe him to performe the contents of your lordship's severall orders or before your lordship do certifie unto England the state of this cause by your suppliant whome it neerelie concerneth, as your lordship hath don in the like causes, or that your lordship doe graunt forth a Commission *Ad Melius Inquirendum* of the premisses.

The aunswer of Tady Doyne to the objections
of Charles Doyne against his Particular.

For the 4 first objections, being all of one nature *viz.* that certaine lands conveied to the said Charles by his father should be freed from the rents and Cheifferies due to Teig, the said Teig doth yeald thereunto for as much land as is lawfully conveied unto him by his father without rent reserved, for which ther maye be a speciall clause in the letters Patents.

For the 5 objection that there was an Adward made between them in the Contrie, to that Teig aunswereth that the arbitrators went beyond the submission, and therefoee the adward voyde in lawe as also for other causes. And further aunswereth that Charles hath comenced suite in the Chauncery against Teig uppon an obligation of a thowsand pounds for not performinge the said adward, in which suit both parties are at issue and his majestie hath directed by his letters that the matter of that adward and land shall be determined accordinge lawe where it is depending or in any other his Majesties Courtes of Record and not otherwise.

For the 6, 7, 8 and 9 objections *viz.* that Charles is in Remaynder, Teig aunswereth that that is but a devise to uphould the barbarous Custome of Tanistrie and his supposed Remaynder is also but for lif after twoe others that are yet livinge, as likelie to live as Charles. But further saieth the same is avoyded by precedent Conveyaunce, besides if the Custome did hould there was no libertie or power in the father to dispose of any Cheifferie or services or any hereditaments belonginge to the Cheiftayne.

For 10, 11 and 12th objections for conveyances of any part of the Cheifferies, if any such was, which Teig denieth, there was no attornement of the freeholders thereunto so as the Chiefferies could not pass. Besides Teig hath a former Conveyaunce well and dulie executed by liverie and seissin and attornement which was alredie shewed before your lordship. The said Teig also denieth any such oath to have bene given by him as Charles hath scandalouslie chardged him withall, neyther was ther any cause whye he should give oath for that Charles did oppose as much as he might at the taking of the office against Teig, as all the contry can wittnes.

For the 13 and 14th objections for his succession and portion by the Custome, Teig aunswereth that there was noe such Custome used for the lands belonging to the Cheftayne in that Contrie but a continuall descent from the Cheiftayne to the succeeder, and if there had beene such Custome the same is against the lawe and is abolished longe since by Statute and power given to the possessor of the Contrie for the time being to surrender and take estate in fee simple, and in this speciall case there are speciall letters directed to you from the kinges Majestie.

For the 15th that his surrender wilbe to the prejudice of the freeholders, Teig aunswereth that it canot be to their prejudice for that he canot surender anythinge but what himself hath rightfully, for if he should surrender other men's lands and the Kinge regraunte other men's lands by Patent the same would be meerelie voyde. Besides this Teig hath the consent of all the freeholders except Charles and his brother, as he can shewe by their deedes. Your lordship also hath taken that Care for these freeholders that you doe for all others in like case by incertinge a proviso in the Patent that it shall not be prejudiciall to any man's tytle or right.

For the 16th concearninge the tythes of Iregan, that they canot pass to Teig for that they are alredie passed to Charles, he thereunto aunswereth that seeinge his Majesties pleasure appears by his letters that the same should be past to Teig, he humbly praieth your lordship to follow that direction preceeding of his Majesties bountie in recompence of his service. And if Charles have right the nowe passing of the tithes canot prejudice him, and for the diminishinge of his Majesties Rent it is not an objection to be made by any reasonable man, consideringe that the like maye be made against everie estate of Fee Simple graunted by his Majestie to any other, so Teig beseecheth likewise your lordship to consider of the Conynge used by Charles in passing the same tythes, which meriteth litle favor.

For the 17th that Charles and his brother would be excepted frome Courte of leets and Courte Baron, thereunto Teig aunswers that it shewes a strange disposition in Charles, beinge a Professor of Lawe and pretending so much Sivillitie, will seeme to be against lawlike Courses and proceedings and especially against Courts of Justice, beinge the likliest meanes to bringe the inhabitants there to Civill and lawlike cariadge, but for havinge any dependancye of the inhabitants Teig disclaimeth except onely the payments of such smale rents and the services are due unto him, nor is ther any thinge he desires so much as the reformation of the said Contry, his education beinge alwaies amongest the Englishe, whereby he can easely distinguishe betweene barbarssie and civillitie, and the king's Majestie beinge signified that such Courts should be graunted to Teige, he thinketh the objection idle against that authoritie.

For the 18th that the order of your lordship and the rest of the Commissioners of surrenders was that Teig should not be admitted to surrender without ensuringe the 4th part of the Contrie and seignorie to Charles, to that Teig answeres that he must have yealded to any order your lordship and the rest would be pleased to laye downe whylest he proceeded in that Course, but nowe his Majestie having signified his pleasure that it should pass in another course and not upon that Commission of Surender, that order is of no more force nor is it any conclusion against Teig in especiall, there beinge noe consideration or cause whye he should be tyed to give awaye the 4th part of his owne lands to Charles above others of his brethren that elder by birth then Charles.

The said Teig therefore humbly beseecheth your lordship that seeinge his desarts, and hath beene at leaste equall to others of his Ranke, he maye have no less favor or respect then they have had and that his surender may be accepted and his patent past, especially his highnes havinge signified his express pleasure for him therin above others of his sorte, which, as your suppliant knoweth, in your lordship is good Judgement and consideration is cause rather to favor your suppliant than to hinder him (as Charles hath objected), he humbly also desireth your lordship to consider that if everie objection maye[20] against the kinge's direction few or no patents should pass, for that in everie such case one or other adversarie doth alwaies doth pretend som cause of grievance, whereof there is no regard to be had, especially when they that pretend a right are not satisfied with the savinge of there right by especiall words, which ever your lordship since your prosperous and happie government hath bene pleased to provide for, and in this case is offered.

Memorandum. That the inquisition findeth that there was an adward betweene the said Teig O Doyne and his brother Charles that the said Charles for certaine respects in the order mentioned should have the 4th part of all the lands and seignories. The inquisition also findeth that there aunswered out of the contry of O Regaine upon all generall hostings a risinge out of 24 footmen, and a Composition of three pound ten shillinges st. in money. And that these lands are houlden of his majestie by what services the jurie know not.

This particuler is drawen for Mr. Teig O Doyne, accordinge your lordships warrant for me in that behalf.

Ex. per Willelmum Parsons supervisor generalis.

---

20 There is a word omitted here.

LETTER DIRECTING ATTORNEY–GENERAL TO DRAW UP
FIANT FOR LETTERS PATENT. 26 NOVEMBER 1608.

By the lord Deputie.

To the attorney general.

We greete yow well. Where the King's most excellent Majestie by his highnes letters under the signet dated the 29th of July 1608 hath signified unto us his Majesties pleasure on the behalf of Capten Thady Doyne esquier Cheiffe of his name, that his highnes is graciouslie pleased in Consideration of the said Tady is good service heretofore done to his highnes to graunt unto the said Thady his heyres and assignes the Contry of Iregaine and all the lands, tenements, tythes and hereditaments therein and thereto belonginge and all fellons goods and deodands therein happeninge, to be held of his highnes, his heyres and successors in Free and Comon Soccadge as of his Majesties castle of Dublin. And further to graunt full power and authoritie unto the said Thady, his heyres and assignes at his and their will and pleasure to hould and keepe within the said Contry of Iregaine in such fitt places at such convenient time Courte Leete and Courte Barrons, marketts and Fayres, as to us shalbe thought fitt. Theise are therefore to will and requier yow forthwith to make a Fyant or Fyants in due forme of Lawe of the particuler appearinge under Mr. Surveyor's hand in the scedule hereunto anexed, and all other lands of right the said Thady hath or ought to have in the said contrey of Iregaine, Tythes, felons goods, deodans, Fayres, marketts, and other the premisses unto the said Thady his heyres and assignes to be houlden of his highnes as aforesaid. Incertinge therein such further ordinary Clauses as in such letters Patents are usuall. And leavinge blanks for the times and places for the said Courts, Fayres, marketts. And such Fiant or fiants so made to send unto us fayer written ingrossed in parchment under your hand that wee maie give further order for passinge the same unto the said Thadye under the greate seale of this Realme. And for your doeinge thereof this shalbe your warrant. Given at his Majesties Castle of Dublin this 26th of November 1608.

To our welbeloved his Majesties Attornie generall or Solicitor or to eyther of them.

> Exceptions exhibited by Charles Duinn against the fiant signed by your lordship for Thady Doyne concerninge the contry called Iregaine in the Queene's Countye.

First, that the said Tadye hathe no power in him to surrender the lands and Cheiffries contayned in the said fiant nor by vertue of his surrender ought to have the same againe passed unto him, his heyres and assignes, by cause your suppliant and som of his brothers to stand seised of the same as feoffees to certaine uses by force of a deed made by their father the 20th of July 1590. And that the deede produced by the said Thady before your lordship dated the 28th of Aprill 1593 made by his father to his owne use for life, with remaynder to the said Tady and after him with remaynder to his sonn Teig Reoghe and the heyres males of his body, and after them with like remaynders to your suppliant and others his brethren before him, the said remainders are taken away contrary to Justice if the said land and Cheifferie be graunted to the said Thady and his assignes.

2. That your suppliant by vertue of the said deed of 1590 is in remaynder of the townes and maners of Castlebracke and Tenahinsy, and of all the lands to them belonginge and of the woods called Mucluain and the forest, and of all the rents and Cheifferies contayned in the said fiant, after the death of the said Thadye.

3. That your suppliant hath an estate to him, his heyres and assignes of the rents and cheifferies issuing out of the quarters of Ririe More and the Lackagh and one quarter in Moyntaghe Milicke by a deede made by his father dated in July 1593. And of 30 acres of land called Naculagha in the quarter of Clann Carroll, 15 acres of land in the quarter of Moyntaghe millocke and 90 acres in Ririemore, which the said Thady confessed in his letter to your lordship to be well conveyed to your suppliant. And of 10 other acres in the said Ririemore and of 24 [acres in] Garrygallaruid and fearan hychristine in the quarter of Moyntaghe millicke and 3 acres in the quarter of Lackaghe, all of which lands were founde by office four your suppliant. And of the villadges of Lackaghbegg, Gurtin, Ballyvonell, Ballyvickena and Scraduffe and of all the lands that his father had in the said quarter of Ririmore, Lackaghe and Moyntaghe millicke. Yet notwithstandinge, all the cheifferies of the said three quarters are contayned in the said fiant to be passed by letters Patents unto the said Thady, his heyres and assignes, contrary to the said deed and the intent of your suppliant's said father. And wheras the said lands assured to your suppliant by the said deed, if any Cheifferies were formerlie due uppon them, were extinguished by vertue of possession in your suppliant's said father, and freelie by the said deed conveighed to your suppliant, yet nevertheless the said Thady doth chardg them with such cheifries and exactions in the said fiant as they are not able to beare nor yealde any profitt thereunto coerespondent.

4. That if your suppliant had no such estate passed unto him by his father by the said deede, yet by the custome of Iregaine if his brother Brien concluded himself by an order if not by his assignment, he ought

immediately after the death of the said Thady to have all the said cheifferies and what lands besides belonged to the name of O Doyne or
Chieftaine of Iregaine. And by the like custome of the said contry thone
moytie of all the lands contained in the said fiant and founde by office
for the said Thady, resemblinge the custome of Gavelkinde. All which
deeds and customes making for your suppliant he did forbere to urge or
cause to be found by an office taken at Marybroughe before Sir Henry
Power and his Majesties surveyor, by the earnest persuasions of the said
Thady, lest any yarre then fallinge betweene him and your suppliant
the Contry of Iregaine should be thereby encouradged to diminish the
cheiffry, unto which persuacions your suppliant did then yealde, by
cause the said Thady then undertooke upon his salvacion to make good
unto your suppliant the 4th part of the lands and Cheifferie contayned in
the said fiant accordinge the order taken betweene them by their friends.

5. That the said Thady, perceivinge the force of the said deeds and tytle
which your suppliant had to the said Iregaine, used what means he could
devise to drawe your suppliant to an order, as it may appeare by his
letters, and at length your suppliant by his earnest intreaties yealdinge
thereunto it was ordered by their friends by theire arbiterment dated the
xith daye of Aprill 1607 that your suppliant should have the 4th part of
all the lands and Cheifferie in Iregaine in Controversie between them.
Unto the performance of which order the said Thady bound himself
first by his bond and afterwards by his corporall oath, and several protestations taken uppon his salvation, as it may appeare by his letters.

6. That if your suppliant by your lordship's favor could enjoye the
performance of the said order and thereby setle himself in Iregaine he
would likelie if any Rebellion had fallen in the contries neere about it
keepe in their fidelitie to the Crowne the most part of the natives of the
said Iregaine, as he hath kept many of the best sort thereabouts in the last
generall Rebellion in the their fidelitie [and] subjection.

7. That of all the like Contryes as Iregaine is, a division between such as
had right thereunto was hertofore thought by the state to be the fitt
meanes to setle them in quietnes, which division was accordinglie done
betweene the nacions of the Farals, Relyes, McGuyers and MacMahons, in
the countries called Rann McWilliam Iacdar, Tyreawly and Ranalaghe and
many the like territories. And therefore the like division beinge done
betweene your suppliant and the said Thady by their mutuall consents
and the orders taken by their freinds uppon good consideration your
lordship is to maintayne it.

8. That Iregane as well within it as rounde about it beinge full of boggs,
woods, glins and montaynes, and scituated betweene Leishe and Offalye,
is one of the fittest and strongest contries in Lenster of the quantitie of

it to maintayne rebellion, and therefore might be thought a surrer course to tye them to continue in their loyaltie still hereafter unto the Crowne, that more then one should beare some swaye in it.

9.   That the said Thadye his eldest sonn Teig Reoghe, sonn to Margarett daughter to Shane O Neyle and mother to Cuconnaght oge McGuyer, deade beyond the seas, is not a fitt ruler over so stronge a Contrye and so fitt for rebellion as Iregaine, both by reason that for his said allyaunce with the O Neylls and McGuyers he furthered the drawinge of forces in the last rebellion out of the North to Lenster, to the greate Charge of the Crowne.   And was then in Companie with Brian Reoghe at the Burninge of his Majesties fort of Phillipstowne and the next daye at the Burninge of Kilcullen in the Countie of Kildare, and in Company with the said Brian when he was kild, and in Bonaght with Owny mcRorie riflinge the Towne of Marybroughe, and havinge not since, beinge now aboute 37 yeares of age, much bettered or altered his course, will likelye returne to his wonnted practise if the like times doe happen.   And therefore not secure for his Majestie that any of so suspiciouse a behavior should commaund alone the said Contry beinge so stronge or so fitt for rebellion.

10. That the said Margarett mother to the said Teig Reoghe and the gentlewoman nowe kept by the said Thadie in his howse and by whome he hath many sones beinge both alive, the issue begotten by the venter of one of them is illegitimate, yet by vertue of the estate passed unto him and his assignes by the said fiant may leave the said lands and Cheifferie to his unlawfull issue and to disinherit his owne heyre your suppliant, his brother and Nephewes, where as for these many hundred yeares no bastard atayned to the Chieferie of Iregaine.

11. That if the said fiant goes forward by pretense of his Majesties letters to your lordship, your suppliant can prove the letter to be undulie obteyned and his Majestie in grauntinge it to be deceaved, which otherwise may be collected by the service therin mentioned to be done by the said Thady and untrulie informed, for his onely service and the same not origionally proceedinge from himself was the sendinge of xx^tie Cowes or thereabouts to the fort of Marybroughe, not past three miles distant from Iregaine, with three men in the night, Cows beinge then in the generall rebellion of smale value.   And if he supposed service be an inducement to disregard your suppliant, he can prove by the testimonye of noblemen and the best Neighbors to Iregaine that his sarvices done in the last insurrection did farre exceed any sarvice done by the said Thady.

12. That his losses missinformed by the letter, in comparison of the rest like unto him in the kingdom then for wealth and stimation farre from the protection of Citties and garisons were but verie smale, havinge lost none of his catle in the rebellion.   And beinge then by Chaunce taken prisoner

by the Bonaghs of Conne base sonn to the Earle of Tyreone in Iregaine and his Castle delivered unto him, he was lett at suddenlie lett at [*sic*] libertie and his castle and goods restored unto him by the said Conne, who intended to put to death the said Bonaghes for that there fact done without his consent.

13. That the letter in most points in contrary to the Commission of accepting surrenders of Irishe tenures and lands not yet surrendered, formerlie sent over to your lordship and the rest of the Commissioners for increasinge of his Majesties rents and setlinge the kingdome in tranquilitie by cause thereby his Majesties rents are not augmented, nor Iregaine in any likelyhood wilbe setled in quetnes.

14. That a Commission of Inquirie should issue forth uppon the said letter, what lands and cheiffries the said Thady might surrend[er], before the surrender should be accepted of, whereby your suppliant and the rest of the freeholders of Iregaine might not be thus prejudiced by his surrender, by reason that your suppliant in the former Commission and office taken at Marybroughe was abused and deceaved as it is layde downe in the 4th exception.

15. That the cheifrie and exaction layde downe in the said fiant should be reduced to a certaine value of rent in money for the ease of the free[hol]-ders before the patents should be graunted unto the said Thadye, whereby he might not have libertie to double or treble the value of the said Cheifries and exactions at his pleasure, as it hath beene done heretofore to the impoverishment of the inhabitants of Iregaine.

16. That if the said fiant goe forward all the concealments in Iregaine doe pass to the said Thadie, which may reward good servitors and yield his Majestie more rent then the said Thadye doe paie for the whole contrye, when he should have not more passed unto him by the letter then he could lawfully surrender.

17. That if letters Patents be graunted unto the said Thady in the tenures of Soccage and fee, such a precident and gappe beinge opened to the rest of his sorte in the kingdome that would surrender, they wilbe suttors to his Majestie for the like tenure to his highnes' trouble and smale benefitt hereafter.

18. That his Majesties pleasure signified by the letter to accept the said Thady is surrender, etc. And that the controversie dependinge betweene him and some of his brothers, which is your suppliant, in his highnes' Court of Chauncery or in some other Court of record should receave a finall end, it seemeth to be the best construction hereof agreeinge to his Majesties meaninge and equitie that the suite begunne in the Chauncery

should be first determined byfore the surrender should be accepted of, both of them concerninge one matter, and without limitation of tyme. And that for twoe causes; the one is that if the surrender be first accepted, the letters Patentes accordinglie graunted, and your suppliant afterwards recover in the said suite, then the said Thady did surrender that which he ought not to surrender and had that passed unto him which he ought not to have. The other cause is that if your suppliant doe recover in the said suite, yet nevertheless the said Thadie by colour of the said letters Patents maye againe comense a new suite against your suppliant, to your suppliant's further vexation.

19. That by these words 'as we are credibly informed' it may be argued his Majestie to be missinformed by cause the informers are not particularly named in the letter, whereby they might be accordinglie censsured if the information were found to be untrewe. And that as it may be gathered his comendation issued not from your lordship nor any of his Majesties Councell here.

20. That his highnes beinge trulie informed would not likely requier your lordship without some restriction to accept the said Thadie is surrender of all Iregaine and the same to pass to him and his assignes to the intollerable hindraunce of your suppliant, his brother and Nephewes and many others besides.

21. That in the said letter, after these woordes, 'to accept the surrender of the said Thady of all the lands, tenements and hereditaments, etc. And thereuppon to make a graunte of all the lands, tenements, tythes and hereditaments, etc.' the woord tythes being not in the surrender was interposed handsomly in the graunte betweene the woords tenements and hereditaments, so that by coursorie reading it might be perceaved, thereby to deceave the kinge in his graunte where by trewe construction of the letter his Majesties meaninge is not to graunt any more lands unto the said Thadye then he could lawfullye surrender.

22. That many of the Councell are of opinion that it was a wrong done unto your lordship and to them, your suppliant's cause dependinge before you and havinge taken severall orders therein, that any such letter should be procured unknowen to you and therefore might fitly be answered if it might so stand with your lordship's pleasure.

23. That there is above an hundred persons by office taken at Marybroughe in the Queenes Countie the 15th of September 1607 found to be seised of lands in Iregaine by inheritance, whose estats are licke to be hasarded to their discontentment and disquetnes hereafter, if the said fiant and surrender doe goe forward, whose disabilitie is an impediment unto them nowe for not appearinge byfore your lordship to plead their right.

24. That by the said office taken at Marybroughe the hariott as a part of the Chiefrie with a relation from the quarters in Iregaine uppon which the hariott is dew had,[21] to the quarter of Ririemore is found to be dew onely uppon the keannfynye, which woord signifieth the head or the chef of his nation. There [be] many such keannfinies in Iregaine which hath hariotts paied unto them after the death of the freehoulders that be next of kine to them or lived under them, as the keannfinies hariot was dew to O Duinn, yet in many places in the said fiant the woord keannfinie is translated to be *libere tenens* or a freehoulder, and by this mistakinge or translation of this word, the keannfinies doth loose his hariott dew unto him uppon the freehoulders by cause that all the freeholders' hariotts ar graunted by the said fiant to the said Thady and his assignes.

25. That the Castle and 60^{tie} acres in Rosskyne found by the said office for your supliant's mother, the remaynder for Donnell O Doyne your supliant's Nephew, and his heyres are by the said fiant graunted to the said Thadie and his assignes by culler that the same should be assured unto him by his mother, who before many wittnesses the xith of this month of J*anuary* did openlie denie that she made any such assurance to the said Thadie or ever gave her consent or was privie thereunto.

26. That the woords of the letter beinge "to accept a surrender of the said Thadye of the contrie of Iregaine and of the lands within the said contrie whereof he and his auncestors have beene possessed" the possession ought to be first in his auncestors and in him by lineall descent or other lawfull mens from them. And yet in the said fiant without limitation of the said Contrie and lands to be in his possession, whereof the best and most part is the possession and inheritance of others, all is graunted to the said Thady his heyres and assignes.

27. That the clause that his Majestie shall maintayne and defend the said Thadie in all the lands to be graunted unto him by vertue of his surrender is contrary to the clause of savinge the right of your supliant contayned in the said fiant.

28. That by your lordship's order of the 15th of February, 1607, your supliant ought to have the 4th part of all the lands and chieferie in contro-versie betweene him and the said Thadie, with which order the said Thadie thought himself well contented and to have received an extraordinary favor by reason that your supliant making the division he was to have twoe choyses before him when the order made by their freinds in that case gave him but the first choyse only. And thereuppon the said Thadye sent a note of his lands for your supliant and perswaded him earnestly by his letter to make the division.

---

21 *Sic.*

29. That the said Thady ought in equitie to make aunswer to these exceptions and your supliant to have a Copie of his aunswer and to have a time for replie uppon his answer. And on both sides to proceede forward until they be at issue and prove their allegations before letters Patents be graunted unto the said Thadie.

30. It may therefore please your lordship in tender consideration of the premisses so farr to respect your supliant as to certifie into England the state of his cause, as your lordship hath done in the like cases. And to make stay of the surrender of the said Tadie untill uppon knowledg of truth his Majestie's further pleasure be signified to your lordship, or els to cause the said Thadie to performe unto your supliant eyther the said order taken by your lordship, or the order taken in the contrie by their freinds.   And to requier and aucthorise the lord Chauncellor to make staye of the said letters Patents from the broade seale untill the said Thady make answer to these exceptions and ioyne issue with your supliant in the materiall poynts of the premisses.   And your supliant shall praie for your lordship, etc.

The 23rd of January 1608.

Mr. Thadie Doyne: these exceptions are taken to the fiant of your intended patent by your brother, of which you are to consider and to cleere them before your grant pass the seale.

The answer of Thadie Doyne to the exceptions
taken by Charles Duinn against the fiant.

1. To the first objection he saieth that the deeds herein mentioned were alredie showen before your honnor, and for wittnes then appearinge were accompted of no validitie, so as the supposed estats derived by them to Doctor Doyne and his brothers are voyde.   And if they bee good the defendant his surrender and takinge of a Patent cannot hinder them, for their Rights are saved by the fiant.

2. To the second he saieth as to the first and further that the defendant canot surrender but his owne estat and neyther his surrender nor his Majestie's Patent can any waye prejudice any estat in possession or remaynder that the said Charles justly hath.

3. To the 3 he saieth that if any such conveyance be extant that the same was and is avoyded by former conveyance sufficiently perfected.   And withall there is a clause in his Patent for saving any man is right whereof the Doctor may take advantadg (if Right he hath) and to the chiefries the defendant saieth that if they were formerlie extinguished his Majestie's Patent canot revyve them nor Chardg the said Charles is land.   And ther-

fore thoughe there be any such rent graunted by the said fiant (as the
defendant thinketh there is not) neyther the said Charles nor any other
can be prejudiced thereby.

4. To the 4th he saieth that the custome of Tanistrie is taken awaye by
statute so as none have the chifrie or lands pertayninge to the name of
O Doyne but he that cometh in by letters Patents, and denieth that there
is eyther deed or custome that maketh for the complainant. And if there
were, yet is the same voyde in Lawe. He saieth also that before the
Commissioners for takinge the office at Marybroughe the complainant
opposed himself accordinge his accustomed manner against this defendant
to the uttermost of his Power. The defendant further denieth that ever he
gave such oath to the complainant as untrulie is surmised or had any
speeches with him as the objection importeth.

5. To the 5 the defendant saieth and denieth that ever he feared the
complainant his tytle but rather feared his polecie and greate Countenance
and for that cause he was at the Complainant and his freinds' entreatie
drawen to submit himself to the order of certain gentlemen in certaine
poynts, but the orderers therein went beyond his submission and therefore
the order voyde, and if the complainant thinketh the order avaylable for
him, let him benefitt himself therein at the Comon Lawe which alredie
he hath attempted.

6. To the 6th the defendant saieth that since his cominge to mannes
state he was the chiefest staye for keepinge that contrie in obedience and
remembrance of their duties in all Rebellions and times of trouble, not the
Complainant. And if the Complainant be desirous to dwell in that Contrie,
he hath better meanes to dwell there then the defendant hath, for he hath
all the tythes in the contrie, worth an hundreth pounds sterling at the least
per annum, bysides the portion of land given by his father unto him.

7. To the 7th he saieth that if such as have right to the lordshipp of
Iregaine are to have the division thereof and none other, by that conse-
quence the Complainant can have no Partition thereof, for their be twoe
elder brethren then he is and divers others also. And as to the devision
of other contries *viz.* the Farrals, Reyles, Mc Mahon, etc, the Complainant
seemeth more ambicious or covetous then skillfull in these causes, for if
there [be] twoe O Farrals, etc, and in many otheres one onely is the
Chief, and so it is with McCoghlane, O Caroll and others. And god
knoweth that to be Cheif of Iregaine, not half so greate as the least of
those contries, is but a poore dignitie, the Chiefrie whereof is scarse
worth 40^{tie} pounds by the yeare.

8. To the viiith what may be hereafter the defendant knoweth not but
when [he] or his heyres fayle in doeinge their dutie to their Prince lett

the Complainant sue for the livinge. In the meantime the defendant praieth the benefitt of his Majestie's letters, and that the complainant's palpable ambition may not hinder the same.

9. To the 9th the defendant will not denie but that the said Teig Reogh did mightilie forgett himself, which he did by the procurement of the complainant his brethren that conspired not onely the overthrowe of the defendant is estate but also pulled awaye his sonn from him. But, God be thanked, if that contry be as stronge as the complainant allegeth, this defendant so kept and governed the same as verie fewe entered there unto Rebellion. And withall the said Teig Reogh gryved at the forgettfullnes of his dutie to his prince, amended the same then after with good service in sheddinge four of the Rebell is bloode. And whether he shalbe the defendant his heyre or not God knoweth.

To the 10th he saieth that he keepeth his lawfull wife in his house not-withstanding the complainants slanderous speeches. And let not the Complainant take any greate care howe the defendant shall dispose his inheritans but let him assure himselfe that none shall e[n]ioye the same by discent or conveyance from the defendant but the most legitimate and that shalbe most faithful to his Prince, the complainant is ydle and vayne Imaginations notwithstanding.

11. To the xith the defendant his faithful service is so well knowen and allredie testified by men of no smale accompt as he will not nowe bragge thereof nor wilbe the trompet of his owne fame as the complainant is, whoe beinge at Tenahensye when the Rebells came he ther did give speciall chardge to the warders of the Castle that none of them should dischardge one shott at the Rebells. And withall if the kinge be deceaved in his graunte it is a good cause to voyde the letters Patents and so no hindrance to the plaintiff.

12. The complainant mightelie abuseth your lordship by his information and less wrongeth the defendant, for the defendent referreth his losses to the Report of his neighbors and although the Complainant his spite and malice to this defendant requirth at his dischardge and libertie gotten from the Rebells yet doth the defendant humbly thanketh god for the same. And if his services and losses had bene less then they were, yet is not the kings bontie and favour extended towards him to be taken from him.

13. To the 13th he saieth no more but that the complainant would seeme verie officious in controllinge the kings majestie and curbinge his bountie, and whether the comissions or letters agree or vary it is impertinent.

14. To the 14th all this is performed and every man is right saved by the

woords of the patents which is apparent (if the Complainant is blind malice could affoord him sight to see). And it appeareth by those ydle excepcions that the plaintiff his whole drift is to put the defendant to charges and delayes.

15. To the 15th all is verie certaine and done at the request of the free-houlders and by their owne confession will not have the service altered, also the Chieffries in the said fiant mencioned are the auncient chifries of Iregaine which by letters Patents or otherwise maye not be altered untill by agreements and conveyances betwixt the lord and the tenaunts.

16. To the 16th he saieth that he knoweth no concealed lands in that contrie and surrendered no more then was in his possession at the time of his surrender, and if there were any concealed, as in truth there are not, yet hopeth to deserv them as well as another. And withall his Majesties pleasure is that a surrender shuld be accepted of any such lands as his subjects here had in his possession at his cominge to the kingdome, what-soever tytle he had thereunto.

17. To the 17th he saieth that the Complainant ought not be herd in diswadinge a most mightie kinge from his wonnted gracious Bountye.

18. To the 18th the Complainant is meaninge is never to have an end of his suite to the end the defendant shuld never surrender. And therefore the defendant referreth the said vayne frivolous exposicion of the kings letter to your honnors. Also if the plaintiff shuld recover in the Chaun-cerye, he recovereth no land but the forfayture of his bond and as that rather proweth the land to be the defendants then plaintiffs, where the assurance is to be made by the defendant.

19. To the 19th he saieth that whosoever informed the matter it skilleth not. And saith also that it is strange that the complainant shuld make so many ydle constructions of the kings letters and utter so many vayne excepcions as he hath done.

20. To the 20th the same is not worth answeringe, for it is comen that ever heretofore and yet the like was and is used. And all Patents made to Irishe lords of their contries the same are generall without restrictions.

21. To the 21th it is ydle for there are no tythes mencioned in the fiant.

22. To the 22th saieth that the same hath bene severall times urged and by your honnor overruled.

23. To the 23th the informacion is most untrue and withall no man his Right is hurt or extinguished by his Patent.

24. To the 24th he seeketh nothing but what is his owne just and trewe inheritance and not the porcion of any keannfinie, for the keannfinies hariot is onely graunted where a keannfinie is. But where no keannfinie is, the freehoulders paie hariots to O Doyne and there only is *libere tenente* mencioned and not the word keannfinie translated to that word as the plaintiff well knoweth or ells is too ignorant in the state of that contrie.

25. To the 25th he saith that his mother graunted her lands unto him by good conveyance well testified, and is assured that his mother never denied nor thought to denie her said assurance (as is surmised) and if the defendant is estat be not good therein, the said Daniell havinge the better right canot be hurt by the letters Patents, as is oftentimes declared.

26. To the 26th the Contrie of Iregaine consisteth of demean lands and services, which altogether is meant to be graunted to the defendant, and not the freehould of any (as is presupposed) no more then if the kings majestie would graunt a maner or one of his contries there passeth nothinge by this but what [was] in his highnes.

27. The Complainant mistaketh the lawe in this objection, for that the king is graunte extendeth no further then to mantayne, warrant and defend what was justly surrendered unto his highnes, and graunted backe by him notwithstanding that woords.

28. To the 28th there was no reasone whye the arbitrators shuld adward the 4th part of the deffendants inheritance unto the complainant, and as little reason for the complainant to demaund the same uppon which order your honnor grounded the said order. But consideringe that the arbitrators order could not binde, alter or change the defendants inheritance, your honnors order grounded uppon the same could be of no more validitie then the same arbiterment and this objection hath beene severall times before made and reiected by your honnor.

29. To the 29th that the former objections are so ydle and frivolous as there is no equitie to compell the defendant to answer unto them and less equitie to give the plaintiff time to Replie, least of all to delaye the defendant is Patent, which is the only drift of Plaintiff.

30. And lastly, in so much as it appeareth to your honnor as well by these exceptions as by the last exceptions preferred by the Complainant before your honnors at the Councell Table that the complainant his only drift is to weary the poore defendant and to weare him out by delayes in such sort as he shall not be able to follow the suinge of his letters Patents which is almost alredie done. And withall that no man havinge right to anything to be graunted by the said letters Patents is no waye to be hindered

by them. That it may please your honnors in your grawe consideracions to keepe and use that speedie course of justice yow use to all subjects in grauntinge him the benefitt and that your honnour will give indelayed order for accepting his surrender and passing his patent. And he shall alwayes pray, etc.

FIANT FOR LETTERS PATENT FOR THADY DOYNE, 7 MARCH 1608/9

Arthur Chichester.

Deliberata fuit in Cancellario Hibernie septimo die Martii anno regni Regis Jacobi Anglie Francie et Hibernie sexto et Scotie xlii^{do} ad exequendum. Fiant litteres Domini Regis patentes in debita juris forma tenore verborum sequentium, viz:

Jacobus Dei gratia etc, Omnibus ad quos etc. Cum nos per literas nostras manu nostra propria signatas et sub signeto nostro gerentes, datas apud Pallaceum nostrum de Westminster vicessimo novo die Junii anno Regni nostri Magne Brittanie Francie et Hibernie sexto predilecto et fideli Consiliaro nostro Arthuro Chichester milite deputato nostro generali Regni nostri Hibernie et Cancellario nostro ibidem modo existenti, aut alicui alio Deputato aut alio Capitali gubernatori sive gubernatoribus et Cancellario sive custodi magni sigillii eiusdem Regni nostri imposterum pro tempore existenti, ac omnibus aliis quibus attinet sive pertinere debeat et eorum Cuiuslibet directas, ad humilem peticionem dilecti et fidelis subditi nostri Tadei O Doyne per *nominem Capitanei Tadei Doyne armigeri sue nacionis principalis, et in Consideracionem boni et fidelis servitii per prefatum Thadeum O Doyne Corone nostre Hibernie in bello et guerra nuper in eodem Regno excitatis impensis et prescitis voluntatem nostram Regiam significaverimus et per easdem litteras nostras predictis Deputato, Cancellario ac ceteris personis predictis mandaverimus et authoritatem dedimus ad acceptandum de eodem Tadeo O Doyne sursumreddicionem Patriae de Iregaine ac omnium terrarum tenementorum et hereditamentorum in eadem patria scituatarum in Comitatu Regine in dicto Regno nostro Hibernie, de quibus ipse et antecessores sui fuerunt possessionati. Ac super inde ad faciendum pro nobis, heredibus et successoribus nostris Concessionem sive Concessiones eidem Tadeo O Doyne in debita Juris forma per literas patentes sub magno sigillo nostro dicti Regni nostri Hibernie dicte patrie de Iregan ac omnium terrarum, tenementorum, decimarum et hereditamentorum in eadem patria et eidem pertinentium sive spectantium ac omnium Cattallorum fellonium et deodandi in eodem patria contigentium, Habendum eidem Tadeo heredibus et assignatis suis imperpetuum in feodo simplice, Tenendum de nobis, heredibus et successoribus nostris in libero et Communi soccagio ut de Castro nostro Dublinii, Ac etiam per easdem literas nostras authoritatem et licentium dedimus et eisdem Deputato, Cancellario et aliis personis predictis mandaverimus quod in eisdem literis nostris patentibus sic ut prefertur prefato Tadeo O Doyne conficiendis plena authoritas et potestas de nobis, heredibus et successoribus nostris concederetur prefato Tadeo O Doyne, heredibus et assignatis suis ad eius et eorum voluntatem et placitum ad tenendum infra predicta patria de Iregan in talibus convenientibus locis et temporibus sic et talis Curiam Letam, Curiam Baronam et mercata et nundines quot et qualis prefatis deputato, Cancellario et Ceteris personis predictis videbitur expedire prout per easdem literas nostras in Cancellaria nostra dicti Regni nostri Hibernie irrotulatas et de Recordo remanentes plenius liquet et apparet, Cumque etiam prefatus Tadeus O Doyne per scriptum suum genertem datum decimo die Januarii Anno Regni nostri Anglie, Francie et Hibernie sexto et Scotie quadragesimo secundo in dicta Cancellaria nostra Hibernie irrotulatum secundum tenorem et effectum dictorum literorum nostrorum dedit, concessit et in *manuas nostras sursumreddidit Totum illud Castrum et 60 acras terre mensure in dicta patria de Iregan usitate Cum pertinentiis, iacentes et existentes in villa et Campis de Bolinumer alias Tenehinsy[1] in territorio sive precincta de Iregan in Comitatu Regine predicta, Ac etiam 7 acras terre mensure predicte cum pertinentiis iacentes in villa et Campis de Monyquid[2] in territorio predicto in Comitatu predicta, Ac etiam 20 acras terre mensure predicte cum pertinentiis in villa, hamlet' sive parcella terre vocata Achmore[3] in quarter de Killtegrallaghe in territorio predicto in Comitatu predicta, Ac etiam unum *castrum, [et] 215 acras terre mensure predicte Cum pertinentiis in villa et Campis de Castlebreake alias Ballincastlebrack[4] in territorio et comitatu predictis, Ac etiam 60 acras terre mensure [predicte] Cum pertinentiis in villa et Campis de Ballinvonyne[5] in quarter de Clancowy alias Clanchowyn in territorio et Comitatu predictis Ac etiam 20 acras terre mensure predicte Cum pertinentiis in villa et Campis de Aghvane[6] in quarter de Clanchowmoye predicta et in Territorio et Comitatu predictis, Ac etiam 30 acras terre mensure predicte Cum

---

1 In margin, in Gaelic script: buali an u*mair* 60 acra.

2 Margin: muini cuid 7 acra.

3 Margin: ac*h*a mor 20 ac[ra].

4 Margin: caislen breac 219 ac*ra*.

5 Margin: balinm*h*onin 60 acra.

6 Margin: aca a*n* b*h*ab*h*ai*n* 20 ac*ra*.

pertinentiis in villa et Campis de Ballygarvan[7] in quarter de Clancarroll alias Kilkevan in Territorio et Comitatu predictis, Ac etiam 24 acras terre mensure predicte Cum pertinentiis in villis et Campis de Aghanecrosse et Cowlicknawle[8] in quarter de Dery alias Dromnebehy in territorio et comitatu predictis, Ac etiam 20 acras terre mensure predicte Cum pertinentiis in villa et Campis de Fearan Clankein[9] in quarter de Moyntaghe Mellecke in territorio et Comitatu predictis, Ac etiam 5 acras terre mensure predicte cum pertinentiis in villa et Campis de Ardarraghmoyle[10] in quarter de Moyntaghe Millick predicta in Territorio et Comitatu predictis, Ac etiam 6 acras terre cum pertinentiis in villa et Campis de Garrycoacha alias Garryconghe[11] in predicta quarter de Moyntaghmilick in territorio et Comitatu predictis, Ac etiam 51 acras terre mensure predicte cum pertinentiis in villa et Campis de Cappabrogan[12] in Territorio et Comitatu predictis, Ac etiam 5 acras terre mensure predicte cum pertinentiis in villa et Campis de Knocke Choncloghane alias Cnockachorloghan[13] in quarter de Moyntaghe milicke predicta in territorio et Comitatu predictis, Ac etiam 30 acras terre mensure predicte cum pertinentiis in Lakamore alias Lackaghemore[14] in quarter do Monyquid in Territorio et Comitatu predictis, Ac etiam quandam parcellam sive precinctam terre pasture, bosce et subbosci vocatam O Doynes Forest[15] iacentem et existentem in territorio et Comitatu predictis, Ac unum Castrum et 60 acras terre Cum pertinentiis in villa sive villata et Campis de Roskine[16] in territorio et Comitatu predictis, Ac etiam 43 acras terre cum pertinentiis in villa sive villata et Campis de Reurybegge[17] in territorio et Comitatu predictis, Ac etiam 20 acras terre cum pertinentiis in villa sive villata et Campis de Agheny[18] in territorio et Comitatu predictis, Ac etiam 20

---

7 Margin: bali garbhain 30 acra.

8 Margin: acha na cros agus culic an abhaill 24 acra.

9 Margin: fearann cloinne cinn 20 acra.

10 Margin: ard darach moile 5 acra.

11 Margin: garri comhc (? ?) 6 acra (the letter or letters between the o and c of the second word are obscure).

12 Margin: ceapa brogain 51 acra.

13 Margin: cnoc a corrclochain 5 acra.

14 Margin: Lacagh mor 30 acra.

15 Margin: an fhoraois.

16 Margin: Roscaoin 60 acra.

17·Margin: Ririe beag 43 acra.

18 Margin: acha an fheich 20 acra.

acras terre cum pertinentiis in villa sive villata et Campis de Lawaghe[19] in territorio et Comitatu predictis, Ac etiam Insulam de Loughduffe[20] cum pertinentiis in territorio et Comitatu predictis. Necnon omnes et singulos annuales Custumos et Redditos Argenti bovium avenarum panis butirie et brasii et Corradia et opera Custumaria et cetera omnia onera et profitua subsequentes Crescentes emergentes seu exeuntes de vell ex Castris, mesuagiis, terris, tenementis et hereditamentis subsequentibus viz. de et ex parcella sive precincta terre vocata *the quarter of Rerymore* in territorio et Comitatu predictis per Annum 8s, duos boves, xxiiii mensuras avenarum Communiter vocatas *Cronocks of oats,* 40 pecias panis, Anglice *Cakes of bread,* 13 mensuras butiri, Anglice *dishes of butter,* 18 mensuras brasii Communiter vocatas *Carnes of maulte,* et unum herriott past mortem cuiuslibet Canfynnye in dicta quarter de Rerymore, unum precarium Anglice a *hookedaye* in Autumpno ex singulis 20 acris terre in eadem quarter de Rerymore, duos dies arature pro quolibet Aratro in eadem quarter de Rerymore viz. unum in estate et alterum in hieme, et 4s in pecunia pro Cibis pediseyquiarum, anglice *horsboyes dyett,* annuatim, Ac etiam de et ex parcella sive precincta terre vocata *the quarter of Bally-knyen* in territorio et Comitatu predictis per annum duos boves, 24 *Cronokes* avenarum, 12 *Cakes* panis, 4 *dishes* buttiri, unum herriot post mortem cuiuslibet libere tenentis in eadem quarter de Ballyknyen unum precarium anglice a *hookedaye* ex singulis 20 acris terre ibidem, duos dies aratri pro quolibet aratro ibidem viz. unum in estate et alterum in hieme, et 4s pro Cibo peditum, anglice *for horsboyes dyett,* Ac de et ex parcella sive precincta terre vocata *the quarter of Cappabrogan* in territorio predicto in comitatu predicta per annum duos boves, 24 *Cronokes* avenarum, 24 *Cakes* panis, 8 *dishes* butiri, unum herriott post mortem cuiuslibet libere tenentis in eadem quarter de Cappabrogan, unum precarium, anglice a *hookedaye,* ex singulis 20 acris terre ibidem, duos dies aratri pro quolibet aratro ibidem, unum in estate et alterum in hieme, ac 4s Currentis monete Hibernie pro Cibo peditum, anglice *horsboyes dyett,* *annuatim, Ac de et ex parcella sive precincta terre vocata *the quarter of Garroughe* in territorio predicto et in Comitatu predicta per annum duos boves, 24 *Cronocks* avenarum, 24 *Cakes* panis, 8 *dishes* butiri, unum herriott post mortem cuiuslibet libere tenentis in dicta quarter de Garroughe, unum precarium anglice a *hookeday* ex singulis 20 acris terre ibidem, duos dies Aratri pro quolibet Aratro ibidem, viz. unum in estate et alterum in hieme, et 4s Currentis monete Hibernie pro cibo peditum, Anglice *horseboyes dyett,* annuatim, Ac de et ex parcella sive precincta terre vocata *the three quarters of Moyntaghe Mellicke* in Territorio et Comitatu predictis per annum 6 boves, 72 *Cronoks* avenarum, 72 *Cakes*

---

19 Margin: leam*h*ac*h* 20 ac*ra.* 696.

20 Margin: oilea*n* loc*h*a duib*h.*

panis, 24 *dishes* butiri, unum heriott post mortem Cuiuslibet Canfynny ibidem, unum precarium, anglice *a hookeday* ex singulis 20 acris terre ibidem, duos dies Aratri pro quolibet Aratro ibidem, viz. unum in estate et alterum in hieme, 12s Currentis monete Hibernie pro Cibo peditum, anglice *horsboyes dyett*, annuatim, Ac de et ex parcella sive precincta terre vocata *the quarter of Sraghleighe* alias *Glannruishe* in territorio et Comitatu predictis per annum duos boves, 24 *Cronocks* avenarum, 12 *Cakes* panis, 4 *dishes* butiri et unum herriott post mortem Guiuslibet libere tenentis in dicta quarter de Glanruishe, unum precarium, anglice *a hookedaye* ex singulis 20 acris terre ibidem, duos dies aratri pro quolibet Aratro ibidem, unum in estate et alterum in Hieme, et 4s Currentis monete Hibernie pro Cibo peditum, anglice *horsboyes dyett*, annuatim, Ac de et ex parcella sive precincta terre vocata *the quarter of Killnegrallaghe* alias *Kiltegralaghe* in territorio et Comitatu predictis per annum duos boves, 24 *Cronoks* avenarum, unum heriott post mortem Cuiuslibet libere tenentis, et 4s currentis monete Hibernie pro Cibo peditum, Anglice *horsboyes dyett*, annuatim, Ac de et ex parcella sive precincta terre vocata *the quarter of Boell* alias *Boeman* in territorio et Comitatu predictis per annum 4s Currentis monete Hibernie, duos boves 24 *Cronoks* avenarum, *quatuor quarter unius bovis, 52 mensuras brasii Communiter vocatas *Barins of mault*, quarum 4 barreins forent brasii hordei, Anglice *of beare mault*, 12 barreins tritici, unum herriott post mortem Cuiuslibet Canfynny ibidem, et 4s Currentis monete Hibernie pro Cibo peditum, Anglice *horsboyes dyett*, annuatim, Ac de et ex parcella sive precincta terre vocata *the quarter of Ryrybegg* in territorio et Comitatu predictis per anum 10s duos boves, 24 *Cronoks* avenarum, 12 *Cakes* panis, 4 *dishes* butiri, 6 *Carnes* brasii, unum heriott post mortem Cuiuslibet libere tenentis ibidem, 4s Currentis monete Hibernie pro Cibo peditum, Anglice *horsboyes dyett*, annuatim, Ac de et ex parcella sive precincta terre vocata *the quarter of Dyrry* alias *Dromnebehy* in territorio et Comitatu predictis per annum duos boves, 24 *Cronocks* avenarum, unum heriott post mortem Cuiuslibet libere tenentis ibidem, et 4s Currentis monete Hibernie pro Cibo peditum, Anglice *horsboyes dyett*, annuatim, Ac de et ex parcella sive precincta terre vocata *the quarter of Corbolly* alias *Glanmylle* in Territorio et Comitatu predictis per annum duos boves, 24 *Cronocks* avenarum, 18 *Cakes* panis, 6 *dishes* butiri, unum herriott post mortem Cuiuslibet Canfyny ibidem, et 4s Currentis monete Hibernie pro Cibo peditum, Anglice *horsboyes dyett*, annuatim, Ac etiam de et ex parcella sive precincta terre vocata *the quarter of Tenyle* in territorio et comitatu predictis per annum duos boves, 24 *Cronoks* avenarum, 12 *Cakes* panis, 4 *dishes* butiri, unum herriott post mortem Cuiuslibet Canfyny ibidem, et 4s Currentis monete Hibernie pro Cibo peditum, Anglice *horsboyes dyett*, Annuatim, Ac de et ex parcella sive precincta terre vocata *the quarter of Cloenmachowe* alias vocata *Ballintegart* in territorio et comitatu predictis per annum xx^{d}, duos boves, 24 *Cronoks* avenarum, 12 *Cakes* panis, 4 *dishes* butiri, unum herriott post mortem Cuiuslibet libere tenentis ibidem, et 4s Currentis monete Hibernie pro Cibo peditum, Anglice *horsboyes dyett,* annuatim, Ac de et ex parcella sive precincta terre vocata *the quarter of Clanmorchowe* alias *Cowlevoghlan* in territorio et comitatu predictis per annum, 10s, duos boves, 24 *Cronoks* avenarum, unum herriott post mortem Cuiuslibet libere tenentis ibidem, et 4s currentis monete Hibernie pro Cibo peditum, Anglice *horsboyes dyett,* annuatim, Ac de et ex parcella sive precincta terre vocata *the quarter of Lackaghe* in territorio et Comitatu predictis per annum duos boves, 24 *Cronoks* avenarum, 12 *Caks* panis, 4 *dishes* butiri, unum herriott post mortem Cuiuslibet libere tenentis ibidem, et 4s currentis monete Hibernie pro Cibo peditum, Anglice *horsboyes dyett,* annuatim, Ac etiam de et ex parcella terre vocata *the quarter of Monyquid* in territorio et Comitatu predictis per annum unum denarium ex qualibet acra terre arrabilis infra eandem quarteriam pertinentis ad aliquen libere tenenti ibidem (exceptis sexaginta acris terre pertinentibus Briano mcRory, que sunt liberis) et unum herriott post mortem cuiuslibet libere tenentis ibidem, Ac de et ex parcella sive precincta terre vocata *the quarter of Clancarroll* in Territorio et Comitatu predictis per annum unum denarium ex qualibet acra terre arrabilis pertinentis ad aliquen libere Tenenti ibidem, et unum herriott post mortem cuiuslibet libere tenentis ibidem, Ac de et ex parcella sive precincta terre vocata *the quarter of Clancowmoye* alias *Clancoomwy* in territorio et comitatu predictis per annum unum denarium ex ex qualibet acra terre arrabilis pertinentis ad aliquem libere tenentis ibidem, et unum herriott post mortem cuiuslibet libere tenentis ibidem, Ac de et ex parcella sive precincta terre vocata *the quarter of Castlebrack* alias *Ballycaslanbracke* in Territorio et Comitatu predictis per annum unum denarium ex qualibet acra terre pertinentis ad aliquem libere tenenti ibidem, et unum heriott post mortem cuiuslibet libere tenentis ibidem, Ac de et ex parcella sive precincta terre vocata *the Shissaraughe of Fassaghe Elly* in Territorio et comitatu predictis unum herriott post mortem cuiuslibet libere tenentis ibidem, Ac de et ex parcella terre sive precincta terre vocata *the quarter of Cloneheene* in territorio et comitatu predictis per annum tresdecim solidos et quatuor denarios, duos boves, sex *dishes* butiri, octodecim *Cakes* panis, triginta et quatuor *Cronoks* avenarium, Ac omnia et singula alias terras, tenementa et hereditamenta que fuerunt prefati Tadei O Doyne, aut de quibus ipse idem Thadeus seisitus fuit tempore Concessionis sive sursumreddicionis predicti iacentes et existentes in vell infra predictam patriam sive territorum de Iregan predicta,[21] Necnon omnia et singula Castra, mesuagia, Grangia, molendina, Stagna, Domos, edificia, structura, stabula, columbaria, horta, pomaria, gardina, terras, tenementa, pratas, pascua, pasturas communas, terras dincolas, terras vastas, montanas, Iampuum, brues, moras, marisca, boscos, subboscos, liberes warrenas, aquas, aquarum Cursus, gurgitos, piscaria,

---

21 In margin: A surrender in generall terms of all whereof he was seised at the tyme of the surrender.

piscaciones, sectas, mulcturas, vivaria, stagna, mineras, querria, Redditus, Reverciones et servicias, Redditus oneris, Redditus siccos, Annuitates ac omnes Redditus Custumarios et servicias tam liberorum quam Custumariorum, opera tenentium, firmas, escaeta, relevia, herriotes, fines, amerciamenta, Curias Baronis, Curias letas, Visas France plegie ac omnia ad Curiis letiis et Visis France plegie pertinentia, ac nativos et nativas, villanos cum eorum sequelis, estoveras, teluetas, Theolona, Custumaria Iura, Iurisdicciones, Franchesas, privilegia, regalitates, proficua, commoditates, advantagia, emolumenta et hereditamenta quecunque predicto Thadeo O Doyne aut de quibus idem Thadeus O Doyne seisitus fuit tempore Concessionis sive sursumreddiciones predicte, cum eorum pertinentiis universis cuiuscunque fuit generis, nature seu specie seu quibuscunque nominibus sciantur, Censentur, nuncupantur seu Cognoscantur, scituata, iacentes et existentes, provenientes, crescentes sive emergentes in, ex vell infra predictam patriam sive territorium predictum de Irgan[22] et in, ex vel infra omnia et singula predicta Maneria, Castra, mesuagia, terras, tenementa et hereditamenta et eisdem vel alicui inde parcella *quocunque modo spectantes vel pertinentes sive ut pars, parcella sive membrum earundem sive earum alicuius accepta, reputata aut Cognitata existere, Ac totum ius, Clameum, Statum, titulum, interesse, Revercionem, Remanera et demanda prefati Thadei O Doyne quecunque ad et in premissis et in aliquid inde parcella et ad vel in totum predictum, Habendum, tenendum et *gaudendum omnia predicta patriam, territorium, Maneria, Castra, messuagia, terras, tenementa, Redditus, hereditamenta ac cetera omnia et singula premissis cum pertinentiis suis universis nobis, heredibus et successoribus nostris imperpetuum prout per predictum scriptum sursumreddicionis in Cancellaria nostra dicti regni nostri Hibernie irrotulatum et de Recorda remaneum plenius liquet et appareat, Ea tamen intencione ut nos predictam patriam sive territorium ac omnia et singula predicta Maneria, Castra, terras, tenementa et hereditamenta ac cetera premissa Cum pertinentiis prefato Thadeo O Doyne, heredibus et assignatis suis Concedere dignaremur.

Sciatis igitur quod nos pro et in Consideracione boni et fidelis servitii per prefatum Thadeum O Doyne Corone nostre Hibernie in bello et guerra nuper in eodem Regno nostro excitatis impensis et presiti de gratia nostra speciali ac ex certa scientia et mero motu nostris, de advisamento et concensu predicti consiliarii nostri Arthuri Chichester militis deputati nostri generalis dicti Regni nostri Hibernie, Necnon in Complementum dictarum literarum nostrarum manu nostra propria signata et secundum tenorem et effectum earundem, Dedimus et Concessimus ac per presentes pro nobis, heredibus et successoribus nostris damus et concedimus prefato Thadeo O Doyne totum predictum Castrum ac 60 acras terre mensure in

---

22 *Sic* MS.

dicta Patria de Iregan predicta usitate cum pertinentiis, iacentes et existentes in villa et Campis de Bollinummer alias Tynehenche in territorio
sive patria de Iregan predicta in Comitatu Regine predicta, Ac etiam
predictas 7 acras terre mensure predicte cum pertinentiis iacentes et
existentes in villa et campis de Monyquid in territorio predicto, Ac etiam
predictas 20 acras terre mensure predicte cum pertinentiis in villa, hamleta
sive parcella *terre[23] vocata Aghemore in quarter de Kiltegrallaghe in
territorio predicto in comitatu predicta, Ac etiam predictum Castrum et
215 acras terre mensure predicte cum pertinentiis in predicta villa et
Campis predictis de Castlebracke alias Ballencaslanbreake in territorio
et Comitatu predictis, Ac etiam predictas 60 acras terre mensure predicte
cum pertinentiis in villa et Campis de Ballinmonyne in predicta quarteria
de Clanchowmoy alias Clanchomwy in territorio et comitatu predictis,
Ac etiam predictas 20 acras terre mensure predicte cum pertinentiis in
villa et Campis de Aghevane in quarter de Clanchowmoye predicta et in
territorio et comitatu predictis, Ac etiam predictas 30 acras terre mensure
predicte cum pertinentiis in villa et Campis de Ballygarvane in quarter de
Clancarroll alias Killkevane predicta in territorio et Comitatu predictis,
Ac etiam predictas 24 acras terre mensure predicte cum pertinentiis in
villis et campis de Aghenecrosse et Cowlickinowle in predicta quarteria de
Dery alias Dromnebhehy in territorio et comitatu predictis, Ac etiam
predictas 20 acras terre mensure predicte cum pertinentiis in villa et
campis de Farrinclankeine in predicta quarter de Moyntagh Milicke in
territorio et comitatu predictis, Ac etiam predictas 5 acras terre mensure
predicte cum pertinentiis in villa et campis de Ardorraghe Moley, in
quarteria de Moyntaghmillicke predicta in territorio et comitatu predictis,
Ac etiam predictas 6 acras terre cum pertinentiis in villa et campis de
Garrichoughe alias Garry Conghe in predicta quarter de Mointaghmeelicke
in territorio et comitatu predictis, Ac etiam predictas 51 acras terre
mensure predicte cum pertinentiis in villa et campis Cappabrogan in
territorio et comitatu predictis, Ac etiam predictas 5 acras terre mensure
predicte cum pertinentiis in villa et campis de Cnockechoncloghane
alias Cnockachorcloghan in quarter de Moyntaghe Millicke predicta in
territorio et comitatu predictis, Ac etiam predictas 30 acras terre mensure
predicte cum pertinentiis in Lakamore alias Lakaghemore in quarter de
Monyquid predicta in territorio et comitatu predictis, Ac etiam predictam
parcellam sive precinctam terre pasture bosci et subbosci vocatam O
Doynes Forest iacentem et existentem in Territorio et Comitatu predictis,
Ac predictas Castrum et 60 acras terre cum pertinentiis in villa et campis
de Roskyne in territorio et comitatu predicto, Ac etiam predictas 43
acras terre cum pertinentiis in villa sive villata et Campis de Rirybegg in
territorio et comitatu predictis, Ac etiam predictas 20 acras terre cum
pertinentiis in villa sive hamleta et campis de Agheny in territorio et

---

23 territorio MS.

comitatu predictis, Ac etiam predictas 20 acras terre cum pertinentiis in villa sive villate et campis de Lawaghe in territorio et comitatu predictis, Ac etiam predictam Insulam de Loughduffe cum pertinentiis in territorio et comitatu predictis, Necnon omnes et singulos annuales customos et Redditus argenti, bovum, avenarum, panis, butiri et brasii et Corrodias et opera Custumaria et cetera omnia onera et proficia subsequentes Crescentes, emergentes seu exeuntes de vell ex Castris, mesuagilis, terris et hereditamentis subsequentibus, viz. de et ex predicta parcella sive precincta terre vocata *the quarter of Ryrimore* in territorio et Comitatu predictis per annum 8s, duos boves, 24 mensuras avenarum Communiter vocatas *Cronocks of oats,* 40 pecias panis, anglice *Cakes of bread,* 13 mensuras butiri, anglice *dishes of butter,* 18 mensuras brasii, Communiter vocatas anglice *Carnes of malt,* et unum herriott post mortem cuiuslibet Canfynny in dicta quarter de Ryrimore predicta, unum precarium, Anglice *a hooke daye* in autumpno ex singulis 20 acris terre in eadem quarter de Rerymore, duos dies aratri pro quolibet aratro in eadem quarteria de Rerymore, viz. unum [in] estate et alterum in Hieme, quatuor solidos in pecunia pro Cibo peditum, Anglice *horsboyes dyet,* annuatim, Ac de et ex predicta parcella sive precincta terre vocata *the quarter of Ballyknien* in territorio et Comitatu predictis per annum duos boves, 24 *Cronoks* avenarum, 12 *Cakes* panis, 4 *dishes* butiri, unum herriott post mortem Cuiuslibet libere tenentis in eadem quarter de Ballyknein, unum precarium, Anglice *a hooke day* ex singulis 20 acris terre ibidem, duos dies aratri pro quolibet aratro ibidem viz. unum in estate et alterum in Hieme, et 4s pro Cibo peditum, Anglice *for horsboyes diet,* annuatim, Ac de et ex predicta parcella sive precincta terre vocata *the quarter of Cappabrogan* in Territorio predicto in Comitatu predicta per annum duos boves, 24 *Cronocks* avenarum, 24 *Cakes* panis, 8 *dishes* butiri, unum herriott post mortem Cuiuslibet libere tenentis in eadem quarteria de Cappabrogan predicta, unum precarium, Anglice *a hooke day* de singulis 20 acris terre ibidem, duos dies Aratri pro quolibet Aratro ibidem, viz. unum in hieme et alterum in estate, ac 4s Currentis monete Hibernie pro Cibo peditum, anglice *horsboyes dyett,* annuatim, Ac de [et] ex predicta parcella sive precincta terre vocata *the quarter of Garoughe* in Territorio predicto et in Comitatu predicta per annum duos boves, 24 *Cronoks* avenarum, 24 *Cakes* panis, 8 *dishes* butiri, unum herriott post mortem cuiuslibet libere tenentis dicte quarter de Garroughe, unum precarium anglice *hooke day,* ex singulis 20 acris terre ibidem, duos dies Aratri pro quolibet aratro ibidem viz. unum in estate et alterum in Hieme, et 4s Currentis monete Hibernie pro Cibo peditum, anglice *horsboyes dyett,* annuatim, Ac de et ex predicta parcella sive precincta terre vocata *the three quarters of Moyntaghmillicke* in Territorio et Comitatu predictis per annum, sex boves, 72 *Cronocks* avenarum, 72 *Cakes* panis, 24 *dishes* butiri, unum heriott post mortem Cuiuslibet Canfynny ibidem, unum precarium, anglice *a hooke daye* ex singulis 20 acris terre ibidem, duos dies Aratri pro quolibet aratro ibidem, viz. unum in estate et alterum in hieme, Ac 12s Currentis monete Hibernie pro Cibo peditum, anglice *horsboyes dyett*, annuatim, Ac de et ex predicta parcella sive precincta terre vocata *the quarter of Shraghlieghe* alias *Glanruish* in territorio et Comitatu predictis per annum duos boves, 24 *Cronocks* avenarum, 12 *Cakes*, 4 *dishes* butiri, unum herriott post mortem Cuiuslibet libere tenentis in dicta quarter de Glanruishe, unum precarium, anglice *a hooke daye* ex singulis 20 acris terre ibidem, duos dies aratri pro quolibet aratro ibidem, unum in estate et alterum in Hieme, et 4s pro Cibo peditum, anglice *horsboyes dyett*, annuatim, Ac de et [ex] predicta parcella sive precincta terre vocata *the quarter of Killngrall-agha* alias *Kiltegrallaghe* in territorio et Comitatu predictis per annum duos boves, 24 *Cronoks* avenarum, unum herriott post mortem cuiuslibet libere tenentis ibidem, et 4s pro Cibo peditum, Anglice *horsboyes dyett*, annuatim, Ac de et ex predicta parcella sive precincta terre vocata *the quarter of Boell* alias *Boeman* in territorio et Comitatu predictis per annum 4s, duos boves, 24 *Cronocks* avenarum, quatuor quarter unius bovis, 52 mensuras brasii Comuniter vocatas *barrins of mault,* quorum quatuor barrins forent brasii hordii Anglice *beare maulte,* duodecim barrins tritici, unum herriott post mortem Cuiuslibet Canfynnye ibidem et 4s. pro Cibo peditum, Anglice *horsboyes dyett,* annuatim, ac [de] et ex predicta parcella sive precincta terre vocata the quarter of Rerybegge in Territorio et Comitatu predictis per annum 10s, duos boves, 24 *Cronocks* avenarum, 12 *Cakes* panis, 4 *dishes* butiri, 6 *Carnes* brasii, unum herriott post mortem cuiuslibet libere tenentis ibidem et 4s. pro Cibo peditum, anglice *horsboyes dyett,* annuatim, Ac de et ex predicta parcella sive precincta terre vocata *the quarter of Dyrry* alias *Dromnebehy* in territorio et Comitatu predictis per annum duos boves, 24 *Cronoks* avenarum, unum herriott post mortem Cuiuslibet libere tenentis ibidem, et 4s. pro Cibo peditum, anglice *horsboyes dyett*, annuatim, Ac de et ex predicta parcella sive precincta terre vocata *the quarter of Corbolie* alias *Glanmille* in territorio et Comitatu predictis per annum duos boves, 24 *Cronocks* avenarum, 18 *Cakes* panis, 6 *dishes* butiri, unum herriott post mortem Cuiuslibet Canfynny ibidem et 4s. pro Cibo peditum, anglice *horsboyes dyett,* annuatim, Ac de et ex predicta parcella sive precincta terre vocata *the quarter of Tenyll* in Territorio et Comitatu predictis per annum duos boves, 24 *Cronocks* avenarum, 12 *Cakes* panis, 4 *dishes* butiri, unum herriott post portem cuiuslibet Canfynny ibidem, et 4s pro Cibo peditum, Anglice *horsboyes dyett,* annuatim, Ac de et ex predicta parcella sive precincta terre vocata *the quarter of Cloenmachowe* alias vocata *Ballin-tegart* in Territorio et Comitatu predictis per annum, 20d., duos boves, 24 *Cronocks* avenarum, 12 *Cakes* panis, 4 *dishes* butiri, unum herriott post mortem cuiuslibet libere tenentis ibidem, 4s. pro Cibo peditum, anglice *horsboyes dyett,* annuatim, Ac de et ex predicta parcella sive precincta terre vocata *the quarter of Canmorchow*[24] alias *the quarter*

---

24 *1. *Clanmorchow.*

[of] Cowlevoghelane in territorio et Comitatu predictis per annum 10s, duos boves, 24 *Cronocks* avenarum, unum herriott post mortem Cuiuslibet libere tenentis ibidem, et 4s pro Cibo peditum, anglice *horsboyes dyett,* annuatim, Ac de [et] ex predicta parcella sive precincta terre vocata *the quarter of Lakaghe* in Territorio et Comitatu predictis per annum duos boves, 24 *Cronocks* avenarum, 12 *Cakes* panis, 4 *dishes* butiri, unum herriott post mortem cuiuslibet libere tenentis ibidem, et 4s pro Cibo peditum, anglice *horsboyes dyett,* annuatim, Ac etiam de et ex predicta parcella sive precincta terre vocata *the quarter of Monyquid* in Territorio et Comitatu predictis per annum, unum denarium ex qualibet acra terre arrabilis infra eandem quarter pertinentis ad aliquem libere tenenti ibidem (exceptis sexaginta acris terre pertinentis Briano mcRory que sunt libere) et unum herriott post mortem cuiuslibet libere tenentis ibidem, Ac de et ex predicta parcella sive precincta terre vocata *the quarter of Clancarroll*[25] in Territorio et Comitatu predictis per annum unum denarium ex qualibet acra terre arrabilis pertinentis ad aliquem libere tenenti ibidem, et unum herriott post mortem cuiuslibet libere tenentis, Ac de et ex parcella sive precincta terre vocata *the quarter of Clanchowmoye* in Territorio et Comitatu predictis per annum unum denarium ex qualibet acra terre arrabilis pertinentis ad aliquen libere tenenti ibidem, et unum herriott post mortem Cuiuslibet libere tenentis ibidem, Ac etiam de et ex predicta parcella terre vocata *the quarter of BallyCaslanebrack* alias *Castlebrack* in territorio et Comitatu predictis per annum unum denarium ex qualibet acra terre arrabillis pertinentis ad aliquem libere tenentis ibidem, et unum herriott post mortem Cuiuslibet libere tenentis ibidem, Ac de et ex precicta terre vocat *the Shesseraghe of Fassaghe Elye* in Territorio et Comitatu predictis unum herriott post mortem Cuiuslibet libere tenentis ibidem, Ac de et ex predicta parcella sive precincta terre vocata *the quarter of Cloneheine* in Territorio et Comitatu predictis per annum 13s 4d, duos boves, 6 *dishes* butiri, 18 *Cakes* panis, et 24 *Cronocks* avenarum, Ac omnia et singula alias terras, tenementa et hereditamenta que fuerunt prefato Thadei O Doyne aut de quibus ipse idem Thadeus seisitus fuit tempore Concessionis vell sursumreddicionis predicte, iacentes et existentes in vel infra predictam Patriam sive Territorium de Iregan predicta, Ac omnia et singula bona et Cattalla felonium quorumcumque et deodanda provenientes, emergentes sive contingentes in vell infra predictam Patriam sive Territorium de Iregan predicta, Necnon omnia et singula Castra, messuagia, gragia, molendina, stagna, domos, edificia, structura, stabula, Columbaria, horta, pomaria, gardina, terras, tenementa, pratas, pascua, pasturas Communas, terras dincollas, terras vastas, montanas, Iampuum, bruerias, moras, mariscas, boscos, subboscos, libera varenas, aquas, aquarum Coursus, gurgitos, piscaria, piscaciones, sectas, socas, mulcturas, vivaria, stagna, mineras, quarrias, Redditus, Reverciones et servicias, redditus oneris, redditus siccos, imunitates ac omnia redditus, Custuma

---

25 Apparently corrected from *Clanchowmoye.*

et servicias tam liberorum quam Custumariorum tenentium, opera tenentium, firmas, Escaeta, Relevia, herrott, fines, amerciamenta, Curias Baronas,
Curias leete, visa France plegie, Ac omnia ad Curiis lete et visis France
plegie pertinentes, ac nativos, nativas, villanos cum eorum sequelis,
estovera, toluetas, Theolona, Custumaria Jura, Jurisdicciones, Franchesas,
privilegias, regalitates, proficua, Comoditates, advauntagia, emolumenta,
et hereditamenta nostra quecunque cum eorum pertinentiis universis
cuiuscunque fuit generis, naure seu speciei seu quibuscunque nominibus
sciantur, censentur, nuncupantur seu cognoscunt, scituata, iacentes et
existentes, provenientes, crescentes seu emergentes de, ex, in vel infra
predictam Patriam sive Territorium de Iregan, predictis Maneriis, Castris,
mesuagiis, terris, tenementis, et hereditamentis sepius per presentes
preconcessis vel alicui inde parcella quoquomodo spectantes, pertinentes,
incidentes vel appendentes aut ut membrum, pars, partes vel parcella
eorumdem aut eorum aliquorum vel alicuius unquam vel ad aliquod
tempus ante hac habitata, occupata, acceptata, rogata, dimissa, usitata
seu reputata, possessionata aut estimata existentes, Ac Revercionem,
Reverciones, Remanere et Remaneria nostra quecunque omnium et
singulorum premissorum eorum cuiuslibet parcella Cum pertinentiis
expectandum sive dependum in et super aliquam dimissionem aut
dimissiones, Concessiones vel Concessiones pro termino vite vel vitarum
vel feodo talliato tam de Recorda quam non Recorda existentes aut aliter
qualiter eumque seu quomodocunque, Ac omnia et Singula Redditus,
Reverciones, servicias, Custuma, opera et alia debita reservationes super
aliquem dimissionem sive dimissiones, Concessionem vel Concessiones de,
ex aut pro premissis per presentes preconcessis ante hac reservatas sive
factas, Necnon totum et omnia Jus, titulum, Clameum et enteresse nostra
quecunque ad et in omnibus et singulis premissis et qualibet inde parcella
adeo plene, libere et integre et in tam amplius et beneficialis modo et
forma prout ea, omnia et singula premissa aut aliqua inde parcella ad
manis nostris seu ad manis aliquorum progenitorem aut antecessorum
nostrorum aliquo modo devenit seu devenerunt vel devenire vel advenire
poterit vel poterint racione vel pretextu predictis idem Concessionis
et sursumreddicionis aut alicuis exchambii vel proquissicionis vel alicuis
attincture vel Forisfacture vel racione alicuius acti parliamendi aut
aliquorum actium Parliamenti, aut racione Escaeti vel legitime prescrip-
cionis sive Consuetudinis aut in jure Corone nostre aut antique hereditatis
nostre seu quorumque alio bono et legali modo iure vel titulo superius
recitato aut non recitato vel male recitato aut in manibus nostris iam
existit vel existimis[26] aut existere debet vel debent vel debeat aut fore
*Contigerint[27] aut in manibus vel possessione aliquorum tenentium,

---

26 *l.* existerint?

27 Conrigerint MS.

occupatorum vel firmanariorum nostrorum aut aliquorum progenitorem
nostrorum sive antecessorum nostrorum vel aliquarum aliarum personarum
sunt aut unquam aliquo tempore fuerunt ante hac, estiamsi possessio,
jus, titulus vel interesse nostrum qualitercunque vel qualiacunque in
premissis vel aliqua inde parcella in his presentibus non recitata vel male
recitata sit vel existit, Salvo[28] semper et ex hac Concessione nostra
exceptis et forsprisis omni jure, statu, titulo et interesse Caroli O Doyne,
armigeri, Donelli mc Cormock O Doyne et Brieni O Doyne et eorum
cuiuslibet et omnium aliorum subditorum nostrorum ad et in omnia et
singula premissa sive ad et in qualibet sive aliquem inde parcella,
Habendum, tenendum et gaudendum omnia et singula predicta maneria,
Castra, mesuagia, terras, tenementa, privilegia, Comoditates, advauntagia,
Iura, hereditamenta ac cetera omnia et singula premissa quecunque
superius expressa, specificata aut per presentes preconcessa, cum eorum
juribus, membris et pertinentiis quibuscunque, Ac revercione et Reverciones, Remanere et Remaneria nostra quecunque eorumdem cum pertinentiis prefato Tadeo O Doyne, heredibus et assignatis suis imperpetuum
ad solum et proprium opus et usum ipsius Thadei, heredum et assignatorum
suorum imperpetuum, Tenendum de nobis, heredibus et successoribus
nostris, ut de Castro nostro Dublin in libere et Comuni socagio per fidel-
itatem tantum et non in Capite nostre per serviciam militariam, Ac ulterius
de ampliori gratia nostra speciali ac ex certa scientia et mero motu nostris
pro nobis, heredibus et successoribus nostris damus [et] concedimus
prefato Tadeo O Doyne, heredibus et assignatis suis quod ipse prefatus
Tadeus O Doyne, heredes et assignati sui de cetero imperpetuum habeant,
teneant et gaudeant, ac habere, tenere et gaudere possint et valeant unum
visum France plegie seue Curiam lete ac omnia ad visis France plegie et
Curiis lete seu eorum alteri pertinentes, tenendum apud villam de Tenehinche predicta in Territorio et Comitatu predictis ad duos separales dies
annuatim viz. infra unum mensem proximum post Festum Pasche et
infra unum proximum post Festum Sancti Michaelis Archangeli, coram
Seneschalli vel seneschallis per prefatum Thadeum O Doyne, heredes et
assignatos suos vel per eorum alterum de tempore in tempus constituendi
imperpettum, Qui quidem visum France plegie sive Curiam lete et predicti
Senescallus sive Senescalli modo et forma predictis Constituti vel Constituendi per prefatum Thadeum O Doyne, heredes vel assignatos suos
imperpetuum, habeant plenam potestatem, aucthoritatem et iurisdiccionem
in predictis viso France plegie et Curia lete ad inquirendum de omnibus
et singulis Feloniis, transgressionibus, deceptionibus, delictis, offensis,
nocumentis, purpresturis et omnibus aliis ad visis France plegie et Curiis
lete sive eorum alteri pertinentes, Contingentes sive emergentes in vel
infra patriam et Territorium de Iregane predicta aut in vel infra omnia
Maneria, terras, tenementa et hereditamenta superius preconcessa, iacentes

---

28 In margin: 'Savinge the right of Charles Duinn, Do[n]yll Duinn & Brian Duinn, etc.'

et existentes *in Territorio et Comitatu predictis, que in Curia lete sive viso France plegie inquiri debent aut soleant per leges, statuta sive Consuetudines huius regni nostri Hibernie, Ac ulterius ad faciendum et ordinandum omnia ad quecumque que ad visum France plegie seu Curia lete sive eorum alteri spectantes aut pertinentis aut que in easdem fieri debeant aut soleant, Ac ulterius de ampliori gratia nostra speciali ax ex certa scientia et mero motu nostris dedimus et concessimus, Ac per presentes pro nobis, heredibus et successoribus nostris Concedimus et licentiam damus prefato Thadeo O Doyne, heredibus et assignatis suis imperpetuum, habeant et teneant et habere et tenere possint et valeant unam Curiam Baronam apud Tenehinche predicta, tenendum ad quatuor separales dies annuatim viz. infra unum mensem proximum post Festum Pasche, Nativitatis Sanct Johannis Baptiste, Sancti Michaelis Archangeli et Nativitatis Domini respective annuatim Coram Seneschallo vel Seneschallis per prefatum Thadeum O Doyne, heredes et assignatos suos de tempore in tempus imperpetuum constituendis, Que quidem Curia Barona et predicti Seneschallus et Seneschalli modo et forma predictis constituendi habeant plenum authoritatem, potestatem et Jurisdiccionem in predicta Curia Barona tenenda omnia placita de quibuscunque Debitis, Convencionibus, transgressionibus, Computis, detentis, Causis et Contractis que non attingint ad summum unum xl s vell amplius in vell infra predictam patriam de Iregan predicta, ac cetera premissa, ac in vell infra omnia alias villas, hamletas, terras, tenementa et hereditamenta iacentes et existentes infra precinctam, Circuitum, limites, metas et bundas eorundem seu eorum Dicimus²⁹ facta, Contingentes seu emergentes, Ac ulterius ad faciendum et ordinandum omnia alia quecunque que in Curiis Baronis fieri debeat aut soleat per leges et consuetudinibus dicti Regni nostri Hibernie, Ac ulterius de ampliori gratia nostra speciali ac ex certa scientia et mero motu nostris de assensu predictorum pro nobis, heredibus et successoribus nostris per presentes Concedimus et licentiam damus prefato Thadeo O Doyne, heredibus et assignatis suis quod ipse prefatus Thadeus O Doyne, heredes et assignati sui habeant, teneant et gaudeant ac habere et tenere possint [et] valeant unum liberum mercatum apud Tenehinche predicta in quelibet die Sabbati singulis septimanis imperpetuum tenendum, Ac unum alterum liberum mercatum apud Balliencaslenebrack predicta in Territorio et Comitatu predictis quolibet die Lune in singulis septimanis imperpetuum tenendum, Ac unam Feriam sive nundinam tenendum Tenehinche predicta in Festum die Sancti Luce Evangeliste (dumodo idem Festum dies non contingat in die Sabbati neque in die Dominica) ac per duos dies eundem Festum proprium sequentes duratur annuatim imperpetuum tenendum, Ac unum alteram Feriam sive Nundinam apud Balliencastlanebracke predicta tenendum primo die Augusti (dumodo predictus primus Dies Augusti non contingat in die

---

29 *Sic* MS.

Sabbati vel in die dominico), Ac per duos dies eundem primum diem
Augusti proximum sequentes duratur annuatim imperpetuum tenendum,
Et quotiescunque predicta separales dies in quibus Ferie sive Nundine
predicta tenendo fuerint in die Sabbati vel in die Dominico Contingerint
vell eorum aliquo contingit, Tunc et tocies Ferie sive Nundine predicta
tenent in Crastino predictorum separalium dierum et per duos dies ex tunc
proximos sequentes, Cum curia pulverizata ibidem tenendam de tempore
in tempus durante eisdem Feriis unacum exitibus, profitiis et amerciamentis
de huiusmodi mercatis, feriis et Curiis provenientibus ac cum omnibus et
singulis libertatibus et liberis consuetudinibus, profitiis et emolumentis
ad huiusmodi mercatos et Feria pertinentibus sive spectantibus, Dum
tamen mercata et ferie predicta non sint ad nocumentum viciniorum
mercatorum et Feriarum, Ac ulterius de ampliori gratia nostra [ac ex]
certa scientia et mero motu nostris pro nobis, heredibus et successoribus
nostris damus et Concedimus prefato Thadeo O Doyne, heredibus et
assignatis suis imperpetuum, Quod ipsi habeant et tenant omnia proficua,
amerciamenta, exitus, Forisfacturas, perquisitas et Comoditates de
predicta Curia lete et viso France plegie et Curia Baronis, mercatis, Feriis
et Nundinis provenientes, crescentes seu emergentes infra predictas
patriam, Castra, mesuagia, terras, tenementa et cetera premissa imposterum contingentes, absque aliquo Computo inde nobis, heredibus vel-
successoribus nostria reddendo vel faciendo, Reddendum annuatim nobis,
heredibus et successoribus nostris, pro predictis Nundinis, Feriis [et]
Mercatis ad Receptum Scaccarii nostri, heredum et successorum nostrorum,
dicti Regni nostri Hibernie, scilicet, ad manus vicethesaurarii sive generalis
Receptoris nostri, heredum et successorum nostrorum, dicti regni nostri
Hibernie pro tempore existentium decem solidos legalis monete Hibernie
ad Festum Pasche et Sancti Michaelis Archangeli[30] per equales porciones
annuatim solvendum imperpetuum, Et ulterius de ampliori gratia nostra
speciali ac ex certa scientia et mero motu nostris volimus, *Concessimus,
Ac per presentes pro nobis, heredibus et [successoribus] nostris damus et
Concedimus prefato Thadeo O Doyne, heredibus et assignatis suis, imperpetuum quod nos, heredes et successores nostri, de tempore in tempus
exonerabimus, acquietabimus et indempnes et exonerati Conservabimus
imperpetuum tam prefatum Thadeum O Doyne, heredes et assignatos suos
et eorum quemlibet in frincione[31] premissorum et Cuiuslibet inde parcelle
predicte, quam Castra, mesuagia, terras, tenementa et hereditamenta et
cetera omnia et singula premissa superius mencionata et specificata, Ac
per presentes preconcessa sive mencionata esse concessa et quemlibet inde
parcella, Cum eorum pertinentiis universis, versus nos, heredes et successores nostros et ab omnibus et omnimodis Redditubus et Reservacionibus
nobis vel aliquibus progenitoribus nostris ante aliquod tempus ante hac

---

30 Margin: '10s. Irishe'.

31 *Sic* MS.

pro quacunque Concessione vell Concessionibus vel literis patentibus debitis, solubilibus vel reservatis de, ex vel pro premissis et qualibet inde parcella, Preterquam de Redditibus, Servitiis et tenuris superius pro premissis in his presentibus [nobis], heredibus et successoribus nostris, reservatis ac de arreragiis eorumdem seu aliquibus aliis redditibus sive reservacione exeuntibus seu solubilibus de, ex vel pro premissis racione alicuius dimissionis, Concessionis, reservacionis Cuiuscunque ante hac factirum sive aliquo alio modo quocunque si que sint insolutis et insatisfactis, Ac preterquam de Composicione nostra ac omnibus expedicionibus, anglice *Rysings out,* debita aut solubile de aut pro premissis vel aliqua inde parcella, Volentis insuper et per presentes firmiter iniungatis precipimus tam Thesaurario et Cancellario et Baronibus Scaccarii nostri, heredum et successorum nostrorum, dicti Regni nostri Hibernie pro tempore existentibus, quam omnibus et singulis Receuoribus, auditoribus et aliis officiariis [et] ministris nostris, heredum et successorum nostrorum, dicti Regni nostri Hibernie pro tempore existentibus, quod ipsi et eorum quelibet super solam demonstrationem harum literarum nostrarum patentium vel irrotulamenti earundem absque aliquo alio brevio seu warranto a nobis, heredibus vel successoribus nostris, quoquomodo impetrando vel prosequendo plenam, integram debitamque allocacionem et exoneracionem manifestam de et ab omnibus et omnimodo Corrodiis, feodis, redditibus, annuitatibus, pencionibus, porcionibus denararum summis et oneribus quibuscunque de Premissis seu de aliqua inde parcella nobis, heredibus et successoribus nostris, exeuntibus seu solvendis vel super inde versus *nos[32], heredes et successores nostros, oneratis seu onerandis, prefato Thadeo O Doyne, heredibus et assignatis suis facientes et de tempore in tempus fieri Causabunt et eorum quilibet fieri Causabit, Preterquam de Redditibus, Serviciis et tenuris que antea ut prefertut in hiis presentibus reservatis vel exceptis sint ut prefertur, Ac per prefatum Thadeum O Doyne, heredes et assignatos suos virtute harum literarum nostrarum patentium sive aliquarum aliarum concessionum aut aliquo alio modo quocunque sunt solubiles, faciendum seu performandum et de arreragiis eorundem, Ac de Composicione nostra et expediciones, Anglice *Risings out,* Et quod he litere nostre patentes vel irrotulamena earundem erunt annuatim et de Tempore in tempus tam dicto Thesaurario, Cancellario et Baronibus Scaccarii nostri predicti, heredum et successorum nostrorum, quam omnibus et singulis aliis receptoribus, Auditoribus, et aliis officiariis et ministris nostris, heredum et successorum nostrorum, quibuscunque in dicto regno nostro Hibernie vel alibi ubicunque pro tempore existentibus, sufficientes et perfectes warrantum et exoneracio in hac parte, Ac de amplius gratia nostra speciali ac ex certa scientia et mero motu nostris volumus ac [per] presentes pro nobis, heredibus et successoribus nostris, Concedimus prefato Thadeo O Doine, heredibus et assig-

---

32 nostres, MS.

natis suis, quod he litere nostre Patentes Construentur, adiudicentur et interpretentur in tam favorabilibus et beneficialibus modo et forma ad omnes intentiones et Constructiones prout interpretari, adiudicari vel construi poterint in maximum advantagium et beneficium ipsius Thadei O Doyne, heredum et assignatorum suorum, Et quod he litere nostre Patentes vel irrotulamenta eorundem erunt in omnibus et per omnia firma, valide, bone, sufficiente et effectuale in lege, erga et Contra nos, heredes et successores nostros, tam in omnibus Curiis nostris quam alibi ubicunque infra dictum Regnum nostrum Hibernie vel alibi absque aliquibus Confirmacionibus, licentiis vel toleracionibus de nobis, heredibus et successoribus nostris, imposterum per prefatum Thadeum O Doine, heredes et assignatos suos, procurandis vel obtinendis, Non obstantes non nominacione, male nominacione vel male recitatione Comitatu, Patrie, Territorii, locum, villarum, hamletarum, parochie seu Baronie in quo vel in quibus premissa aut aliqua inde parcella existit vel existint aut existere debet aut deberent, Nec obstantes male nominandum vel male recitandum vel non recitandum predicta messuagia terras, tenementa, hereditamenta et cetera premissa vel aliqua inde parcellam per presentes preconcessa, Et non obstans quod officium aut Inquisiciones premissorum aut alicuis inde parcelle per presentes preconcessorum per que titulis nostris ad premissis inquiri seu invenire debuit ante Confeccionem harum literarum nostrarum Patentium non fuerint cpate, invente aut retournate, Et non obstantes male nominandum, male recitandum, non nominandum vel non recitandum aliquem dimissionem ac dimissiones, Concessionem vel Concessiones pro termino vite vel vitarum vel annorum in feodo Talliato vel aliqua de premissis vel de aliqua inde parcella facte alicui persone vel aliquibus personibus existentibus de *recordis vel non de Reccordis, Et non obstans quod dum omnibus Tenentium, firmariorum seu occupatorum predictorum maneriorum, Castrorum, villarum, villatarum, hamletarum, messaugiorum, Terrarum, pratarum, Tenementorum et hereditamentorum predictorum seu aliquorum premissorum aut aliavis inde parcella plena, vera et certa non fit mencio, et non obstantibus aliquibus defectibus de certitudine vel Computacione et declaracione veri annui valoris, generis vel speciei premissorum aut alicuius inde parcelle aut annualis redditus reservati de, super vel pro premissis vel de et super aliquam inde parcellam in his presentibus expressis et Contentis aut non expressis vel non contentis, Et non obstantibus aliquis aliis deficionibus in non nominandum aut in male nominandum aliquem tenentium, firmariorum seu occupatorum premissorum aut alicuius inde parcelle, Et non obstante statuto in parliamenti domini Henrici nuper regis Anglie sexto antecessoris nostri Anno Regni sui decimo octavo facto et edito ac postea in regno nostro Hibernie inter alios auctoritate parliamenta stabilita et confirmata, et non obstantibus aliquibus aliis deficionibus in non recte nominandum natura, genera, species, quantitates [vel] premissorum aut alicuius inde parcella, Er non obstantes non recitaciones vel male recitaciones Tituli nostri de et in premissis vel aliqua inde parcella aut aliqua variacione in his litteris Patentibus a predictis literis nostris manu nostra propria sub signeto nostro Sequatis aut aliquo decepcione nostra quacunque aut aliquo alio statuto, actu, ordinacione, prehibitacione, restriccione aut promissione antehac facto vel imposterum fiendo infra hoc regnum nostrum Anglie vel infra hoc regnum Hibernie, Aut aliqua alia re, Causa vel materia quacunque In vacuacione seu ad *inhibitacione harum literarum nostrarum Pattentium in Aliquo non obstante. In Cuius Rei testimonium, etc.[33]

---

33 The letters patent were dated March 7, 1608 (N.S.) (*Calendar of the Irish Patent Rolls of James I*, 123).

NOTE BY SOLICITOR–GENERAL COVERING FIANT

May it please your lordship. This fyant contayneth a graunte to Tady O Doine Esqr. and his heyers of all such lands in the Countrie of Iregaine as were found for him by office accordinge to a particular thereof certi-fied by the Surveyor, and of all other land in the said Country whereof the said Tady O Doine is seised. And of all Felons goods and demaunds[1] ther happening. To be holden of his Majestie in Common soccadge with a Courte Leete and Courte Baron to be holden at Tenahinch. And a Fayre and a markett to be kepte at Tenahinch. And other fayer and a markett to be kepte at Ballycaslan Bracke. Renderinge to his Majestie for the said fayers and marketts But Ten shillings. Which graunt is made uppon a surrender of the premisses by the said Tady O Doine to the kinges Majestie accordinge to the effecte of his Majesties letters in that behalf bearing date at Westm*inster* the xxixth daie of June in the sixte yeare of his Raigne of Greate Brittaine and according to your lordships warrante bearing date the xxvith daie of November 1608, Remayninge with me his Majesties Sollicitor generall.

Nicholas Kardiffe.   Rob: Jacob.

---

1 *Sic. Recte* deodands.

LETTER OF PRIVY COUNCIL IN FAVOUR OF TADY DOYNE, 30 JUNE 1608

A letter to the L: Deputie of the realme of Ireland.

Whereas it pleased his Majestie at the humble suite of Captayne Tady Doyne in consideracion of his good service done to that State to authorise your lordship by his highnes letters in June last to accept of a surrender of the said Tady Doyne of the Contrie of Iregaine and of all the lands, tenements and hereditaments in the said Contrie, situate in the Queenes Countie in that realme, whereof he and his auncestors have bene possessed. And thereuppon to make a graunte unto the said Tady and his heyres in due forme of lawe, by letters patents under the seale of that realme of the said Contrie of Iregaine and of all the lands, tenements and hereditaments thereunto belonging, with surrender beinge voluntarilie made by the said Tady Doyne of all the said Contrie and his said lands and hereditaments and letters patents made from his Majestie for the same unto the said Tady Doyne and his heyres according to the tenure of his letters. Forasmuch as wee are informed that the Patent is stayed by reason of som pretended tytle made by Charles Doyne brother to the said Tady Doyne to some parte of the said lands, wee have therefore thought good to let your lordship understand that if thereby no other respect or consideration of state which may be incident unto the passinge of this graunte, whereof we praye your lordship to informe yourselfe, but that it is only upon private suite and at the instance of some particular man whoe maie seeke his remedie by ordinary course of Lawe that then his Majestie is pleased that the Patent shalbe delivered to the said Tady Doyne accordinge to his former gratious intention. And so wee bid, etc.

Signed by the L. Chauncellor. L. Treasurer. L. Privie Seale. L. Chamberlain. Earl of Worcester. L. Wotton. L. Stanhope. Jo: Corbett.
Dated the 30th of June 1609.

BOND OF THADEUS O DOYNE, 8 MARCH 1608/9

Coram Domino Cancellario huius regni Hibernie octavo die Martii 1608.

Thadeus O Doyne de Iregaine Recognovit se debere Carolo Doyne fratre suo 2000 [1] ster. sub conditione sequenti, vix.

The condition is that the said Tady soone after the sealing of his patent now beinge brought to the seale shall pass and confirme to the said Charles his brother such an estate and Conveyance in lawe of all suche lands and Cheeferies in Iregaine as were passed by Teige O Doyne their father to the said Charles by Feoffment as the said Charles learned Councell shall reasonablie devise, according to an agreement passed befor the L. Deputie and Councell on the 9th of this instant under the hand of the said Thady remayninge in the custodie of the L. Chauncellor and anexned to this recognizance that henceforth, etc.

Coram Thoma Dublinensi Cancellario.   Tha: Doyne.
Copia vera Extracta per Pa: Foxe.

COMPLAINT OF CHARLES DOYNE, 25 JULY 1611 (?)

Mr. Secretary. Havinge made choice of you as my dearest friend to assist my unfortunate suite these iii yeares depending before my lord and not yet ended, I thought now *tandem aliquando* to desyre to feele his lordshipes meaninge towarde me, and to acquaint you with what hath bene done alredie, though I forget many of my chefest motives by reason that in a suite so grevous unto me and so ma*teria*llie tuching my estate and credit I tooke forgetfulnes to be the best phisicke to settle my troubled mynde at rest when it did not prosper with mee as I expected. Take choise now *tanquam ad summa rerum Capita.*

First, a Feoffment made by my Father the late deceased O Duinn the xx of July 1590 of all the chiferie and land therunto belonging in the barony of Iregain *alias* Tenehence in the Queens Countie to the use of each of his sonnes successively one after another during their lives, the remainder to the use of the heire of ech of them successively (excepting such parcell as he intended to leave to ech of his sons and their heirs in particular for their livelihood) with a power given to the Feoffees to surrender the said land and the chefrie to the intent to have a reestate to the intent of the feoffment, which left no power in my brother to surrender the same. By force of which feoffment I ought to have the said lands and chefrie imediatly after my brother Teig and my heirs as often as his heirs.

The consideration moving my Father to make that feoffment was the auncient custome of the said Barony which did run after the custome of Tanistie, The suite of the best freehoulders of the said Barony to the effect, The illegitimacion of my said brothers issue (exceptinge one) and the discencion that was like to falle betwene them concerning the said chifrie.

2. A feoffment made by the said O Duinn my Father to me and my heirs and assignes the xiith of July 1593 containing in lands and chifrie not above 379 acres so dispersed up and down and so farr asunder in the said barony that I cannot conveniently build upon them. Which feoffment was indorsed the second of March 1608 by my lord Chauncelor with the words: It is agreed that all the contents of this deed shall stand firme to Charles and his heirs. Arthur Chichester.

3. An order by the earnest suite of my brother made betwene us by Sir Edward fitzGerald, Sir James fitz Pyers, Gerott fitz Phillip and James Terrell, arbitrators chosen with our consent by the Earle of Kildare my brothers earnest friend, whereby they ordered all our lands and chiefry to be devided in four partes, eyther by my brother or me at his election, and I [and] my heirs to have one parte and he three partes and if he had made the division, I was to have the first choice or if I had devided he was to take the first choice and I the second choice of the said foure partes, by which order I could not misse to have one of the best Castles in the said barony. Unto the performance of this order wee are bound one to another in a 1000 *l.* sterling and he booke sworn to mee. He rested so well satisfied with the said order that he refused a good reward of me to give his consent to have it cancelled, and since he heard of the coming over of the commission of surrenders he used what shifts he could devise not to stand to it.

4. When my brother offered a bill containing a surrender of the said barony to my lord and I then shewed the said order my lord demaunded of him which of us should make the division. My brother answered that he would make it, wherupon then my lord conceived an order agreeing with the said order of our friends, and appointed my brother to make the division and I to have the first Choice of the said foure partes.

5. My lord conceived another order the 11th of February 1608 betwene us wherby he appointed me to make the division of the said lands and chiefrie into four partes before Easter then next following by our instrument in wryting and that my brother should take two choices before me and I the third choice only after him, with which order my brother was so well pleased because that he was therby to have the ii Castles in variance betwen us and I to have none of theme when by the order of our friends I could not misse of one of them that he sent me a letter the 16th of the said moneth with a particulare note of all his lands desiring me to make the division in hast. And after I presented the said instrument of division to my lord, he said the fourth parte was but the tenth parte of the whole and nothing worth, or licke unto a division of twenty ˢ· in

foure partes, wherof ech of three partes should have 6^S a peece and the 4th parte but ii^S only, and this was all the excepcion that my brother toke to my division in particular, and his refusall to let me have the 4th parte then if I would accept of it was a sufficient confutacion of that exception.

6. My lord made an order the 9th of May 1609 that the said instrument of division should be delivered to my brother to be delivered of and that upon his refusall to perform the last order or to make his choice I should be permitted to take the best parte of the 3 worst of the said 4 parts, and the same to surrender.

7. The last and worst order of all for me was conceived by my lord the second of March 1609 by which he tied me to the benefits of the said second feoffement only made by my said Father to my use. When I was at studie in Oxen., containing in land and chiefrie but 379 acres so disposed in smale peeces in the said Barony that I can neyther fitly Dwell nor build upon them as I said before, which was intended unto me by my Father besyde the said Barony in my tourn, being scarce the 9th parte of the lands and chiefries in difference betwene us, for my brother hath in lands and chiefrie 2808 acres of which lands I should have the one moity by the custom of the gavelkind now and tyme out of mynde used in the said Barony. My lord did often promise that if my brother would not let me have the full contents of this last feoffment he would draw from him his favour hereafter.

And when my lord did choose Sergent Beere then newly coming over to make upp the wrytings betwene us and referred the perusing of them to my lord Chefe Barron and the Master of the Roles, my brother refused to sign them and so went home. This is the unluckie end of this my long continued and chargefull suite.

Therefore seinge that I ame as willing to doe his Majestie and my lord my best service as be, and that what service he did in the last rebellion, I can prove it proceedes from myself originally and that bastards should not enjoy what my father lefte unto me havinge no better state of living then the same, and that one man should not have the command of that Barony being full of fastnes ²unlesse he were² known well to be true to the Crown. I pray yow once againe to try how you can find my lord in his honorable disposicion towards mee. If you finde his lorship willinge to compell my brother to lett me have the benefit of any of the said orders, to call for him to appear before his lordship upon his return from the north. I would accepte of the last and the worst order of all for me to redeme any quietnes without my journey into England. For the benefit

2–2 *Bis* MS.

of that order would scarce requite my Chardges thither. And yf my lord could not travaile with my brother, my humble suite to his lordship is to wryte on my behalfe into England concerning the order of the 4th parte which I thinke in honnour his lordship is tied to make good unto me, and not to leave me in a worst state then his lordship found me before my matter came to his lordships hearing.

Dabit Deus his quoque finem.

From Trinity Colledge the
25 of July 1619[3].

Your fast and faythful
friend
Charles Duinn.

I thought that this controversie had bene ended long since, but seinge it is not, let Doctor Duinn preferr his bill and his brother shalbe called and concluded withall as shalbe thought fittinge according to former orders.

SUMMONSES FOR APPEARANCES OF THADY DUINN

Whereas complaint hath bene exhibited unto us by our welbeloved Master Doctor Duinn that you have failed in the performance of divers orders made by us in the suite depending betwene him and you, these are therefore to will and require you presently upon receipt hereof to make your personall and undelaied apparance before us to aunswere to the bill of Complainte exhibited against you by Mr. Doctor Duinn remaining with the Clerk of the Councell. Hereof you may not faile. Given at Dublin, the 26th of October, 1611.

To Thady Duinn of Tenenchie in the Queenes County Esquire.

Sir. Wee have heretofore required yow by our warrant bearing date the 26 of October last to make your personall apparance before us at the table to aunswer to the suite and bill exhibited against you by Mr. Doctor Duinn remaininge in the Clerk of the Councells office wherein yow made default of apparance contrarie to the contents of the said warrant, only by a letter yow aleadged that you were sick and so could not come wherof there was noe affidavit made without which your excuse was not allowable in that case. And Forasmuch as Mr. Doctor Duinn doth persist in the

---

3 *Sic. Recte* 1609.

followinge of his suite and that we are informed that yow are recovered
of your former sicknes, we doe therefore hereby require and commaund
yow without further excuses or delaies to make your personall apparance
before us at the Councell Table within 12 daies after the receipt hereof
to make a sufficient answer, to the contrary at your perrill. Given at
Dublin the sixth of Aprill, 1612.

To Thadie Duinn of Tenehinchie in the Queenes County, Esquire,
give these.

> The humble peticion of Doctor Charles Duinn Esqr.
> one of the Masters of his highnes court of Chauncery.
> To the right ho: the L: Deputy and Councell.

Whereas Teig O Duin Esqr. deceased, your supliant's Father, being
chefe of his name and Captain of the Countrey of Iregan in the Queenes
County was seised of divers mannors, lands, tenements and hereditaments in the said Queenes Countie in his demesne as of Fee and of divers
rents and chifries unto the said manors and lands belonging, and so thereof
[seised] by his said deed bearing date the xxi of July 1593 did enfeoffe
Cahir mcFir O Molloy of Ballyboy in the Kinges Countie, gent., and others
and their heirs of the manors, twones,[4] villadges and hamlets of Rery more,
Balle vickena, Racohie, Corilis, Laccagbeg, Sraduffe, Gurtine, Ballironell,
Feran Caro Reoughe, Gary Gallrind, Feran Christen, five acres in Gary
Donogh, Garrykneen, Coulagh in the quarter of Clankeroll and the rents
and signories in the quarters commonly called the quarter of Rerimore,
the quarter of Laccagh, in the one quarter of Moyntegh Mylocke in the
said country of Iregaine, with all the pastures, meddoues, woods, waters,
commons and other the appurtenaunces unto the premises or to any parte
or parcell thereof beloning or appertaining to the use of your said supliant,
his heires and assignes, as in and by the said ded of feoffment made and
readie to be shewed may appeare. And afterwarde the said Teig O Duin
died seised of the residue of divers other manors, lands and chieferies in
the said countrey of Iregan and after whose death Teig Og O Duinn your
supliants eldest brother and son and heir unto the said deceased Father
entered into the residue of the said manors, lands and signories of Iregan
whereof their said Father died seised as aforesaid and into some parte of
the lands also conveied as aforesaid unto the use of your supliant and
indevoured to surrender the whole countrie of Iregan unto the kings
majestie and to take letters patents therof unto himself and his heirs
thereby to defeit your supliant of the said lands to conveied by his said
Father to the use of your supliant, which your supliant opposing the
said Teig Og O Duinn and your supliant for a finall end and a determina-

---

4 *Sic.*

cion of their severall claimes unto the said manors, lands and signories of Iregan by their mutuall consents submitted themselves to thaward, order and arbitrement of Sir Edward fitzGerald, knight, Sir James fitzPiers, knight, Gerald fitzPhillip of Kyllmeage and James Terell of Castlost, Esqr. and the said Teig Oge O Duinn by his obligacion bearing date the 9th daie of Aprill 1607 became bound unto your supliant in 1000^{li}. ster. current money of England to performe the award and order of the said arbitrators in the premisses and your said supliant became bound in the licke bounds unto the said Teg for the performance of the said award on his parte, wherupon afterwarde the said arbitrators by their wrytinge under their hands and seals bearing date the xith daie of Aprill 1607 according the said submission did order and award that all the said tenements and hereditaments within the said countrey of Iregan with all signories thereunto appertaininge except such lands as had bene six daies before the said award purchased by the said Teig or your supliant by their own industrie and the two Castles of Castlebreack and Tenehenchie should be equaly devided into four quarters or partes by your said supliant or by the said Teig at the election of him the said Teig. And if the said Teig would take upon him to make the said division that then your said supliant should have the first choice of the said four partes or porcions to be and remaine to your said supliant and the heirs males of his boddie free and exonerated from any signories, taxacion or rent or other duty or any other charge by the said Teig demaundable, the remainder to the said Teig, and thother 3 partes to be the said Teigs and his heires males as aforesaid. And if by the said Teig his allowance or choice your said supliant should make the said division as aforesaid, then the said Teig to have the first choice of one fourth parte and your supliant to have the second choise to be and remaine to him and his heirs males aforsaid. And the said arbitrators did further order that the said Teig within ten daies after the said award should enter into a bond of a thowsand pounds sterling to your supliant with condicion that at any tyme or whensoever and so after as it should be reasonablie required by your said supliant or his assignes the said Teig his heirs and assignes to pass from them and everie of them a perfect sure and indefeasable estate in law to your supliant and the heirs males of his bodie of the fourth parte or porcion of the said countrey of Iregan which should be chosen and elected by your supliant. And Further tuching any chardge that should be in procuring the setling estate of the said countrey of Iregan from the king upon any surrender to be made by the said Teig, your supliant to be contributory to the fourth parte of the said Teig his chardge and that your supliant should paie a fourth parte of the overplus of the rent to be reserved out of the said countrey of Iregan unto the kings majestie exceeding Forty shillings for the said fourth parte, but if the fourth parte of the kings rent exceede not fortie shillings then Teig his three partes to be chardged with the whole and your supliants parte to be free from the said rent, as by the said order and award among other things therein contained may appear.

Which order and award the said arbitrators made known unto the said Teig Oge O Duinn befor they published the same as their award, and demaunded of the said Teig if he would allow therof and the said Teig did read and peruse the same and gave his full consent therunto before the publishing therof and afterwards the xith daie of Aprill 1607 published the same award under their hands and seales and delivered one parte therof unto the said Teig and the other parte therof unto your said supliant. And afterward according to the purporte of the said order and award your supliant caused a draught of an obligacion to be made frome the said Teig unto your supliant for his assuring of the 4th parte of the said lands according to the said award and sent the same unto the said Teig. Whereupon the said Teige did write his letter unto your supliant excusing himself from sealing the said obligacion and desyring your supliant to joyn with him to surrender the said lands unto his Majestie and tooke upon his salvacion that the estate being setled in himself he would make good unto your supliant in all that the order did importe and that he was content to give bond to fullfill the same. And the said Teig also tooke a voluntarie oath to performe the same not withstanding[5] afterwarde the said Teig semed to dislicke of the said award and became a suter to this table to surrender to the king and take a patent of all the said lands to himself, whereupon it was ordered the 15th of February in the fift of his Majesties raign by your lordship and the commissioners upon hearing of both parties and view of the said award that before Easter daie then next coming, your supliant should make an instrument in wryting purporting a division of foure partes of the said chiefries and lands and that the said Teig thereupon should have his election first of two partes and that your supliant should have election of the third parte for his porcion and the said Teig thother fourth parte, and that they should both surrender and a patent to be graunted to the said Teig[6] to be bound in a statute staple of 1000[li] to make a perfect estate to your supliant and the heirs males of his body of the third parte which your supliant should choose, the said statute to be lefte in your lordships hands. With which order the siad Teig seemed to be well pleased and sent a note to your supliant of the particulers of the said signories and lands requesting your supliant to make the said division which division your supliant made accordingly and presented the same to your lordship. Wherupon your lordship and the other commissioners the 9th of May in the sixth year of his Majesties raign did order that the said booke of division should be delivered unto the said Teig to consider therof and to redeliver the said booke within 3 days and if he should refuse to performe the said former order that your supliant should be allowed to chose one of the three worst partes of the said foure and the fourth and best parte to be reserved for the said Teig and upon

---

5 *Sic.* Probably the words 'the same' should be repeated twice.

6 Some words have been omitted here.

such choise to be made by your supliant he to be permitted to surrender and to have new letters patent granted upon the same. Which booke of division was accordingly delivered to the said Teig who intending never to performe the said former order tooke some nyce exception unto the said division to delay your supliants choise. And in the meane tyme procured a letter frome the kings majestie dated the nine and twentieth of June in the sixth year of his highnes raign requiring and aucthoriseing your lordship to accept of a surrender from the said Teig of the said countrey of Iregaine and grant the same by letters patents unto the said Teig and his heires with a grant of a Court leete and a Court barron which your supliant opposing for that the said Teig had not performed your lordships said orders which the said Teig refused to performe your lordship then gave directions that the said surrender and patent should be made to the said Teig with a saving of your supliants right and Further directed that the said Teig not having performed the former orders should after the said Patent convey unto your supliant and his heirs all the lands and chiefries contained in the said deed of the 22th of July 1593 conveied to your supliants use by his said Father. The said surrender and Patent were made accordingly and the conveyance intended to be made frome the said Teig to your said supliant was drawen, ingrossed and tendered unto the said Teig to be sealed, who thinking the contents contained in the said conveyance to strict, your lordship referred the consideracion thereof unto my Lo: Chefe Barron and the master of the Rowles who considered of the said conveiance in the presence of both parties and expressed somme particuleres whereine they would have the said conveyance altered if the said Teig would consent to sealle the same, but the said Teig tould them plainly that he would not convey the said lands and signories unto your supliant and his heyrs, whereupon the matter hath ever sythence bene rested and your supliant hath bene ever sythence disturbed and kept out of possession of the greatest parte of the lands by the said Teig to his greate damadge and impowrishinge.

In tender consideration of all which premiss and for that the said lands are the whole estate lefte unto your supliant by his said Father and for that the said award was made by the consent and agreement of the said Teig both before and after the making therof and hath bene confermed by two orders at the councell table that your supliant should have one fourth parte of the said lands and chiefries of the said countrey of Iregaine, May it please your lordship to call the said Teig before you to answer the premiss and the same appearing to be true to order the said Teig to assure the said fourth parte of the said lands and chiefries unto your supliant and his heiers dischargd of any tenure, rent or service to the said Teig according to the said award and your lordshipes order of the 9th of May in the sixth year of his majesties raign together with the moste[7] profitts thereof ever

---

7 *Sic. Read* mesne.

sythence, and your supliant shall pray, etc.

The answer of Thadie Duinn to the bill of
Complaint of Charles Duin.

The defendant saieth that he is continuallie vexed by the plaintif without cause, and all these of purpose to putt the defendant to chardge, his dwellinge beinge farr of and his estate much weackned by the plaintifs hard dealing and trouble, and further the defendant for answer saieth that the matter in the bill contained are matters meerlie determinable by course of common law, for that they concern matters of frehould and inheritance, and ought not to be determined at this honourable boord, and after the supposed order said to be made by Sir Edward fitzGerrald and others, which is the matter whereupon the plaintif doth relie in this bill, the defendant saieth that the plaintif brought that matter in question in the high court of Chauncerie about three or foure years sithence and sued the defendant upon the forfeture of a recognizance of one thowsand pownds for not performinge the said supposed order, Wherunto the defendant pled to the matter and the cause hath and still doth depend undertermined. And further the defendant saieth that his most gratious Majestie hath by his letters bearinge date the 29th of June 1608 signified his highnes pleasure that the said controversie arisinge upon the said order should receive a judiciall hering and determinacion in his highnes courte of justice of record and not otherwise, upon which letters and upon other letters also of the 30th of June 1609 from the lords of the Councell signifieng his highnes pleasure in the premiss the defendant was dismissed formerlie by your honour and thes borde of the plaintifs former suite in this matter, and your supliants patent was delivered unto him by your honors direction which was before that time staied from him upon pretence of the said order and other matters. And the plaintiff lefte to his remedie by the ordinarie course of law, as everie other suter ought to be, upon all which matters the defendant praieth to be dismissed of this vexacion.

RECORD OF PROCEEDINGS IN CHANCERY (LAW SIDE)
BETWEEN CHARLES AND THADY DUINN

Comitatus Civitatis Dublinensis.

Memorandum quod alias, scilicet terminus Sancti Michaelis ultimo praeterito coram Domino Rege in Cancellaria sua Hibernie apud domum communiter vocatam *the Ins* Carolus Duinn armiger unus magistrorum Curiae Cancellariae iuxta libertates et privilegia eiusdem curiae pro huiusmodi magistris et aliis ministris de eadem curia a tempore quo usu *extra memoria usitata et approbata presens his in curia propria persona sua queritur per billam de Thadeum Duinn de Tenahence in Comitatu de la Queenes, armigerum, in custodia mariscalli mariscalcie domini Regis coram Domino Rege in Cancellaria sua existente de placito debiti et sunt plegii de prosequandi, Johannes Doe et Richardus Roe. Quo quidem billa sequitur in hec verba: Comitatus Civitatis Dublin'. Carolus Duinn armiger unus magistrorum curiae cancellariae iuxta libertates et privilegia eiusdem curiae pro huiusmodi magistris et aliis Ministris de eadem curia a tempore quo non memoria usitata et approbata queritur de Thadeo Duin de Tenahinsi in comitatu de la Queenes Countie armigero in custodia mariscalli mariscallcie domini regis coram Domino Rege existente in Cancellaria sua de placito quod reddat ei mille libras bone et legalis monete Anglie quas eu debet et iniuste detinet pro eo quod cum predictus Thadeus per quiddam scriptum suum obligatorium curia his ostensis cuis datum est apud Draynenston in Comitatu Kildarie nono die Aprilis Anno Domini 1607 cognovit se deberi et firmiter obligari prefato Carolo in predictis mille libris solvendis eidem Carolo heredibus executoribus administratoribus et assignatis suius ad voluntatem suam predictus tamen Thadeus licet seipsum requisitus predictas mille libras prefato Carolo non solvit sed illas et hac usque solvere contradixit et ad hic contradixit, unde prefatus Carolus dicit quod deterioratus est et damnum habet ad valenciam centum librum et inde producit sectam. Et modo ad hac diem scilicet diem mercurii proximum post xv^{tam} Pasche isto eodem termino usque quem diem predictus Thadeus dudum habuit licentiam ad billam predictam interloquendem et tunc ad respondendem etc. coram dicto domino rege in cancellaria sua apud *the Kinges Courts* venit tam predictus Carolus in propria persona sua quam predictus Thadeus per Jacobum Newman attornatum suum et idem Thadeus defendit vim et injuriam quando etc et petit auditum scripti etc *as in the answer.*

Et predictus Thadeus Duinn per Jacobum Newman suum attornatum verum etc petit auditum scripti predicti et ei legit in hec verba: Noverint universi per presentes me Thadeum alias Teig O Duinn de Tenahince in Comitatu de le Queenes Countie armigerum teneri et firmiter obligari Carolo Duinn alias Cahir O Duinn armigero [*etc, as recited in the Inquisition, p. 11*]. Petit etiam auditum condicionis eiusdem scripti et ei legit in hec verba: Whereas controversie hath bin and is dependinge betweene thabove bounden Thadie alias Teig O Duinn on the one partie and Charles alias Cahire O Duinn on thother partie [*etc, as recited in the inquisition, pp. 11-12, with some variations in spelling. Note the following variants in the spelling of place-names:* Iregaine, Castlebrecke, Rerrimore, Tycroghan, Kilmag, Castlelost. *There is also an additional witness:* Garrett Claby].

Quibus lectis et auditis idem Thadeus[8] quod predictus Carolus accionem suam predictam versus eum habere seu manutenere non debet quia dicit quod predicti arbitratores post datum predicti scripti obligatorii non publicaverint in scriptum indentatum sub manibus et sigillis dictorum arbitratorum aliquid arbitrium adwardum seu ordinacionem inter ipsos prefatum Thadeum et Carolum de aut super premissis in condicione predicta specificata secundum formam et effectum Condicionis et submissione predictis ad vel ante dictam xii die Aprilis Anno Domini 1607. Et hoc paratum est verifacere unde predictum iudicium si predictus Carolus accionem suam predictam versus eum habere seu manutenere debeat, etc.

Will: Talbott.
Copia vera extracta per
Fra: Edgworth.

BOND OF THADY DOYNE, 16 NOVEMBER 1593

Noverint universi per presentes me Thadeum[9] de Castlbreack teneri et per presentes firmiter obligari fratribus meis Cormako et Briano O Don in mille libris bonae et legalis monetae Angliae soluendis eidem Cormaco et Briano heredibus et assignatis suis ad suam voluntatem ad quam quidem solucionem bene et fideliter faciendam obligo me heredes et executores meos firmiter per presentes in cuius rei testimonium sigillum meum apposui. Datum 16 die Novembris Anno Domini 1593 et anno regni reginae nostrae Elizabethe tricesimo quinto.

The condicion of this obligacion is that if the said Thadie O Duinn shall of his parte performe, accomplish and fullfill in all partes such order, arbitrment and finall determinacion as Sir Piers fitz Gerald, knight, Teig O Duinn, chief of his name, James Terrell of Castlelost, John fitzPatricke of Garran and Neyll mcGeoghegane of Moycashell shall take or anie three of them for and concerning all maner of debats, quarrells, contencions, strife, suite or other matters whatsoever betwist him and his said brethren Cormock and Brian O Duinn, that then this obligacion to be voyd otherwist to stand in full force and efecte in lawe.

Thady Doyne.

---

8 Dixit *omitted.*
9 *Sic.*

Signed sealed and delivered in presence of us whose names be subscribed: John Eustace. James Eustace. Patrick Frayn. Geffrie FitzPat:

Articles of agrement betwixt Teig O Duin of Castlebreacke of the one parte and his brethren Cormocke, Brian [and] Mortagh O Duinn of the other parte ... [*as recited in the Inquisition, pp. 27-8, with minor variations of spelling, including* O Duinn, O Duinnes *for* O Doyne, O Doynes. *This version gives the word* corkesur *where that in the Inquisition has a blank space.*]

> Reasones and causes shewinge whie Teig Og O Duin should not perfect a feofement to Doctor Charles Duinn according the drawght latelie by him drawen and presented to the right ho: the L: Deputie and councell.

First, for that in that draught is contained several lands of freholders within the countrey whoe long before this agreement betwixt Charles and Teig did voluntarilie agree with Teig to paie out of their lands a certaine yearlie rent in lyew of some Irish customes and dueties which they paied formerlie to his father and himself. And have therof past estats in fee symple to Teig upon confidence that he shall repasse the same to them and their heirs reserving a yearlie rent according the English maner. Soe as if he doe perfect that deede to Charles according this drawght he shall breake the trust in him reposed and overthrowe the poore freholders, besydes the losses which himself shall sustaine thereby.

Secondlie, there are in the drawght contained many covenants and clauses verie preiudiciall to Teig if he should perfect it *viz.* first, a bargaine and sale of all evidences concerning the lands by him requiered to be assured. Whereas many parcells of them belonginge in truth to freholders, the evidences of that parcell doe belong to them lickwise and therefore Teig ought not to deliver or sell them. Alsoe a covenante that all these lands are free of all former bargains, uses, etc., whereas — bysydes the uses and confidence betwixt Teig and the freholders for their lands past unto him (as aforesaid) — all the lands which Teiges father had were conveyd to certaine feoffees to the use of Teig and the heirs males of his bodie with divers remainders over, soe as hosoever Teig during his own life may binde the feoffees yet after his death it is not in his power to restraine them from reviving the use to his son and others in remainder of his brothers which are inheritable to that use before Charles.

Thirdlie, there is a covenant that the lands are dischardged of *joyntors, dowers, recognizances, etc, which covenants are impossible to be kept by Teig yf therbe titles of ioynters, dowers or recognizances alredie wherunto the same is liable as out of doubt there is.

Fourthlie, a covenant that Teig and his heirs shall from time to time make further assurance to Charles and his heirs (whereas in troth there is contained in this drawght severall lands belonging to the said Teig his brethren and their children whoe are in possibilitie to be heires to Teig before Charles. And therfore it were inconvenient to Teig to be bound that they[10] should passe anie lands or interests they have or may claime.

Fiftlie, a covenant that the feoffees hereafter to be seised to the use of Charles shall not alter or extinguish etc the uses now to be raised for Charles by his deede, but shall continualie stand seised to him and his heires which were a hard matter to Teig to be tyed herunto, considering that it lyeth not in his power to binde those foeffees now nominated by Charles himself from making what convenant they please.

Sixtlie, a covenant that the seignories are not at present extinguished or suspended etc whereas in troth (if these Irish customes may beare the name or be in the nature of signories) they are extinguished by the feoffment of the freholders made to the said Teig (as aforesaid) upon confidence.

Seventlie, a covenant that the inhabitants of these lands shall not be soe moved or called to anie courts to be holden before Teig or his senescalles, whereas in troth there is a *courte leete* graunted to Teig to be holden before his senescall within that precinte, from which (beinge the kings courts) Teig seeth noe reason whie Charles his tenants should be exempted.

Alsoe, the recognizance bindeth Teig to passe nothing to Charles but what was passed formerlie unto him by Teig his Father. And in the drawght there are severall lands and services contained which were never past to Charles by his Father. Also for the agreement betweene Charles and him which hath words that Teig should passe all that was meant to be past to Charles by his father and that his father had power of himslefe to passe in so ample and beneficiall maner as his Father would passe the same, Therunto Teig saith that his Father had noe power to passe the lands of the freholders nor yet himself to passe such lands and services as he had onlie in use for life. And for anie thing else Teig wilbe reddie to make anie conveyance that shalbe reasonable.

And wheras Charles doth much insist uppon a supposed of[11] his Father bering date in Julie 1593 Teig saith that the same is not to be regarded. First, for that the same was not perfected. And also for that the same was not upon anie good grounde or consideracion beinge made

---

10 *Sic.*

11 *Sic.* The word 'conveyance' has been omitted.

by him by the procurement of his yonger sonnes whoe beinge discontented the Father had formerlie entailed his lands to the heires males of his bodie successivelie accordinge the English lawes, they persuaded the father to make an other deede wherby he should limitte the lands to passe according the Irish custome of Tanistry and having noe meanes to avoyd the former deede of feofment made to the uses in taile, they procured him to make a resitall in that latter deede that the former was contrarie to his meaninge and that he understoode it not, laing the imputacion upon Teig that he Inveighed him therin. But after, the matter beinge brought in question in the Chauncerie, the father surseased that suite and being moved in *conscience did declare before divers men of greate worth and honestie that the first was trulie and sincerelie made *Bona fide* by his own direction and that the latter was procured by the earnest perswacion of his other children of purpose to discredit the former deede whereat they were agreved.

All which Teig humblie praieth may be examined to avoyd such imputacion as Charles laid upon him for that ded and that therby it may appeare what the Fathers true meaninge was, what lands should passe to his yonger children and in what maner. And where it is urged by Charles that the meaning of my lo: deputye and councell was that Teig should passe all expressed or nominated in that deede dated in July 1593, Therunto Teig aunswereth that there was noe such order made by the lo: Deputy and Councell, Neyther is there any thing to binde him but his own agreement made before their lordshippes. By the words whereof it will appeare what was meant to be passed. And soe much Teig will performe, Protesting that he never meant to passe anie more than accordinge as in that agreement is laid down.

Teig humblie therefore beseecheth your lordshippes that seinge his desarts hath bin better than many whoe had benefitt of his Majesties bountie in passing of their lands and that seing his highnes hath bin *gratiouslie pleased to give speciall direction by his letters to passe his letters Patents and that there is noe wrong done nor any preiudice can arise to Charles his right therby (his beinge saved both by law and by speciall words in the patent) it may please your honor to deliver him his Patent and that he may have benefitt of what his highnes hath bin pleased gratiouslie to bestowe upon him. And he shall allwaies praie etc.
The 13 of No: 1609.

I pray you the L. Chife Justice and L. Chefe Baron and Mr. of the roulles or any two of yow to consider of the drawght drawn by the councell of Doctor Doyne and of Mr. Teig Doyne's exceptions and to reconcile the difference if possibly you can or to certifie what yow thincke fitt for us to conclude for a finall end of the cause.
Arthur Chichester.

I wilbe presente after diner tomorrow being thirsdaie in the councell Chamber before this cause and the rest of the referries then reddie at that place.

H. Winchr.

The humble petition of Art O Doyne to the right honorable the L: Deputie.

Shewinge unto your honorable lordship that where your supliant past an estate by Conveyance bearinge [date] sesimo octavo octobris 1608 unto Thady Doyne of all his lands, tenements, etc in the territorie of Iregaine otherwise called the baronie of Tenehensie to thend amonge other the lands of the said Thady these lands should in letters patents be graunted unto the said Thady by his Majestie and it was covenaunted betweene your supliant and the said Thady that after the passinge of his said patent a re-estate should be made unto your supliant which the said Thady hath not performed as yet. And in as much as your supliant his father and grauntfather was seised in his demesne as of fee of x1 acres with the appurtenances in the towne and fields of Gurtin and Ballironell in the three quarters of Moyntegh Milicke and that his father and grand-father died therof seised and your supliant was therof seised in his demesne as of Fee at the tyme of the making of the said conveyance to the said Thadie, your supliant most humblie praieth your lordship to call before you the said Thade and to cause him to make a re-estate to your supliant of the said 40 acres according his covenant and he shall pray, etc.

16th of November 1612.

The defendant is commaunded to perfect such a conveyance as is desired unto the peticioner if he be tyed theruntoe by conveiance, or failinge therof to appeare and shewe by his aunswere good cause whie he should not and that without delay.

Ar: Chichester.

The aunswere of Thadie Duinn to the bill of complaint of Arte O Duinn.

The defendant for aunswer sayth that true it is that the peticioner his father and grandfather were seised of the said fortie acres in Gurtin and Balleronill in the bill mencioned and that the peticioner did passe the said fortie acres unto the defendant with purpose to re-estate that unto the peticioner againe after the defendant should obtaine letters patents therof

in maner and forme as in the peticion is sett forth, which to performe the
defendant had a firme purpose, but soe it is that long after when the
defendant was about the passing of the letters patents Mr. Doctor Duin
giving opposicion therunto produced at this honorable burd a feoffment
bering date the twelth of July 1593 before then not known to the defendant wherin is mencioned that Teig O Duin father to the defendant did
amongest other things convey the said 40 acres unto the said doctor,
wherupon it was agreed that the defendant should passe unto the said
doctor all such lands as the said Teig the father did convey and of himself
had power to convey unto the said doctor by the said deede of feoffment,
for the performance wherof the defendant entred into a recognizance of
2000^{li}. By reason wherof and for avoyding anie pretence of suite that the
said doctor might conceive against the defendant upon the recognizance
the defendant hath hitherto deferred the repassing of the said lands unto
the plaintif to thend that before the passing therof it should be examined
whether the said Teig the father did convey or had anie power of himself
to convey the same unto the said Doctor. Wherefore the defendant
humblie praieth that as well for the righting of the plaintif as for the
securing of the defendant against the said doctor your lordship wilbe
pleased to call the said Doctor Duinn before your lordship that the said
matter may receive full examinacion and therunto to take such order as to
equitie appertaineth which to performe the defendant wilbe allwaies reddie.
21 of November 1612.
Doctor Duinn is required to replie unto this.
Arthur Chichester.

The declaracion made by Doctor Charles Duinn of
the state of the cause betwene Art O Duinn plaintif and Teig O Duinn defendant.

Doctor Charles Duinn being required by the right honorable the lord
Deputy to replie to the aunswere of Teig O Duinn to a bill brought against
him by Art O Duinn declareth that Teig O Duinn his father was in his
lifetime quietlie seised in his demeasin as of Fee of the lands in the bill
mencioned and being soe seised Conveyed the same amongest other
thinges to the said Charles Duinn and his heirs, according to which conveyance the said Charles was seised therof in his demeasin as of fee which
being well known to Teig O Duinn his brother, and the said Teig being
willing to defeate the said Charles his estate therin combyned with the said
Arte O Duinn the complainant that the said Arte should passe an estate in
the premisses to him the said Teig, wherby he might surrender the same
amongest the rest of his lands to the kings majestie to take the same backe
againe to him and his heirs wherby if his highnes had any precedent title
therunto the same beinge granted unto the said Teig he might thereby
overthrowe the said Charles his estate therin and if the said Teig O Duinn
the father had the rightfull estate therof the said Teig the sonne would

defeate the said Charles his tytle by the precedent pretended estate made therof by the said Teig the father to the use of the said Teig the sonne, upon oppening of which matters and of divers other controversies depending between the said Charles and the said Teig O Duin his brother it was ordered by your lordship and by the rest of the councell that his said brother should convey the said lands in complaint amongest other things to the said Charles and his heires for ever. Wherefore and because the said Charles verielie thinketh that he will sufficiently prove that this suite nowe brought by the said Arte against the said Teig is upon a combynacion betwene them to overthrowe the said Charles his estate therin, he humblie praieth that your lordship would be pleased not to make any order betweene them that might be preiudiciall to him the said Charles.

OPINION OF JUDGES UPON THE ABOVE CASE, 9 DECEMBER 1612

9 die Decembris 1612.

Right honorable. Upon the hearing of this cause it seemeth unto us that the peticioner Art O Duinn and his father did occupie the land in question by custome of Tanestrie painge a chiefrie out of the same unto the father and auncestors of Thadie Duinn and Doctor Charles Duinn, whoe also held by custome of Tanestrie. This custome of Tanestrie is utterlie voyd in lawe (as wee take it) soe as all the said parties have occupied as intruders upon the kings majesties possession untill the late patent frome his majestie to Thadie, in which there is a saving of the right of others, by which saving it seemes to us that Thadie should graunt a goode estate to everie one to whome anie former estate was Inteyned by tanestrie. And soe consequentlie he ought to assure the lands in the peticion unto the peticioner painge the accustomed chifrie.

And for that Doctor Duinn sheweth a grant frome old Teig their auncestor of the town of Gurtine and all the lands and tenements therin, wherof the land in question is parcell, it seemeth to us that the chifrie therof should be assured to Doctor Duinn yf that the title and right of the doctor against Thade shalbe adiudged by your lordship to be within the savinge of the said patent. And soe in all humblenes wee leave it to your lordshipes censure.

Ger: Lowther   Ussar R:

A true coppie of the certificate made by us uppon a reference from the Lord Deputie for hearing of certaine controversies betweene Arte O Duinn plaintiff *versus* Thadie O Duinn.

SCHEDULES OF ACREAGES INVOLVED IN THE PLANTATION OF IREGAN, 1622

1622 for plantation.

1. Iregan surveyed to		12,103
2. Patent lande		2195
3. After deductinge patent lande		9908
4. Undertakers have thereof		5,768
5. Remayninge to Natives but		4140
6. Undertakers have more then natives besides Patent lande by	a.	1628
7. When they should have but the 4th parte which is but		2477
8. And they have more than a 4th part by	a.	3291
Iregan		12,103

Patent lands

n. acres	o. acres		o. acres	n. acres
435	80	Buollynumer	60	326
673	80	Kilnagrealcha	20	168 (200)
275	80	Derry	24	84
466	120	Rerybeage	63	244
1359	240	Moynteagh	36	204 (389)
542	240	Munyquid	57	127 (50)
524	240	Castlebracke	215	454
487	240	Clancowoy	170	346 (38)
354	80	Keapabrogain	55	243
			ac:	2196

Undertakers.

		acres
1.	Lord of Dunsauny	500
2.	Lord Burke of Bryttas	1000
3.	Sir Robert Loftus, knt.	848
4.	Sir Robert Pigott, knt.	500
5.	Gilles Rawlins	600
6.	Patricke Hussey	600
7.	Marmaduk Nelsone	300
8.	Robert Kennedye	400
9.	The Church	620
10.	Walter Greames	400
		5768
		6760

o. acres[12]		n. acres
80	Corbowly	596 – 394
80	Tenyle	396 – 384
80	Gleanruish	541 – 310
80	Clowinhyne	871 – 864
240	Mointeagh	1359 – 1214
240	Castlebracke	524 – 319
240	Munyquid	542 – 342[13]
240	Clancowoy	487 – 446
240	Clancarroll	362 – 361
120	Ririebeage	466 – 462
80	Ririemore	682 – 620
80	Dirrie	275 – 275
80	Buollynummar	435 – 430
80	Kilnagrealcha	673 – 673
180	Boell	719 – 719
120	Garrough ⎫	
80	Keapabrogan ⎬	1062 – 1025
80	Lackaghe ⎭	
80	Cowilbouchlane	463 – 462
80	Ballintagart	669 – 651
80	Ballykneein	363 – 362
120	Fasaghely	620 – 608

12 The heading of this page has been cut away in rebinding.
13 Corrected from 'the same'.

[¹⁴] my Lord Chancelor

	ar.	w.
Clouenehyne	77 —	56
Tenyell	200 —	416
Glanruishe	079 —	107
Corbolie	096 —	101
Moyntaghe Milicke	188 —	181
The wood of Killmilicke	221 —	100
Moare in Moyntaghe	048 —	030

320	Garrough, Lackagh	162	340	1062		
240	and Cappabrogan					
240	Moyntagh	1369	180	989		
240	Monyquid	342	42	94		
80	Cloneheyne	871	10	$108\frac{4}{3}$		
80	Rerymore	680	80	680		
120	Rerybegg	466	12	$69\frac{4}{3}$		
80	Derry	275	50	172		
80	Killnegrallaghe	673	30	252	$\frac{4}{1}$	$\frac{9}{1}$
180	Boell	719	110	370		
80	Ballykneene	363	20	90	$\frac{2}{1}$	$\frac{4}{1}$

(End of manuscript)

---

14 Lost in rebinding.

APPENDIX I

HISTORICAL NOTES ON IREGAN

The territory of Uí Riagain (Iregan, Iregaine, Oregan) took its name from its ruling lineage, the descendants of a Riagán who was a near descendant of Flann da Congal, king of Uí Failghe in the eighth century and the ancestor of all the dominant clans of that area in the later period. The genealogical sources differ as to Riagán's precise descent, but the version[1] which makes him a son of Cinaedh, king of Uí Failghe 806-829, who was a son of Mughron (slain 782), also king of Uí Failghe and a son of Flann da Congal, is certainly the correct one. Another version, which makes him son of Cinaedh, son of Mughron, son of Oenghus, son of Flann da Congal, is certainly erroneous, although also found in early sources[2]. There is no Oenghus among the list of Flann da Congal's sons, and it seems that the name of Oenghus, king of Uí Failghe (died 803), another son of Mughron and elder brother of Cinaedh, has been intruded into the line[3]. Some late collections[4] make Riagán the son of another Cinaedh, king of Uí Failghe, a son of Flann da Congal who died in 770, but this is certainly

---

1 M.A. O'Brien, *Corpus Genealogiarum Hiberniae,* I (Dublin, 1962), 60, 65, quoting Rawl. B 502 and *Book of Lecan,* 90 c-d; *Book of Uí Maine,* 12r b. For the death of Cinaedh, 829, see *Annals of Ulster;* according to the king-list in the *Book of Leinster* (40 c) he was the immediate successor of Flaithnia macCinaedha, slain in 806. For Flann Da Congal and his immediate family see G. MacNiocaill, *Ireland before the Vikings* (Dublin, 1972), 113, 127.

2 O'Brien, *op.cit.,* 11, from Rawl B 502. There is, however, no Oenghus among the sons of Flann da Congal listed in the same source *(ibid.,* 59). See next note. This same defective version is found also in the *Book of Leinster,* 314 c-d.

3 The explanation of this intrusion would seem to lie in a confusion between Mughron son of Flann da Congal and his grandson of the same name, Mughron son of Oenghus. This latter Mughron was the father of Maelsinchill, whom the *Book of Leinster* king-list makes the immediate successor of Cinaedh macMughroin as king of Uí Failghe (829); there is perhaps a lacuna in the list at this point. There is no Cinaedh among the four sons (of whom Maelsinchill was the eldest) of Mughron macOenghusa listed in the text from Rawl. B 502 reproduced in O'Brien, *op.cit.,* 64; cf. 59.

4 See Appendix II.

mere telescoping. Of Riagan and his descendants nothing is known besides their bare names, nor did they ever produce a king of Uí Failghe. Donn, the eponym of the surname Ó Duinn, was a great-grandson of Riagán. The only reference to his descendants which I have been able to find before the Anglo-Normal invasion is that to Aedh Ó Duinn (not in the genealogies) who in 1155 slew Muircheartach (an t-aithcleireach) O Connon, king of Uí Failghe[5]. The history of the area, remote and woody, remains obscure throughout the middle ages, and its settlement was probably of comparatively late date. The identity of the boundaries of the barony of Tinnahinch – which are those of the O Duinn lordship as it existed in the sixteenth century – with those of the parish (Oregan formed until 1639 only a single parish of that name, centred at Rosenalis, see Appendix III) show that the limits of the lordship could not have changed between the early thirteenth century – when the ecclesiastical divisions were established – and the sixteenth, and this stability, so rare in late mediaeval Ireland, is a striking testimony to the remoteness of the area and its consequent immunity from political changes.

At the Norman conquest of Leinster the whole of Uí Failghe (Offaly) was given to Robert de Bermingham, whose daughter and heiress Eva brought it to her first husband, Gerald fitzMaurice (died 1203), and to their descendants[6]. It was probably Gerald who enfeoffed his younger brother, Thomas fitzMaurice, of the *tuath* of Oregan[7] and it was probably Thomas who bestowed the tithes of the area, some time before 1213, on the Hospitallers of Kilmainham, though in later times the Hospitallers claimed Maurice fitzGerald, baron of Offaly, the son of Gerald and Eva, as the donor (see Appendix III). He had probably confirmed an original grant by his uncle Thomas. The latter died in or around 1215; his son and heir John fitzThomas, a great man in Munster, was slain together with his son and heir Maurice at the battle of Callan in Desmond in 1261, and his grandson heir, Thomas fitzMaurice, was an infant. On the coming of age

---

5 *Book of Leinster,* facs. ed., 40 c = *Book of Leinster,* ed. Best, Bergin and O'Brien, I, p. 188: *A.F.M.,* II, p. 1114

6 G.H. Orpen, 'The Fitz-Geralds, Barons of Offaly', *R.S.A.I. Journal,* xliv (1914), 99-112; *idem, Ireland under the Normans,* III, p. 113; *Register of the Hospital of St. John the Baptist,* ed. E. St. J. Brooks (Dublin, Irish Manuscripts Commission, 1936), no. 332. I am not convinced by the argument of Professor A.J. Otway-Ruthven (Knights' Fees in Kildare, Leix and Offaly', *R.S.A.I. Journal,* xci (1961), 178) that Robert must have had more than one daughter.

7 See Nicholls, 'Some Place-Names from Pontificia Hibernica', *Dinnseanchas,* III,4 (1969), 89.

of Thomas a series of inquisitions *post mortem* were taken on his grand-father's lands. One of these, taken at Tully in County Kildare on April 13, 1282, found that John fitzThomas had held a theodum (*tuath*) called Oregan in Offaly, held of Maurice fitzGerald by the service of half a knight and suit at Maurice's court of Geashill. The theodum was then worth £45 yearly and no more because the whole had been destroyed and laid waste by the war of the Irish, but in time of peace it was worth £90 13s 4d. Nicholas fitzAlexander held 6 carucates of John fitzThomas's heir in fee by the service of rendering the half knight's service due to Maurice fitzGerald whenever royal service was proclaimed[8]. It is pretty certain that some sort of fortification and settlement – perhaps even a 'rural borough' of the type so common in the south of Ireland – had been erected at Castlebrack (which is called the manor of Courtbrake in 1421, *infra*) in the first half of the thirteenth century and the dedication of the church there to St. Mary *may* reflect a Norman foundation[9]. It is probable, however, that after the death of Thomas fitzMaurice (II) in 1296 Oregan was effectively lost to the Irish, and unlikely that his son Maurice, first earl of Desmond (1329) ever gave it any attention. An inquisition taken at Naas on January 14, 1421 (N.S.), found that John, earl of Desmond, who died on October 12, 1398, had been seised of the manor of Courtbrake and the lordship of Oregane in County Kildare, which he held of the King *in capita* (*sic*), and which were worth nothing because of the Irish enemies[10].

In 1306 the then Ó Duinn, Amhlaibh, *taoiseach* of Uí Riagáin, was in alliance with (Muircheartach) O Connor of Offaly and others against the English of County Kildare and their Irish allies, the O Dempseys. He was slain at Geashill by Finn O Dempsey and the English at some time before June 9 of that year, when O Dempsey and his lord John fitzThomas, baron of Offaly (afterwards first earl of Kildare), had a reward of £40 for the beheading of O Doyng and other felons[11]. Amhlaibh was the grand-father of David O Duinn who ends the genealogy in the *Book of Uí*

---

8 *Calendar of Inquisitions post mortem*, II, no. 437; *Calendar of Documents, Ireland*, II, 424.

9 For the dedication see *Dinnseanchas*, II,2 (1966), 32. The castle and church of Castlebrack were, however, said to have been built by Tadhg macLaighnigh Uí Duinn in the late fifteenth century (*infra*).

10 N.L.I., D. 1571; *Calendar of Ormond Deeds*, III, 31, where the first name is misread as 'Courthrad'.

11 *Annals of Inisfallen*, ed. S. Mac Airt (Dublin, 1951), p. 396: *Calendar of Justiciary Rolls, Ireland, 1305-1307*, (London, 1914), 215, 270; *The Annals of James Grace*, (ed. R. Butler, Dublin, Irish Archaeological Society, 1852), 48-9, are corrupt, but give the place.

Maine and who is probably the David Ua Duinn, chief (*taoiseach*) of
Uí Riagáin, who was slain by the son of Cearbhall Ó Duinn in 1379.[12]
The genealogy in the *Book of Lecan* ends with a brother of David,
Donnchadh, perhaps the chief of Uí Riagáin of that name who was slain
in 1381 by Aedh son of Muircheartach O Molloy while raiding Fercal[13].
The later line of Ó Duinn was descended from Donnchadh's son Ruaidhrí,
almost certainly the *taoiseach* of Uí Riagáin of that name who died in
1427[14]. Karoll (Cearbhall) and Owen, sons of Donogh O Doyne, who
were slain in a conflict between MacMurrough and the English in 1398[15],
were presumably his brothers. In 1443 O Doyn and his forces joined
MacGillapatrick, O More, Conn O Donnor of Offaly and William fitz-
Thomas of the Geraldines in an expedition against the Butlers which
plundered Slieveardagh but was heavily defeated by Edmond macRichard
Butler[16].

Tadhg macLaighnigh Uí Duinn, a grandson of the Ruaidhri mentioned
above, was ruling the territory in 1475[17]. A contemporary note in praise
of him[18] credits him with the building of the castles of Tinnahinch

---

12 *A.F.M.*, IV, 672-3; *A. Clon.*, 306.

13 *A.F.M.*, IV, 685 *n.* ; cf. *ibid.*, 682-3, and *A. Clon.*, 307.

14 *A.F.M.*, IV, 870-1.

15 *A. Clon.*, 322.

16 'Annales Anonymi', in British Library Add. MS 4793 f. 74; cf. P.R.O. (London), S.P.
63/214 f. 304v. O Doyn is not mentioned in the notice of this event in 'The Annals
of Ireland, from the year 1443 to 1468', in *Miscellany of the Irish Archaeological
Society*, (Dublin, 1846), 201.

17 'Tadhg mcLaig*nigh* mcRuadri ina hua Duinn', in the list of Irish lords prefixed
to the Gaelic version of the Travels of Sir John Mandeville ('The Gaelic Maundeville',
ed. Whitley Stokes, *Zeitschrift für Celtic Philologie*, ii, 6).

18 This note is found in two versions: 1) in Merchants' Quay (*now* Franciscan
Library, Dun Muire, Killiney) MS XXXI, from which it is printed by the Rev.
Cuthbert Magrath, O.F.M., in *Collectanea Hibernica*, ii, 15-6; 2) in a nineteenth-
century copy in Royal Irish Academy MS 24 P 61 (d). This copy is accompanied by
a note which implies that it was copied from the commencement of a manuscript
then in private hands. Unfortunately there is no clue to the owner's identity. That
the source in question was not the Merchants' Quay MS is evident, not only by some
significant differences in the texts, but by the fact that the writer of the 23 P 61
note was unable to place the Tadhg in question in the O Duinn genealogy, only the
MacFirbisigh version of which was available to him (the Merchants' Quay text is
accompanied by detailed genealogies). While in the Merchants' Quay text, too, he
is called Tadhg mcLaighnigh mcRuaidhrigh hI Duinn, that in 23 P 61 calls him Tadhg
mac Amalguigh mic Ruaidrigh. It seems to me that Amhalghaidh must have been
the true name of Tadhg's father, whom the genealogies and other sources call Laigh-

(*Caisleán na hinnsi*) and Castlebrack and the churches of Castlebrack, Reary[-more] and Kilmanman, all of which he provided with vestments, books and other necessary alter furniture; he also gave a missal to the church of Rosenalis and books to the monastery of Killeigh, as well as patronising the copying of many tales both religious and secular. The ascription to him of the building of Castlebrack — although there had certainly been some earlier mediaeval structure on the site — also occurs in the report of the jury for the plantation of the territory in the time of James I, who declared that it had been the original occasion of the exactions levied by the subsequent O Dunnes[19]. According to the genealogy drawn up in 1634 he was twice married, his first wife being a daughter of Lord Power and his second a daughter of the earl of Kildare, perhaps a natural daughter of the seventh earl. The next notice of the O Duinns is in the Rental Book of the ninth earl of Kildare, whose compilation commenced in 1518. In O Regane, O Dones countre, the earl had six 'rudders' (beeves) yearly upon Twosmere, two rudders from the vicar, and 3 rudeers from Cayre [Cathaoir] O Doyn, which he had covenanted to pay during his life by indenture dated February 24, 1525 (N.S.)[20].

neach.   Laighneach, although it appears in use as a proper name from the fifteenth century, must have been originally a simple epithet, the Leinsterman. A late fifteenth century genealogical collection ends the line of O Duinn with *Amhalghaidh son of Ruaidhrí, but in the full list of Ruaidhrí's sons which is given in another collection no Amhalghaidh appears, the list being headed by Laighneach (see Appendix II). I have printed below the version of the note on Tadhg O Duinn as it appears in 23 P 61; the reader may compare it with that printed by Fr. Magrath, although I have indicated a few readings from the latter where these are manifestly the correct ones. Oradh do Thadhg mac Amalguigh mic Ruaidrigh hi Duinn *araile.* Ni fagham scriobhtha a leabhraibh airisne no annálta go dtáinic isin tir sin hi Dhuinn riamh tighearna bodh mó sochar do cill agus do tuaith ná é, óir is lais do righneadh caislén na hinnsi agus in caislén breac, agus teampull Ruighri, teampull na mbanbán, agus teampull in caislein breic; agus ro cuireastair aidhmhetealta in ccach eaclais diobh sin, do leabhraibh aifrinn agus cailísibh aitfrinn agus d'eideadh aittfrinn, agus do chlocaibh, agus do fportamhsaibh.   Ro cuireastar leabhur aitfrinn go Rosfinnglaisi, agus leabhur mór^a agus stolící^a cco cilleich. Agus is do ro scriobhadh *Vita Christi,* eidir páis agus eiseirgi, agus freasgabail agus páis na napstall, agus beatha pfattraig *agus* Brigde *agus* Martain agus beatha fresgabáil^b agus longaireacht in soisgeal naomhtha, agus stair mac n-Israhel, agus stair *Alexandair, agus stair na Machabda, agus toraigheacht na croiche, agus stair na ^c rideradi trapesa sgeala^c, agus in cruthughadh, in boraime *agus* agallamh na senorach, bruighin mic Dato, agus mórán fosgél agus *aislinntibh^d, agus leabhr^e naimhseancusa, agus trac^f, agus lín meic^g, agus feis tigi Conáin. a-a) i. catolícon, M.Q.   b) Fhineinn, M.Q.   c-c) ridearaidh trai cona sgelaibh, M.Q. d) cislinntp '(*or* -tibh)' (*sic*)   e) *Sic*   f) traoe, M.Q.   g) míon, M.Q.

19 See Introduction.

20 *Journal of the Kilkenny and South-East of Ireland Archaeological Soc.* (N.S.), V, 1867, (= *R.S.A.I. Journal, viii*) 125. This rent of six beeves *per annum* out of Towsmeare in O Doyne's Country is mentioned in an early seventeenth-century list of possessions claimed by the Kildares which were to be 'sued for, recovered and divided' between the then earl and Lady Lettice Digby (British Library, Add. MS 19,937, f. 4).

This Cathaoir, who thus paid for the earl's *slánuigheacht* or protection, must have been the person of that name who was Tadhg macLaighnigh's son by his Geraldine wife.

On August 30, 1540, Thadeus O Dyn, Captain of Oregan, Thadeus Fuscus (*Tadhg Riabhach*) O Dyn, his son, 'and others of his followers' entered into indentures of treaty with the Lord Deputy, Sir Anthony St. Leger, by which they bound themselves to be faithful to the King, whom, and not O Connor of Offaly or any other, they acknowledged to be their sovereign lord. They agreed, among other clauses, to serve in person in every hosting when commanded by the Deputy, with 24 footmen with arms and provisions, and also to serve for two or three nights with their full force ('rising out') of horse and foot when required. They and their successors, possessors of the lordship of Castlebreke, otherwise called Toghesuier, were to pay a yearly rent to the King of six good plump kine, with the arrears for three years up to Michaelmas next following, 1540. They agreed to deliver as hostages Edmond, son of Thady the captain, and another Thady, son of Thady *Fuscus*, and to change them for other hostages if and when the Lord Deputy required[21]. The clauses of this indenture were identical (except in the number of soldiers to be furnished) with those in that made by St. Leger on the same day with Owen mcMaurice O Connor of Irry, but while the O Connors of Irry were involved in the fall of their kinsmen and overlords of Offaly and were expropriated by the administration at the same time as the latter, the O Duinns not only escaped this fate but profited by the fall of the Offaly O Connors to emancipate themselves from the control which the latter had exercised over them. The Survey of Offaly made after the fall of Brian O Connor, on November 2, 1550, found that Brian had been in possession of certain lands 'out of the countrey of Offaly in Oregan in O Doynes country'[22] and that he also 'had yerelie the thirde parte of Canes, casualties and like perquisites for defence of O Doyne over all his lordship and lands', worth 10s *per annum*[23]. On October 25, 1551, Thady O Doyn, gent., had a grant of the privileges of English liberty for himself and his issue[24], one of a number of such grants made to members of the clan at this time[25]. This was probably the Thady *Fuscus*

---

21 *Calendar of Carew Manuscripts,* ed. Brewer and Bullen, I, 163-4. 'Toghesuier' is certainly to be read *Toghesmer. Cf. the 'Parochia de Tuaghe Smertha' mentioned in the deed printed on pp. 32-3.

22 For these see App. IV, *s.vv.* Roskeen and Kilcavan.

23 'Survey of Offaly, 1550', ed. E. Curtis, *Hermathena,* XX (1930), 368.

24 *Fiants, Edward VI,* no. 864.

25 'Arthur O Doyne of Regan' (perhaps a son to the Cahir mentioned above, see *n.* 73 to Genealogical Tables) had a similiar grant to himself and his issue, May 1, 1550 (*Fiants, Edward VI* no. 478); Mary O Dyn *alias* Moore O Dwyne of Regan had grant of English Liberty to herself and her issue on the same date (*ibid.,* no.477).

(Riabhach) of 1540; his father, the elder Tadhg, Tadhg macLaighnigh's son, being probably dead by this date. He would appear to have resigned or been deposed, as on 4 June 1558 his son Thady Oge O Doyne (the hostage of 1540), 'son of Thady Riough O Doyne's had a grant of the office of captain of Iryegane, to hold during good behaviour with the accustomed powers and profits[26]. On 30 November 1572 Gerald, eleventh earl of Kildare granted the castle and lands of Ballenkeslan-vrekye [Castlebrack] in the territory called Twosmerye to Pierce Boyce of Calgagh and Thomas Nugent of Carne, to hold to the use of Thade O Doyne 'the younger' and Margaret Neyle his wife, and the heirs male of their bodies lawfully begotten remainder in default to his father Thade O Doyne of Sralye, and the heirs male of his body, and reserving the rent of six beeves already mentioned[27]. There is little to record of the career of Tadhg Óg, who survived until 1606 and whose troubles with his eldest son and namesake will be found recorded in the text above. In 1570 he was involved in a dispute, resulting in 'burnings, murther and other disorders' with his subject Tirrelaugh O Doyne of Garryheder, who rejected O Doyne's claim to impose exactions upon him[28]. The country seems to have remained in general obedient to the Queen's government, and not until James fitzPiers FitzGerald of Ballysonan (County Kildare), whose aunt was old Tadhg's wife and the mother of his sons, revolted in 1598 did the O Doynes break their loyalty and join him[29]. Most of Iregan, except old Tadhg and his son and namesake, revolted again when the Earl of Tyrone entered the territory early in 1600, although the earl wasted and plundered the country and, according to a report of a government spy, put many of the poor inhabitants to the sword[30]. Tadhg Riabhach Ó Duinn, grandson of the old chief and son of the younger Tadhg by his first wife, the daughter of the great Seán O Neill, who had separated from Tadhg O Duinn to become the wife of Sir Cúchonnacht Maguire of Fermanagh, had been a rebel for some time before this but, with the rest of his family and many of the inhabitants of Iregan, was included in the general pardon issued to Tadhg Ó Duinn and his followers on May 14, 1601[31].

For some clerics of the family, including 'Rory O Doyn of Castelbracke, chaplain', who had similar grants at this period see App. III.

26 *Fiants, Philip and Mary*, no. 223.

27 Original deed among Leinster estate papers abstracted in Lord Walter FitzGerald's collections, T.C.D.

28 See App. IV, *s.v.* The Shisseragh of Fasaghely.

29 *Cal. S.P.I., 1596-1598*, 375.

30 *Ibid., 1599-1600*, 439, 464.

31 *F.E.*, no. 6523. For the doings of Tadhg Riabhach see the statements made by his uncle Charles, in Text, above; on April 10, 1595, a reward was proposed to be offered for him and his mother, Maguire's widow (*Cal, S.P.I., 1592-1596*, 311). He was half-brother to Cuchonnacht Óg Maguire who fled with the Earls of Tyrone and Tyrconnell in 1607.

APPENDIX II

GENEALOGIES OF THE O DUINNES

(The earlier genealogies of the Uí Riagáin will be found printed in *Corpus Genealogiarum Hiberniae,* ed. M.S. O'Brien, (1962), pp. 11, 59, 60, 65. They are therefore not reproduced here.)

BOOK OF LECAN, 90 c-d.

Dondcad[1]
mc Amalga
mc Amalga[2]
mc Thaidc
mc Conmuigi
mc Duindslebe
mc Conmuigi
mc Cerbaill
mc Conbladma
mc Conallad
mc Fidallaich
mc Duind[3]
mc Duibgilla
mc Mailfhindi
mc Riacain[4]
mc Cinaith[5]

---

1 Probably the lord of Uí Riagáin of this name who was slain by Aedh (son of Muircheartach) O Molloy while raiding Feara Ceall, 1381 (*A.F.M.,* IV, 685 *n.;* cf. 1682-3 and *A. 'Clon.,* 307). This genealogy has been copied into MacFirbisigh's Book of Genealogies, p. 479 a.

2 Probably the Amhlaibh, chief of Uí Riagáin, slain in 1306 (*Annals of Inisfallen;* see App. I).

3 Eponym of the surname *Ó Duinn.*

4 Eponym of the territory-name *Uí Riagáin.*

5 King of Uí Failghe, died 829.

mc Mugroin[6]
mc Floind da *Con*gal

BOOK OF UÍ MAINE, 12v a.

Do genelogia I Duind
Dauid[7]
mc Amlaib
mc Amlaib
mc Conmuigi
mc Dui*n*dsleibi
mc Conmuigi
mc Cerbaill
mc Conbladma
mc *Con*allad
mc Indillaig
mc Duind[8]
mc Duibgilla
mc Mailindi
mc Riagan
mc Cinaeta
mc Mugroin
mc Aengusa
mc Flaind da *con*gal.

R.I.A. MS 23 Q 10 (*An Leabhar Donn*)[9], 43v. 9

Genelach I Dui*nn*
Ruaid*ri*[10]
mc Donch*adha*

----

6   King of Uí Failghe, died 782.

7   Probably the David, chief of Uí Riagain, who was slain by the son of Cearbhall
O Duinn, 1379 (*A.F.M.,* IV, 672-3; *A. Clon.,* 306).

8   *Bis* MS.

9   Although the (incomplete) collection of genealogies in the earlier part of this
volume dates (as can be deduced from internal evidence) 1479-82, the second collection (in which the genealogy reproduced here is included) is of early fifteenth-
century date.

10 This must be the Ruaidhrí, chief of Uí Riagain, whose death is recorded in 1427
(*A.F.M.,* IV, 870-1). This genealogy also appears in *The O Clery Book of Genealogies*
(ed. Pender, *Analecta Hibernica,* 18), p. 132) and in N.L.I. MS G. 192 (see below,
n. 11), 317. The short line found in MacFirbisigh (478 a.), following the genealogy
of Donnchadh O Duinn, *Ruaidhri mc Donncuidh mc Amhalghaidh mc Conmuighe
mc Duinnslebhe*, probably represents a truncated version of the same genealogy.

mc A*m*algaig
mc Amalgaid
mc Taidg
mc Amalgaid
mc *Con*muige
mc Duin*n*sleibe
mc *Con*muigi
mc Ce*r*baill
mc *Con*bladma
mc *Con*allaid
mc Fid*allaigh*
mc Duin*n*
mc Duibgilla
mc Ailfia*n*
mc Riacain
mc Ci*n*aech
mc Flain*n* da *con*gal.

T.C.D. MS H. 1. 12,[11] p. B 32.

Gené*lach* hi Duind
Algaid (*sic*)[12]
m*c* Ruaid*ri*
mc Don*n*ch*adha*
mc A*m*luig*h*
mc Taidce
mc Amluig
mc *Con*muid*h*e
mc Duin*n*slebhe
mc *Con*muid*h*e
mc Cerb*h*al
mc *Con*blad*h*ma
mc Conall*aigh*
mc Fiag*h*ail
mc Duin*n* a quo
mc Dub*h*gall-
mc Maoilfind

---

11 The second half of this MS consists of a very inaccurate copy, by the eighteenth-century scribe Hugh O'Daly, of a collection of genealogies said in the colophon to have been compiled by Seán Ó Maoilconaire in or around 1485. Internal evidence bears out this date.

12 *Recte* Amhalghaidh. For this man, and his identity with the Laighneach of later sources, see App. I, n. 18. It is probably from this source that the name has been inserted in the original of *The O Clery Book of Genealogies* (*loc. cit.*).

mc Riagain
mc Cinnaotha
mc Flainn da con [g] al

N.L.I. MS G. 192,[13] R.

Giunoluidh Ui Duinn
Tadhg O Duinn,[14] Feradac, Diarmuid, da Amhalgaidh, Brian, Sean, Uaithne
agus Failge,
clann Luighnidh
mc Ruaidhrighe
mc Donnchadha.

Laigne, Donnchadha, Cerbhall Óg, Tadhg, Eoghan. Sean, Toirdelbach,
Emonn, Feidhlimidh[15], Failghe,
clann Ruaidrighe
mc Donchadha sin.

Tadhg
mc Laighnigh
mc Ruaidhrighe
mc Doncada
mc Amalguidh
mc Amalguidh
mc Taidg
mc Amalgaidh
mc Conmuidhe
mc Duinn sleibhe
mc Conmuide
mc Cerbuill
mc Blathmhac [sic]
mc Conullaidh
mc Fitcealluid
mc Duinn o bfuil an cine
mc Dubgalluid
mc Maoilfhionn

---

13 This MS was written by Tadhg Ó Neachtain in the early years of the eighteenth
century, but contains much material derived from earlier MSS not now available.
The collection of genealogies of which this forms part was apparently derived from
an exemplar of late fifteenth-century date.

14 Living 1475. See App. 1.

15 Perhaps the Felim O Duinn who was slain by Cuchoigchriche O Molloy, in revenge
for his brother whom Felim had slain, in 1448 ('The Annals of Ireland, from the Year
1443 to 1468', ed. John O Donoovan, *Miscellany of the Irish Archaeological Society,*
I (1846), 221).

mc Riagain o bguil Tuat*h* Riagain.
mc Cinnaet*h*a

The two basic authorities for the later genealogy of the O Dunnes are the genealogy written by Terence O Dunne on February 4, 1633 (O. *or* N.S.?), contained in the MS XXXI formerly in the Franciscan Library at Merchants' Quay, Dublin, and now at the Franciscan College at Dun Mhuire, Killiney (printed by Fr. Cuthbert Magragh, O.F.M., in *Collectanae Hibernica,* 2 (1959), pp. 13-17), and that in the genealogical collections of Sir George Carew, Earl of Totnes (Lambeth MS 626, p. 250, and MS 635, f. 160). These may be added to by, among other sources, the Funeral Entries of William O Dunne of Park (died 1625) and John O Dunne of Kilcavan (died (1636) in the Genealogical Office, Dublin[16], and the settlement made by Teig O Dunne on February 21 1616/7[17], which contains a long list of collaterals in remainder. From these sources the genealogical tables accompanying this Appendix have been constructed. It may be noted, however, that the genealogy prepared by Terence O Dunne inserts a second Ruaidhrí (Ruaidhrí Óg) between Ruaidhrí son of Donnchadh O Duinn and Laighneach, father of Tadhg. In view of the material from N.L.I. MS G. 192, printed above, this is almost certainly incorrect, but the fact that this material is only preserved for us in an eighteenth-century copy does not enable us to speak on the matter with absolute certainty. The Carew genealogy commences with Leynagh (*Laighneach*) O Dunne.

---

16 Funeral Entries, Vol VI, p. 345; Vol. VII, p. 100.

17 P.R.O.I., R.C. 5/10, pp. 338ff.

Descendants of Ruaidhrí Ó Duinn

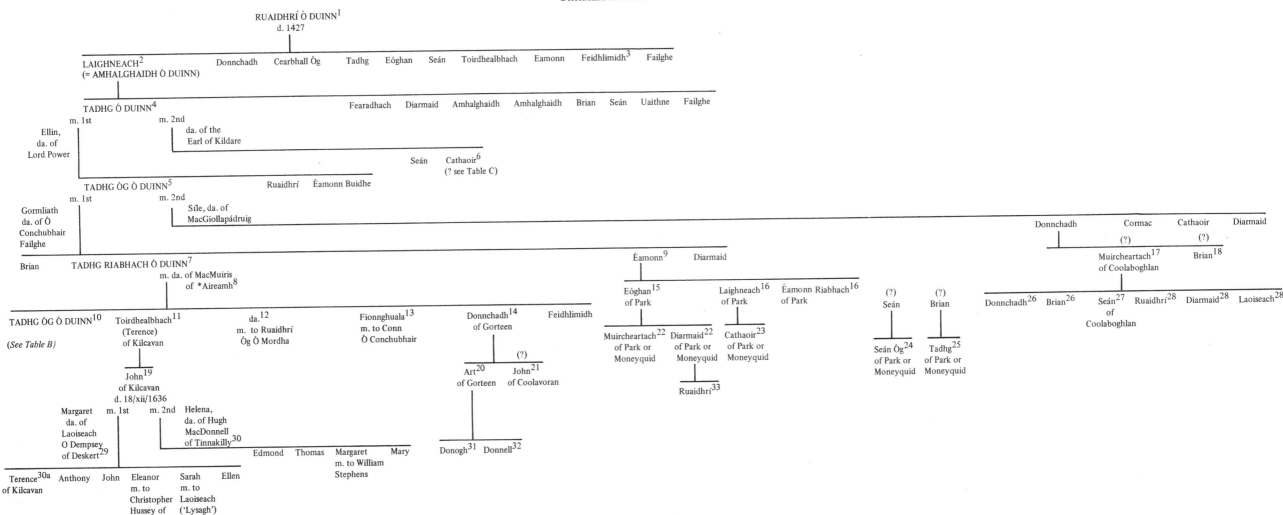

TABLE B

Descendants of Tadhg Óg Ó Duinn

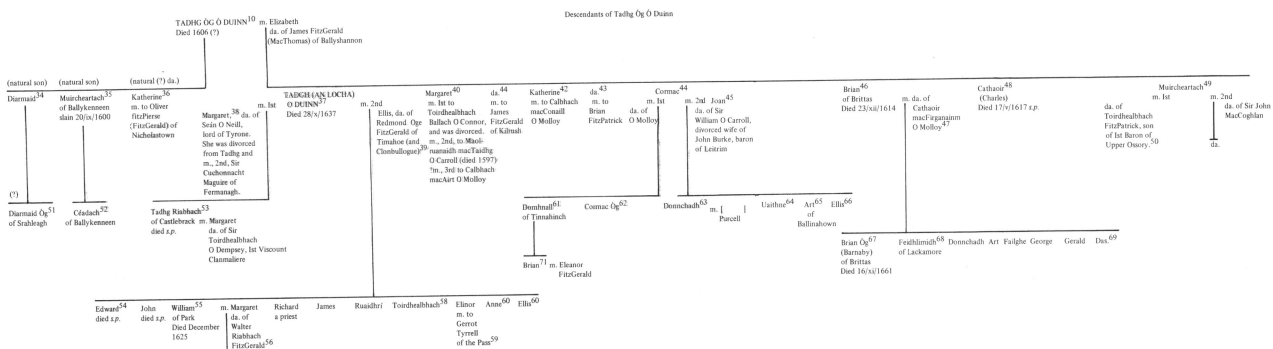

TADHG ÓG Ó DUINN[10] m. Elizabeth
Died 1606 (?) da. of James FitzGerald
  (MacThomas) of Ballyshannon

(natural son)   (natural son)   (natural (?) da.)
Diarmaid[34]   Muircheartach[35]   Katherine[36]
              of Ballykenneen   m. to Oliver
              slain 20/ix/1600   fitzPierse
                                 (FitzGerald) of
                                 Nicholastown

Margaret,[38] da. of   m. Ist   TADGH (AN LOCHA)   m. 2nd   Margaret[40]   da.[44]   Katherine[42]   da.[43]   Cormac[44]   m. 2nd Joan[45]   Brian[46]   m. da. of   Cathaoir[48]   Muircheartach[49]
Seán O Neill,   Ó DUINN[37]   m. Ist to   m. to   m. to Calbhach m. to   m. Ist   da. of Sir   of Brittas   Cathaoir   (Charles)   m. Ist
lord of Tyrone.   Died 28/x/1637   Ellis, da. of   Toirdhealbhach James   macConaill   Brian   William O Carroll, Died 23/xii/1614 macFirganainm Died 17/v/1617 s.p.   m. 2nd
She was divorced   Redmond Oge   Ballach O Connor, FitzGerald O Molloy   FitzPatrick O Molloy divorced wife of   O Molloy[47]   da. of   da. of Sir John
from Tadhg and   FitzGerald of   and was divorced. of Kilrush   John Burke, baron   Toirdhealbhach MacCoghlan
m., 2nd, Sir   Timahoe (and   m., 2nd, to Maol-   of Leitrim   FitzPatrick, son
Cuchonnacht   Clonbullogue)[39] ruanaidh macTaidhg   of Ist Baron of   da.
Maguire of   O Carroll (died 1597)   Upper Ossory.[50]
Fermanagh.   ?m., 3rd to Calbhach
                                                        macAirt O Molloy

(?)   Domhnall[61]   Cormac Óg[62]   Donnchadh[63] m. [ ]   Uaithne[64] Art[65] Ellis[66]
Diarmaid Óg[51]   Céadach[52]   Tadhg Riabhach[53]   of Tinnahinch   Purcell   of
of Srahleagh   of Ballykenneen   of Castlebrack m. Margaret   Ballinahown
                                    died s.p.   da. of Sir
                                                      Toirdhealbhach   Brian Óg[67]   Feidhlimidh[68] Donnchadh Art Failghe George   Gerald Das.[69]
                                                      O Dempsey, Ist Viscount   (Barnaby)   of Lackamore
                                                      Clanmaliere   of Brittas
                                                                            Brian[71] m. Eleanor   Died 16/xi/1661
                                                                                     FitzGerald

Edward[54]   John   William[55]   m. Margaret   Richard   James   Ruaidhrí   Toirdhealbhach[58]   Elinor   Anne[60]   Ellis[60]
died s.p.   died s.p. of Park   da. of   a priest   m. to
                     Died December   Walter   Gerrot
                     1625   Riabhach   Tyrrell
                                     FitzGerald[56]   of the Pass[59]

Edward[70]   James   William   Oliver   Bridget Mary Anne
of Park

TABLE C

Descendants of Cathaoir O Duinn

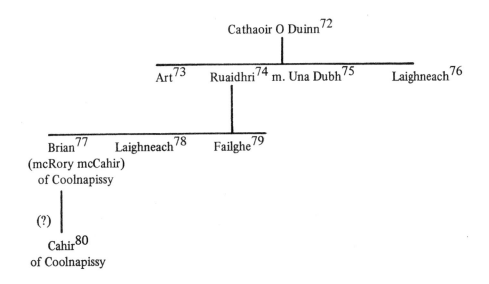

Cathaoir O Duinn[72]

Art[73]   Ruaidhri[74] m. Una Dubh[75]   Laighneach[76]

Brian[77]   Laighneach[78]   Failghe[79]
(mcRory mcCahir)
 of Coolnapissy

(?)

Cahir[80]
of Coolnapissy

Notes to Genealogical Tables.

1 See above, App. II and *n*.8. His sons are listed in N.L.I. MS G.192, p.*R*.

2 See App. I *n*.18. The genealogy in C.626 commences with this 'Leynagh', but erroneously inserts an extra Teig. Laighneach's sons are listed in N.L.I. G.192; MQ names only Tadhg and Failghe.

3 Perhaps the Felim slain in 1448 (App. II *n*.13).

4 Chief in 1475 (see App. I and *n*.18). His marriages and issue are from MQ.

5 Chief in 1540 (App. I). His marriages and issue are from MQ.

6 Probably the Cayre O Doyn who entered into indentures with the earl of Kildare in 1525 (App. I).

7 Occurs in 1540; living 30 November 1572 (App. I). His marriage and four sons are in MQ; the three eldest named also in C.626 and C.635.

8 'McMorish Ire'. For the sept (A branch of the O Connors of Offaly) and territory (in the west of Portnahinch Barony, County Laois) see Lord Walter FitzGerald, 'Notes on the District of Irry', *Kild. Arch. Journal*, IV, 297-9.

9 Hostage for his father, 1540 (App. I).

10 Hostage for his father, 1540; appointed captain of Iregan, June 4, 1558 (App. I). Pardoned, as of Tenehenshia (Tenehensey, Tenyhynch, Tenehinch), chief (or captain) of his nation, 1569, 1570, 1582, 1601 (*F.E.*, 1337, 1570, 3840, 6523). He was apparently still living August 20, 1606, but dead by July 3, 1607 (inquisition).

11 Tirlogh (Terence) O Dun, of Garremore, 1569 (*F.E.*, 1337; of Colmoran in Iregan, horseman, 1570 (*F.E.*, 1570) of Kilkevan, brother of Teig O Doyn, 1582 (*F.E.*, 3840); of Kilkevan, 1601 (*F.E.*, 6523). In remainder in his brother's settlement, 1593 (App. V). Called 'uncle to the now O Doyne, 1636', in the Funeral Entry of his son John. (C.626 interchanges the names of this John and his cousin Art of Gorteen, making the former son of Donogh and the latter son of Tirlogh.)

12 C.626, 635.

13 Con O Conor, of the country of Aregan, and Fenoile O Done, sister

of Thady O Done, chief of his name, had grant of English liberty to them and their issue, March 5, 1569/70 (*F.E.*, 1301).

14 Donogh O Dun of Gortin, 1569 (*F.E.*, 1337); of Balliglas in Iregan, horseman, 1570 (*F.E.*, 1570). In remainder in his brother's settlement, 1593 (App. V).

15 Egidius or Owen O Dun of Parke, gent., 1569 (*F.E.*, 1337); Ouin mcEdmond O Doyn of Parke, 1582 (*F.E.*, 3840). As his sons were next in remainder after the descendants of Tadhg Riabhach, 1616, he must have been son of the Edmond of 1540.

16–16 Lenagh mcEdmond O Doyn of Park and Edmond Reough mcEdmond O Doyn of the same, 'brothers of the said Owin', 1582 (*F.E.*, 3840); Lenagh O Dun and Edmond O Dun of Parke, kerns, 1569 (*F.E.*, 1337).

17 Moriartogh mcDonoghe of O Donne's Country, 1574 (S.P. 63/51, 26, I); Murtagh mcDonoghe in remainder after the sept of Park, 1616. Presumably this is Murtagh (Moriertagh) O Dun (Doyn) of Culboghelan (Culbolan, Coylewochellan, Cowlebohalane), 1569, 1570, 1582, 1601 (*F.E.*, 1337, 1570, 3840, 6523), and 1608 (inquisition).

18 Brian mcDonogh of Castlebrake, gent., 1582 (*F.E.*, 3840). His position here is very doubtful and, indeed, he might not have been an O Duinn at all.

19 John mcTerence O Duinn of Kilcavan, 1601 (*F.E.*, 6523), 1607; (John mcTyrlagh) in remainder 1616. For his death, marriages, and children see his Funeral Entry (VII, p. 100); he was buried in Castlebrack church.

20 Art mcDonogh of Gurtin, freeholder, 1601 (*F.E.*, 6523), 1607 (and see Text of MS; the reference to his having inherited his lands from his father *and grandfather* cannot throw doubt on his being first cousin of the then chief, which is certain). Next in remainder after John mcTyrlagh, 1616.

21 Shane mcDonogh O Doyne of Cappaloghran (or of Couilmoran), 1607 (in connection with Art of Gurtin). The fact that he held only a life-interest in his lands is suspicious.

22–22 Mortagh mcOwin O Doyn and Dermot mcOwin O Doyn of Parke, sons of Owen, 1582 (*F.E.*, 3840); of Parke, freeholders, 1601 (*F.E.*, 6523); of Moniquid, 1607; of Park, in remainder 1616.

23 Cahir mcLynagh of Parke, yeoman, 1601 (*F.E.*, 6523); of Moniquid, 1607; in remainder after sons of Owen, 1616.

24 Shane Oge mcShane O Doyne of Park, next in remainder after Cahir, 1616. It is possible that 'James Oage O Doine' of Moniquid in the 1607 inquisition is an error for the name of this Shane Oge.

25 Teig mcBrian of Moniquid, 1607; Teig mcBrien O Doyne of Park, next in remainder after Shane Oge, 1616.

26–26 Donogh mcMortagh O Doyn and Brian mcMortagh O Doyn, sons of Mortagh of Coylevochellan, 1582 and 1601 (*F.E.*, 3840, 6523).

27 Shane mcMortagh, son of Mortagh of Cowlebohalaine, 1601 (*F.E.*, 6523); of Coolvochelan, had grant of lands there under the plantation, (App. V); of Killevolan or Coulbochlan, 1641 (Depositions, ff. 67, 102v).

28–28 Rorie, Dermot and Lisagh mcMortagh, sons of Mortagh of Cowlebohalaine, 1601 (*F.E.*, 6523).

29 Deskert was a district in Geashill Parish, Philipstown Upper Barony, County Offaly; Ballintemple was in 'the parish of Diskert', according to the 1550 extent of Clanmaliere (abstract in Carrigan MSS (unnumbered volumes), St. Kiernan's College, Kilkenny; the original was destroyed in 1922). A Lysagh O Dempsey died at Deskert shortly before May 2, 1604 (C.P., J, 250).

30 For the family see Lord Walter FitzGerald, 'The MacDonnells of Tinnakill Castle', *Kild. Arch. Journal*, IV, pp. 205-15.

30a 'Late a Protestant, and one of the clerks of His Majesty's Court of Exchequer' (Depositions, f. 63v).

31 Donogh mcArt Doyne of Gortin (or Gortinrath), 1641 (Depositions, ff.10v, 124); Donogh O Dun, had confirmation of Gurtin by Letters Patent, August 15, 1639 (App. VI).

32 Donnell mcArt Doyne of the Gurtin, 1642 (Depositions, f.63v).

33 Rorie mcDermot mcOwen of Parke, yeoman, 1601 (*F.E.*, 6523).

34 His name is only in C.626, but cf. the statement that Tadhg Óg had five legitimate sons and two bastards (App. V); Dermot O Doyn fitzThade, horseman, 1570 (*F.E.*, 1570).

35 C.626, C.635, which says that he was 'slain 1600'; he must be the Moriertagh O Donne of Ballykenin who died September 20, 1600, and who held lands which had been in the hands of Tadhg Óg (inquisition).

36   T.C.D. MS E. 3.2, p. 21. She was pardoned in 1599 with her husband and others of his sept (*F.E.*, 6323). He was a natural son of Pierse Fitz-Gerald, a full-brother of James FitzGerald of Ballyshannon and son of Sir Gerald 'macShane' and had pardons several times from 1548 (*Fiants, Edward VI*, no. 233) onwards.

37   *Tadhg an locha* in MQ genealogy; Teig Oge O Doyn of Castellbrack, 1582, 1601 (*F.E.*, 3840, 6523) 'very aged and sickly', 1626 (*Cal. S.P.I., 1625–1632*, p. 191; for his death, see *Repertorium Inquisitionum ... Lagenia*, Queen's County, no. 27 of Charles I. His sons, MQ and (except Edward and James) C.626; his daughters, C.626. I cannot identify Thomas Ardagh, 'uncle' of Teig Oge in 1601 (*F.E.*, 6523); could 'uncle' perhaps be an error for 'fosterer'?

38   C. 635 (pedigrees of O Doyne, O Neill, Maguire). For this Margaret see also David Greene, ed., *Duanaire Mhéig Uidhir*, (Dublin, 1972), Intro-duction, p. x. On April 10, 1595, it was proposed to offer a reward for her and her son Teig Reogh (*Cal. S.P.I., 1592–1596*, p. 311).

39   C. 626, 635; MQ. Settlement made on her by her husband, October 20, 1583, recited in the inquisition; she was living at the date of the latter (September 22, 1607).

40   C.626; C.617. Her first marriage, to Toirdhealbhach Ballach O Connor was annulled, on grounds of her non-consent, by decree of 24 June 1586 (*Cal. S.P.I. 1575-88* p. 428).

41   C.626. This James was the second son of Sir Maurice fitzThomas of Lackagh (see App. III, *n*. 14 and the references there cited). Either his wife or her sister who was the wife of Brian FitzPatrick may be the sister Grany who was a legatee under the will of her brother Charles O Duinn, April 2, 1616 (App. V).

42   C.626 precises her husband as Callogh mcConell O Molloy C.635 says simply Callogh O Molloy. As neither gives her forename, it is *just* possible that there is a confusion with Margaret, wife of Callogh mcArt O Molloy (*n*.40, *supra*). That the name of Callogh mcConnell O Molloy's wife was Katherine appears from P.R.O.I., C.P., G,389.

43   C.635. This Brian FitzPatrick, afterwards of Garran, County Laois (Records of the Rolls, V, p. 26) was the 4th son of Fineen, 3rd Baron of Upper Ossory.

44   Of Balleknyne, son of Teig, 1582 (F.E., 3840); of Ballyskeanagh (in Ely O Carroll), 1593 (*F.E.*, 5818); of Lisnerode, 1601 (*F.E.*, 6523); 'of Timnelinch and Roskeene' (C.626; these lands were settled on him by his father, 1593, see App. V). He was dead by September 22, 1607. For his first marriage, C.626.

45 C.626, C.635. Joan ny Carroll, pardoned 1593, 1601 (*F.E.*, 5818, 6523). She was living September 22, 1607 (inquisition). For her divorce from the baron of Leitrim (by whom she was the mother of, *inter alios*, Redmond Burke, titular baron of Leitrim) see Morrin, *Calendar of the Patent and Close Rolls of the Irish Chancery*, II, p. 102.

46 Son of Teig, 1582 (*F.E.*, 3840); of Mylick, 1601 (*F.E.*, 6523); of Castle-Brittas (C.626). For the settlement made on him by his father, 1593, see App. V. His death, *Repertorium Inquisitionum ... Lagenia*, Queen's County, For his sons, the will of their uncle Cahir O Doyne (App. V) and (omitting Gerald) C.626.

47 C.626. Cahir mcFir O Molloy was of Ballyboy, Co. Offaly; for him and his brothers see *Analecta Hibernica*, XXVI, p. 113.

48 See Introduction, and, for the settlements made on him by his father, Text. He made his will, April 2, 1617 (App. V) and died *s.p.* on May 17 following (Funeral Entries, iii, p. 64).

49 C.626, 635, MQ. Living in 1593; he was dead *s.p.m.* by September 22, 1607. His first marriage, C.635; his second, C.626.

50 This Tirlogh, a son of the 1st Lord Upper Ossory by Elizabeth, daughter of Brian O Connor of Offaly by the daughter of the 9th earl of Kildare (C.635), was treacherously slain, with his full-brother Dermot, by Donnell O Molloy, 1581 (*A.F.M.*, V, pp. 1754-5; *Cal. S.P.I. 1574-1585*, p. 324).

51 Dermot Oge O Donne of Srahliagh, gent., 1601 (*F.E.*, 6523) and 1607, who was in possession of certain lands which had been bestowed upon him by Teig Oge O Doyne, was probably — because of the adjective *Óg* attached to his name — a son of the latter's son Dermot rather than identical with the latter, but this is not certain, and it is possible that he is the same.

52 Keadoghe mcMoriertaghe, aged 13, 1607. He had a grant of lands in Ballykenneen under the plantation, 1629, and still held them in 1641 (Book of Survey and Distribution).

53 Teig Reogh, son of Teig Oge, 1601 (*F.E.*, 6523); of Castlebrack, 1619 (C.626); living 1626 (*Cal. S.P.I., 1635-1632*, p. 190); dead without issue before his brother William (Funeral Entries, VI, p. 345). His marriage, C.626, C.635.

54 MQ (omitted C.626). Hostage for his father, 1598 (*Cal.S.P.I. 1592-1596*, p. 425; = 'Edmond' mcTeig O Dunne, 'other son' of Teig, 1601

(*F.E.,* 6523); living 1617 (settlement, App. V; he and his next brother dead *s.p.* before their brother William (Funeral Entries, VI, p. 345).

55 Had grant of lands in Park under the Plantation, 1629 (App. VI). His death (at Park), his marriage and children, Funeral Entries, vi, p. 345.

56 Funeral Entries, vi, p. 345; C.626. For Walter Reagh FitzGerald see Lord Walter FitzGerald, 'The Career of Walter "Reagh" (the swarthy) FitzGerald', *Kild. Arch. Journal,* VII, pp. 103-8.

57 A priest and Vicar-General of the diocese of Kildare (MQ). I cannot place in the pedigree Lieut.-Col. Richard Doyne, a native of Iregan and a distinguished soldier (Gilbert, ed., *A Contemporary History of Affiars in Ireland from 1641 to 1652,* III, p. 107).

58 The writer of the pedigree in MQ, February 4, 1633 (O.S. or N.S.?).

59 C.626; Funeral Entries, vii, p. 204. He was son and successor of James Tyrrell of Castlelost (and Pass), County Westmeath, chief of that family, and died April 6, 1637 (Funeral Entries, VII, p. 204).

60–60 Unm. at the date of their father's settlement, February, 1616/7.

61 Donell, son of Cormock, 1601 (*F.E.,* 6523); 'son and heir of Cormock', in remainder, 1617; of Tinnehinch and Roskine, 1619 (C.626; App. V); had grant under the Plantation, 1629, and regrant confirming this and his original lands, March 8, 1637/8 (App. VI); of Tinnahinch, one of the Irish leaders proclaimed by the Lords Justices, February 8, 1641/2 (Gilbert, ed., *A Contemporary History of Affairs in Ireland,* I, p. 388). Is he the Daniel O Doyne who was pardoned with Owny [*Una*] nyne Rory his wife in 1602 (*F.E.,* 6647)?

62 Cormock Oge, son of Cormock, 1601 (*F.E.,* 6523). Not in C.626.

63 Donogh, son of Cormock, 1601 (*F.E.,* 6523); his marriage, C.626. Donnogh mcCormock, allotted 150 acres under the Plantation of Iregan; this is Ballynahown, of which the Book of Survey and Distribution returns him as proprietor. In remainder, 1617.

64 Owny Doyne, brother of Donnell, in remainder 1617.

65 C.626; Art mcCormick, brother of Donnell, 1641 (Depositions, ff. 42v, 63v). Art mcCormick of Ballinehoine, gent., aged about 36, 1638 (*Historical MSS Comm., Reports,* IX, App., p. 309); Arthur Doyne of Ballynehowne (Depositions, f. 108); Art mcCormock Dun, late of the

Island of Drumlin (*ibid.*, f. 61).

66   Ellis Doyne, da. of Cormock, 1601 (*F.E.*, 6523).

67   Son and heir, aged 24 and unm. (inquisition *p.m.*); in remainder, 1617; of Castle-Brittas, 1619 (C.626); Barnaby Donn, had grant under Plantation, 1629, and regrant, 1639 (App. VI); for his subsequent history, see Gilbert (ed.), *A Contemporary History of Affairs in Ireland,* I, p. 129, and Depositions.   His death, *Repertorium Inquisitionum ... Lageniae,* Queen's Co., no. 2 of Charles II.   Richard FitzGerald of Boleybeg, Co. Kildare, a son of the James of Kilrush who married a daughter of Teig Óg O Doyne, refers in his will (dated 5 May 1622) to Barnaby Dunn as his 'brother' [-in-law] (abstract in Lord Walter FitzGerald's genealogical collections, T.C.D.); Was Barnaby's first wife, the mother of his son Charles (who, unlike his Protestant father, was a Roman Catholic (*Cal. S.P.I. 1660-62*, p. 534)), a da. of James FitzGerald of Kilrush (and therefore Barnaby's first cousin)?   Barnaby m. as his 2nd wife Sibell (= Isabel = Elizabeth), da. of Sir Robert Pigott of Dysart and widow of Richard Cosby of Stradbally, who d. 1631 (*Repertorium Inquisitionum... Lageniae,* Queen's Co., no 36 of Charles I).   For documents relating to Charles Dunn of Brittas and his family see *Analecta Hibernica,* XXV, 126 ff.

68   Phelim, C.626 and his uncle Cahir's will; Phelim Dun, brother of Barnaby, 1641 (Depositions, f. 67); of Lackamor, (*ibid.*, ff. 63v, 108).

69   Margaret, Katherine, Ellis and Elizabeth, *sisters,* and nieces of Cahir O Doyne, mentioned in his will, were presumably daughters of Brian.

70   Heir to his grandfather, aged 18 years and 2 months, October, 1637 (inquisition *p.m.*); had regrant of his grandfather's lands and those granted to his father under the Plantation, August 15, 1638 (App. VI); Edward Dun of the Parke, 'a captain of the rebels' 1641 (Depositions, f.69).

71   son of Donnell of *Tenehynns, 1641 (Depositions, f.67); Elenor FitzGarrald, wife to Brian mcDonell (*ibid.*, f.108).   A Francis Dune of Tinehinch, killed at the battle of Aughrim with two of his sons (another son, Daniel O Dune, was afterwards a captain in Dorington's Regiment in France; *Hist. MSS Comm., Report on Stuart MSS,* I, p. 173), may have been a son of this Brian).

72   See Table A and *n*.6.

73   Arthur mcCahir O Doyne of Teaghynishe, pardoned April 10, 1550 (*Fiants, Edward VI,* no.458); ? Arthur O Dyne of Regan, had grant of English liberty to himself and his issue, May 1, 1550 (*ibid.,* 478); of Oregan, pardoned November 7, 1550 (*ibid.,* 623). He might possible have

been the father of Teige, Tirlagh and Owny mcArt O Doyne of Derry (*q.v.*, Appendix IV. A Tirlagh mcArt O Donne was pardoned with Brian mcRory (see *n.*77 below) in 1583).

74 Rory mcCahir O Doyne of Teaghynishe, 1550 (*Fiants*, Edward VI, no.458); ? Rory O Doin of Oregan (*ibid.*, 623); Rory O Doyn of Kollnepesy, 1566 (*F.E.*, 949); Rory mcCahir O Dune, 1578 (*F.E.*, 3170).

75 Owny Duffe, wife of Rory mcCahir, 1578 (*F.E.*, 3170); ? Owny ny Moloy of Ballynestragh, 1583 (*F.E.*, 3949).

76 Leynagh mcCahir O Dune, 1578 (*F.E.*, 3170).

77 Brian mcRory mcCahir, 1607. Brian mcRory O Donne, of Ballynestragh, 1583 (*F.E.*, 3949); Brian mcRorie of Cowlnapissey, freeholder, 1601 (*F.E.*, 6523).

78 Leynagh mcRory O Donne of Ballynestragh, 1583 (*F.E.*, 6523); Leynaghe O Doine, or Leynagh mcRorie, of Killowrine, 1607 (inquisition). Hardly the Leynagh mcRory of Fertire in Geashill pardoned with his brother Owney in 1601 (*F.E.*, 6501).

79 Faly mcRory O Donne of Ballynestragh, 1583 (*F.E.*, 3949).

80. Had a grant of lands in Coolenepish under the Plantation 1629 [App VI] : he and his wife conveyed them to Thomas Weldon by fine levied in Easter term, 1638 (P.R.O.I., Entry Book of Fines, 1517-1648, p. 185).

APPENDIX III

THE RECTORY OF IREGAN; SOME O DUNNE CLERICS

The territory of Uí Riagain, corresponding to the present barony of Tinnahinch, remained as a single undivided parish,[1] with its parish church at Rosenalis, dedicated to St. Brigid and probably the only ancient ecclesiastical site in the area, until the seventeenth century. The churches of St. Mary at Castlebrack, of St. Finian at Rearymore and of Kilmanman[2], which had been erected by Tadhg macLaighnigh Uí Duinn in the late fifteenth century (see Appendix I), seem to have only ranked as chapels. By Letters Patent dated June 13, 1639, it was ordered that 'the old reputed vicarage of Iregan should be dissolved and suppressed and that within the limits thereof three new vicarages should be instituted *viz.* those of Rossenallis, *Killmanavane and Castlebracke'[3]. The erection of Rearymore into a separate parish must therefore be even later.

The ecclesiastical benefices *de Oreugan de Terra Thome filii Mauricii* (see Appendix I) had been granted to the Knights Hospitallers of St. John in Ireland before 1212[4] and the rectory of Iregan was to remain in their possession, although not without challenge, until the dissolution. In 1305 the prior of the Hospital in Ireland brought suit against the bishop of Kildare and David, son of O Doyng, clerk, whom the bishop had instituted to the church of Oregan which the prior claimed as having been given to his house by Maurice fitzGerald and who had, the prior claimed, taken possession of it by force of arms[5]. (As has been seen it had not in fact been given by (either) Maurice fitzGerald but by Gerald fitz-

---

1 In Ireland it is sometimes difficult to establish what was and what was not an independent parish. It seems to me that an area, such as Iregan, which was under the cure of a single *vicar* must be regarded as a single parish.

2 None of these churches are named in the Visitations of 1591 or 1610 (T.C.D. MS E.3.14). For the dedications of Rosenalis, Castlebrack and Rearymore see *Dinnseanchas,* II, 2 (1966), 32.

3 Records of the Rolls, VI, pp. 176-80.

4 *Registrum de Kilmainham,* ed. Charles MacNeill, Irish Manuscripts Commission, n.d., 140, 152.

5 P.R.O.I., Repertory of Plea Rolls, xi (R.C. 7/11), pp. 43, 100 (from Plea Roll no. 74, Trinity Term, 33 Edward I).

Maurice and his brother Thomas.)   On October 26, 1400, Maurice O Duynn, a priest, born of unmarried parents, was collated by the pope to the perpetual vicarage of Oregan, valued at 12 marks yearly, to which he had been already presented by the prior of Kilmainham on the resignation of the former incumbent, John Harper[6]. It would seem that, not content with the vicarage, Maurice made an attempt to secure possesion of the rectory as well (a common happening at this period in the case of rectories within the Irishry impropriate to religious houses within the obedient shires), as he is stated to have obtained provision of it before his death at the papal court[7]. His journey to the Curia was very probably for the purpose of obtining it.   On December 10, 1430, David O *Duynd, clerk, son of unmarried parents related in the 4th degree of kindred (i.e., third cousins) was collated to the rectory of Rosfyndglaisse *alias* Oregan, whose cure was exercised by a perpetual vicar and which was stated to be vacant through Maurice's death and to have been illegally detained for two years by John Muur, commander of Tully (the nearest Hospitaller house)[8]. It would seem, however, that David's attempt failed and that the Hospitallers succeeded in proving their canonical title to the rectory, as we hear no more of it as a secular benefice, and the same David O Duynd, clerk, of a race of dukes and who had studied for about seven years at universities, was provided to the prebend of Ley in the cathedral of Kildare on July 15, 1431; he is referred to as a canon of Kildare in 1443 and, if indeed the same man, in 1464[9]. The latter canon, however, is very probably the David O Duynd, vicar of Kasleaynbreke *alias* Oregan, who in 1466 was delated as an open and notorious fornicator and incestuary who had celebrated mass while under sentence of excommunication by his ordinary by Charles *alias* Culaima [*Cú-Bhladhma*] O Duynd, clerk; on May 20, 1466, the latter (son of unmarried parents related in the 3rd and 4th degrees of kindred (i.e., second cousins once removed) obtained collation to the vicarage in his place[10].

The extent made at Conall in County Kildare on November 23, 1540, found that the Hospitallers of Kilmainham had been possessed of the rectory of Oregan and Rossenall, 'in the country of the Irish called O Dyns', worth in time of peace £8 13s 4d yearly, but then waste.   On

---

6 *C.P.L.*, V, 298.

7 *C.P.L.*, VIII, 201.

8 *Ibid.*, 200-1.

9 *Ibid.*, 337; *C.P.L.*, IX, 373; XII, 220.

10 *C.P.L.*, XII, 480.

January 3, 1543 (N.S.), the tithes of Oregan and Russenall in the country of O Doyn, were leased for 21 years at the rent of £8 13s 4d, to Owen [*Uaithne*] O Doyn *alias* Grene[11]. This lease would appear to have lapsed, perhaps through non-payment of the rent, as in 1552 a new lease for 21 years was made by the Crown to two Welshmen, William Waghan and Greffyth ap David[12]. With the restoration of the priory of Kilmainham under Queen Mary, the rectory reverted to it, and in 1559 it was leased by the priory to Sir Maurice fitzThomas FitzGerald of Lackagh and his wife Dame Margaret Butler for 29 years. On February 18, 1573, Sir Maurice obtained a renewal of the lease of 'the rectories of Oregan *alias* Rossennoles, Rierymore, Kilmonymyn and Castellbreack, with the advowson of the vicarages, to run for an additional 21 years from the determination of the previous lease, at the annual rent of '16 good beeves or marts'[13]. Sir Maurice fitzThomas died on December 26, 1575; by his will he bequeathed his lease of the parsonage of Oregan to his younger son Edward FitzGerald[14]. An undated surviving Chancery Bill of his widow Dame Margaret Butler (who survived until 1601[15]) complains that she had been possessed by lease from the Queen of the parsonage of Rossenall and Oregan in O Doyn's Country, but Teig O Doin *alias* Teig ne Barrowe of Oregan and Terelaghe O Doyn his brother had for the past five years detained the third part of it, worth £20 yearly[16]. It is possible that the third part in question was in fact the vicarage — which would normally have either a third or half of the tithes, the rector receiving the remainder — and that Dame Margaret was in fact attempting to assert in law an usurpation common in Ireland at this period, by which the holders of impropriate rectories, when the vicarages were in their advowson, would neglect to appoint a vicar and absorb the vicarial share of tithes into the rectorial. On the other hand the dispute may have concerned some other issue. The lease of the rectory must have been acquired from the Lackagh FitzGeralds by Charles or Cahir O Doyne, who held it at the time of his dispute with his brother Teig. As the lease would have been due to expire in 1609, he obtained on November 10, 1608, in the name of William

11 *Extents of Irish Monastic Possessions, 1540-1541*, ed. Newport B. White, Irish Manuscripts Commission, 1943, 94; MacNeill, *op.cit.*, 152.

12 *Fiants, Philip and Mary*, no. 1139 (undated, but of 1552).

13 *F.E.*, 2208.

14 For the date of his death, see Lord Walter FitzGerald's article on 'The Fitz-Geralds of Lackagh', *Kild. Arch. Journal*, I, 241ff., and N. ní Sheaghdha, *Catalogue of Irish Manuscripts in the National Library of Ireland*, fasc. 1, p. 93. For his will, see Lord Walter's genealogical collections now in Trinity College, Dublin.

15 See Lord Walter FitzGerald's note in *Kild. Arch. Journal*, VII, 188.

16 C.P., E.180.

Brounckar, a grant in fee of the corn and hay tithes and other emoluments of the rectory of O Regan, commonly called Rossenolles, Rerimore, Kilmanvaine and Castlebracke, with the advowson of the vicarage[17]. By his will Charles bequeathed the rectory, with his lands, to his nephew Barnaby O Dunne, who had a confirmation by Letters Patent on April 13, 1639[18], and who in a deposition made in 1642 complained that Ross Mageoghagan, the Catholic bishop of Kildare, had inhibited the people from paying tithes to him, the impropriator[19].

In 1591 and after another Charles O Doyne, also called Charles mcMorishe, was vicar of Oregan[20]. In 1610 also an O Duinn was vicar[21].

The following clerics of the O Duinn family, besides those mentioned above, may be referred to:

Edmond O *Duynd, scholar, son of unmarried third cousins – and therefore probably brother of the David O Duynd mentioned above – had on December 17, 1430, collation from the pope of the rectory of Cuilbeancair *alias* Ardia (Ardea in Portnahinch Barony, County Laois), which had been detained by the prior of Kilmainham for three years[22]. This attempt to dispossess the Hospitallers of one of their impropriations, like that made by David O Duynd on the rectory of Oregan, seems to have failed.

Cearbhall O Duynn, a priest and canon of St. Mary's, Killeigh, O.S.A., had collation, April 11, 1464, to the vicarage of Nurnaychi *alias* Balyyceyn (Urney or Ballykean, County Offaly), detained by Maurice O Cuynd, priest[23].

---

17 *Calendar of the Irish Patent Rolls of James I*, 131; *Analecta Hibernica*, XXV, 125. For Cahir's interest see the text.

18 Records of the Rolls, VI, p. 228.

19 Depositions, f.107.

20 T.C.D. MS E.3.14, f.107v.; deed of Thadeus O Doine to his son Charles, 1595 (?), witnessed by 'Carolus mcMorishe, viccar' de Oregan' and 'Edmundus Brien, Curatus de Rossenalis' (above, Text).

21 [   ] Duinn (E.3.14 f.37). The forename was first altered with another pen and then effectively erased, so that neither original nor amendment is legible. Could this erasure have been the work of Charles O Doyne, through whose hands the MS passed, and was he endeavouring to conceal the fact that, perhaps, he himself (although a layman) was holding the vicarage? John Durin was curate in 1610.

22 *C.P.L.*, VIII, 202.

23 *C.P.L.*, XII, 220.

Thomas Doyn or Doyng, O.E.S.A., was prior of the Augustinian firary at Dublin, 1519[24].

William Doyn *alias* O Doyn, clerk, had Letters Patent granting English liberty, October 4, 1546[25]. This is perhaps the William Doyne, treasurer of Kildare, who was deprived for treason before October 14, 1547[26].

Patrick Doyne, clerk, had grant of English liberty to himself and his issue, October 24, 1550[27].

Cornelius Doyne, clerk, had grant of English liberty to himself and his issue, October 25, 1550[28].

Rory O Doyn of Castelbracke, chaplain, had grant of English liberty to himself and his issue, November 9, 1550[29].

Patrick Doyne, clerk, had a grant of English liberty, June 17, 1570[30]. He is probably the Patrick Doyne who was prebendary of St. John's in Christchurch, Dublin, at this date[31].

John Doyne was prebendary of Maynooth in St. Patrick's, Dublin, 1571[32].

Robert Doyne was archdeacon of Kildare at some date in the reign of Elizabeth I[33], and Richard Doyne chancellor of Kildare at the same period[34].

---

24 *Calendar to Christchurch Deeds,* nos. 408, 1134.

25 *Fiants, Henry VIII,* no. 503.

26 *Fiants, Edward VI,* no. 112. A William Doyn, vicar of Straboe, County Carlow, was dead by October 25, 1550 (*ibid.,* 582).

27 *Ibid.,* 580.

28 *Ibid.,* 584.

29 *Ibid.,* 609; Morrin, *Calendar of the Irish Patent Rolls,* I, p. 203.

30 *F.E.,* 1566.

31 Cotton, *Fasti Ecclesiae Hiberniae,* V, p. 97. As Sir Patrick Don he signs leases granted by the cathedral in 1570 and 1573 (*Calendar to Christchurch Deeds,* nos. 1319, 1328).

32 Cotton, *op.cit.,* V, p. 126.

33 C.P., H.,27, J.152.

34 *Ibid.,* H.,27.

Barnaby Doyn was ficar of Ardea, 1591[35], and Daniell Doyne held the same vicarage in 1610[36].

---

35 T.C.D. MS E.3.14, f. 107v.

36 Ibid., f. 37.

APPENDIX IV

(Information in this Appendix derived from the inquisition and other documents in the Text above is not referenced and what appears here is only the minimum of information; for *e.g.,* the amount of mortgages and similar details reference should be made to the Text itself.)

CASTLEBRACK QUARTER.

Teig O Donne: the castle and 215 a. in Castlebrack.
   For details see the schedule of partition. Teig O Doyne, in a letter of March 20, 1607/8, divides the quarter of Castlebrack as 120a. that belonged to his father, 80 (*recte* 60) a. in Parkemore 'gotten by myself', 30 a. in Cappacloughan (below) 'and thother 30 that is in the Strade and that belongeth to Dermott mcJames and the rest.'

Edmonde mcJames and Donnell mcMorish: Cappoughlouchane, 25 a., owing a rent to Teig mcEdmonde and Neile mcDermott and his kinsmen[1].
   Genealogy:

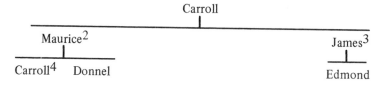

William Reogh of Castlebracke and Donoghe Duffe mcDermott of the same appear as freeholders in the Commission but not in the inquisition; they may possibly have sold their lands to Teig O Doyne in the meantime. Tirrelagh mcOwen O Dun of Capenleg, gent., pardoned in 1569[5], must have belonged to Cappanlug in this quarter. A Gilpatrick O Doyne of Castlebrack was the father of Una, wife of John O Higgin of Kilbegg, County Westmeath (living 1642)[6].

---

1   These were of Clonaghadoo; see Roskeen quarter.

2   Maurice mcCarroll of Castlebrack, freeholder, 1601 (*F.E.,* 6523); of Capullcaghe (*sic),* 1607 (Commission).

3 James mcCarroll of Castlebrack, freeholder, 1601 (*F.E.*, 6523).

4 Carroll mcMaurice of Keppoghloughana, 1601 (*F.E.*, 6523).

5 *F.E.*, 1337.

6 Funeral Entries VI, p. 161.

ROSKEEN OR CLANCOWMEY[1] QUARTER

Teig O Donne: 60 a. in Ballinmunnin, 20 a. in Achuane.
(The schedule of division also gives '10 a. of arable ground and $3\frac{1}{3}$ a. in the village of Cloncaddow and qr. of Clancomey'.)

In 1550 Brian O Connor of Offaly had held 'Agheylarevane and Ayshvave, 60 a. arable and 20 a. pasture, worth 30s *per annum*' and bounded, in length 'from Boerballynycaislan to Bonynacoger, the breadth from thother of the said Botyrs of Ballynycaislan to the ditch that is in the moor between the said lands of Aghenlarvane and Ballykilkevan.'[2]

Elizabeth Fitzgerald, widow: A castle and 60 a. in Roskyne (of which Teig mcEdmond [see below] claimed 12 a.).
This had been settled on her in jointure by her late husband Teig Oge O Doyne, by deed of October 20, 1583, with power to appoint any of their sons she chose as her heir. However, by deed of July 12, 1593, Teig Oge granted the castle and town of Roskyne, with 130 a. arable land in Roskyne, *Ballynuonine, Aghavane and *Cluancaddowe to his son Cormock and his heirs (App. V), and these lands were accordingly recovered in 1618 by Cormock's son and heir Donell O Doyne.

Edmonde mcJames and Donell mcMorish of Cappoghloghan: 20 a. in Achvoan (claimed by Teig mcMorogh and his brother).

Neale mcDermot of Clonaghadow[3]: 20 a. in Roskene (of which Donnell mcCormock claims 7 a. in mortgage), 4 a. in Cloncoddow.

Teig mcEdmond of Clonoghadow: 10 a. called Cosbegge, 20 a. in Fertane, 20 a. in [   ] and 6 a. in Clonecoddow.
He also claimed all the lands in Roskeen in general. He would seem to have afterwards sold or mortgaged Cosbegge and Fertane to Charles Doyne, who bequeathes them in his will, 1617 (App. V).

---

1 Probably Clann *Conmhuighe.

2 *Hermathena*, XX (1930), pp. 347-8.

3 Neale mcDermot of Clonaghdowe, yeoman, 1601 (*F.E.*, 6523). The '20 a. in Roskene' is duplicated in the inquisition.

KILCAVAN OR CLANCARROLL[1] QUARTER

Teig O Donne: 30 a. in Balligarvan.

Charles Donne: 30 a. in Aculagha.
This is in both deeds to Charles from his father Teig Oge.

Brian O Donne [of Brittas] : 3 a. in Garrimore.

John O Donne[2]: 60 a. in Kilkevan (of which Owney O Donne claimed 30 a.), 30 a. in Coolmoran (claimed by Dermott mcJames) and 17 a. in Garrimore (of which Edmond mcDermott claimed half, and Brian O Donne claimed 1 a. in mortgage).
  Brian O Connor of Offaly had held 'Kilkevan Kuregge, 100 a. arable, 1 a. pasture and 20 a. bog and moor, worth £3 5s *per annum'* in 1550; its boundaries are then described as 'in length from Laaghbagandowe to Kyllynacregyr, and in breadth along the botyr going to Ballycaislane to the moor and lake called Laghdyrreneboitteke'[3].

Shane mcDonoughe O Doyne of Cappaloughran: 30 a. in Couilmoran for life, the reversion to Art O Doyne of Gurtin, and claimed by Dermott mcJames and his brothers as their inheritance.

Cahir mcOwny[4] of Clongaghe: 2½ a. in Cloinga.

William mcRosse: 2 a. in Killmacrygarre.
  There is 15½ a. left unaccounted for.

---

1 *Clann Cearbhaill.*

2 John mcTirlagh O Doyne, Commission. See Genealogical Table A and n. 19.

3 *Hermathena,* XX (1930), p. 348.

4 Cahir mcOwen, Commission.

MONEYQUID OR COOLNAPISSY QUARTER

Teig O Donne: 7a. in Moynequid; 30 a. in Lackaghmore.
  This 30 a. in Lackamore was included in the conveyance made by Teig Oge O Doyn to his son Bryan, 1593 (App. V).

Elizabeth FitzGerald, widow: 20 a. in Lawagh.
  Settled on her as jointure by her late husband, Teig Oge, 1583.

Mortagh mcOwen[1]: 10 a. in Parke; 10 a. in Moniquid.

Dermott mcOwen[1]; 10 a. in Parke

Teige mcBrian[1]; 20 a. in Parke.

Cahir mcLeynagh[1]; 20 a. in Parke.

James Oage O Donne[2]; 20 a. in Parke.

William O Boolie[3]; 7 a. in Moniquid.

Morogh mcCahir; 16 a. in Moyniquid (of which 2 a. are in mortgage from Neale mcDermott[4], and 2 a. are claimed by William mcRory[5]).

Brian mcRorie O Donne[6]; 60 a. in Coolenpisie (of which Morough mcCahir holds 3 a. in mortgage).
    This land was free from tribute to O Doyne.

Brian mcRory and Leynaghe O Doine[7] of Killowrine[8]; 4 a. in Moniquid.

1–1   For these see Genealogical Table A and *nn.* They were second cousins of the chief and were all in remainder in his settlement of 1617.

2   Perhaps an error for the *Shane* Oge mcShane O Doyne of Moniquid in remainder in 1617.

3   Probably the William mcEdmond of Monyquid named in the Commission.

4   Of Clonaghadoo (see Roskeen Quarter).

5   Is this William mcRorie of Ballinloigge (in Kiltegrallagh Quarter, *q.v.*) or William mcRorie of Graignefollagh (in Boyle Quarter, *q.v.*)?

6   Brien mcRorie mcCahir in index to MS. For him and his family see Genealogical Table C.

7   Leynaghe mcRory in Index to MS. This Brian mcRory is certainly the same person as Brien mcRorie mcCahir, above.

8   Killurin, in Geashill Barony, County Offaly.

REARYBEG QUARTER

Cooleymy[1] mcTeige: 7 a. in Rirribegge; another 5 a. there, in mortgage from Donogh Reogh.

Moriertagh mcOwen O Donne[2]: 3a. in Cappanskibboll.

Shane mcMorogh: 7a. in Rirrybegge.

Mulmory mcDonogh of Dirrygall[3]: 34 a. in Ballykillkeinroe.

Elizabeth FitzGerald, widow: 43 a. in Reriebegg (of which Edmund mcMelaghlen claims 8 a. as in mortgage from him); 20 a. in Agheny in Ririebegg.

> These lands had been settled on her as part of her jointure by her late husband Teig Oge, 1583. Also in the settlement was 'the parcell of land called the Iland of Loghduffe in the quarter of Rirribegge, valued at 4 a. of arable land' (see schedule of partition).

---

1   *Cú-Bhladhma.*

2   ? of Park.

3   He was allotted 84 a. profitable under the plantation, according to Add. 4756; this may be a mistake for 64 a., as 64 a. profitable in Ballynelogg were confirmed to a Donogh mcMullmory Doyne in 1639 (App. VI) He was no longer proprietor by the time of compilation of the Book of Survey and Distribution.

REARYMORE QUARTER

This quarter possessed a *Ceannfine,* presumably the chief of the O Halagan family, mentioned below.

Charles O Doyne: 16 a. formerly belonging to the heirs of Teige Galogan and Clan Donill Donn[1]; 14 a. called Mecowill[2]; 20 a. called Racowgh; 8 a. more which William mcMorish mortgaged to Teige O Doine, who conveyed it to his son Charles, who retained it although it was redeemed from his father by William.

> For these lands see the deeds of conveyance from Teig to Charles, in which some other place-names will be found.

William mcMorish: 7 a. in Rerymore; another 15 a. mortgaged to Rory Oge O Sten for marriage goods.

---

1   In the second deed of conveyance '16 a. of the sons, successors and heirs of Thady Y Alaguin and Donald *Brondi* alias Domhnaill *Dhuinn hI Alagain, viz.* 9 a. free of charge, ordinary and extraordinary (pp. 32-3, above).

2   In the second deed of conveyance called '14 a. of Mac Comaill of the same family, (i.e., O Alagain).

DERRY OR DRUMNABEHY QUARTER

The quarter of Derry also had a *Ceannfine.*

Teig O Donne; 24 a. in AchneCross and Coolickenoule.
(The schedule of partition makes this only 20 a. arable with 30 a. pasture and 30 a. wood.)

Mulmore mcCarroll: 12 a. in Cappaghroe.
The Commission names, instead of Mulmore, his son Edmond mcMulmorie of the Cappaghroe.

Miagh mcCassin of the Borriesmore[1]: 8 a in Roishnoyer, claimed by Arte O Donne as in mortgage.

Teig mcArt and his brethren Tirlagh[2] and Owny: 36 a. in Dirry, of which Murtagh O Doyne claims 20 a. as mortgaged by himself to their father.

Rorie mcOwen of Dromnebehie is named in the Commission, but not in the inquisition.

---

1   See Introduction, *n.*8.

2   Called in the Commission Tirelaghe mcArt O Doyne of the Dyry. Teige and Tirlagh mcArt O Doyne were pardoned in 1601 (*F.E.,* 6523).

TINNAHINCH OR BOLLINUMER QUARTER

Teige O Donne: A castle and 60 a. in Bollinumer *alias* Tinehinche.
For details see the schedule of partition. The castle and town of Tenahinsie and Aghamore (in Kiltegrallagh Quarter) were conveyed by Teig Oge to O Doyne to his son Cormock in 1593 and were recovered by Cormock's son Donnell in 1618 (App. V).
   The remaining 20 a. of the quarter are passed over in the inquisition. As no chiefry from them is returned they must have been free land. A David Duff mcEdmond of Tenehinch, freeholder, was pardoned in 1601 (*F.E.,* 6523).

KILTEGRALLAGH QUARTER

Teige O Donne: 20 a. in Achmore.
This had been conveyed by Teig Oge O Doyne to his son Cormock in

1593 and was recovered by his son Donnell in 1618 (App. V).

William mcRorie[1]: 14 a. in Ballinloige, claimed by Teige O Doine.

Donogh mcMorish[2]: 6 a. in Coolmonnin.

Dermott mcMorish[2]: 19 a. in Coolemonyne.

William O Divoy (or O Davey): 5½ a. in Coolemonin.

Mortagh mcMorgh: 1 a. in Coolemonyne.

James Oge Carpenter: 3 a. in Coolemonyne.
All these lands in Coolmonnin were alleged to have been only mortgaged by the ancestors of O Doyne.

Moriertagh mcMorrogh of Clarchill[3]: 5 a. in Coolemonyne.
(Described, apparently incorrectly, as in Boyle Quarter.)

Teige mcOwen of Cappanagraige[3]: 7 a. in Ballimickrory.

Donnogh mcMorish of Coolmonnin [see above[2]] : 7 a. in Ballimickmullore.
There is 2½ a. left unaccounted for in this quarter.

---

1   A William mcRory mcJamès and a William mcRorie mcCowleoma, both of Tenehinch, were pardoned in 1601 (*F.E.*, 6523).

2–2   Were these sons of Morish mcDonogh Riegh of Culmonyn, pardoned in 1570 (*F.E.*, 1338)?   Pierce mcMaurice of Cowlemonyne, husbandman, was pardoned in 1601 (*F.E.*, 6523).

3–3   See Boyle Quarter.

BOYLE OR BOEMAN QUARTER

This quarter had a *Ceannfine*.

Dermott mcTeige: 1½ a. in TraghCollen.

Donogh mcMorish: 8 a. in Stragcullen, of which William mcMurtagh claims 2 a.

Owen mcMelaghlin: 3½ a. in Stracullen.

John Fiane: 3½ a. in Stracullen.

Mortagh mcWilliam of the Strathcullen occurs in the Commission. Donogh mcMuimy (*sic*) mcMaurice of Shracullin, husbandman, Murtagh mcDonogh, Murtagh mcWilliam and Tirlogh mcMurtagh of the same, yeomen, were pardoned in 1601[1].

Dermott mcMorish: 5 a. in Coolincossan.

Morogh mcEdmond: 2 a. in Boell.

Donogh mcRory: 1 a. in Boell.

Ferrduffe[2]: 2 a. in Boell.

Davie mcTeige: 1 a. in Boell.
Shane Oge mcShane claimed all the above lands in Beoll.

Teige mcOwen: 42 a. in Cappanagraige, 15 a. in Boell, 10 a. in Coolecossan, 14 a. in Ballinteian, (all of which were claimed by Tirleogh mcColleima, Shane mcShane and their kinsmen as their inheritance).

Genealogical Table:

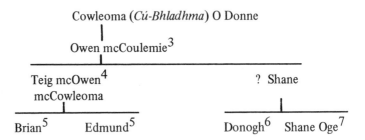

Cowleoma (*Cú-Bhladhma*) O Donne

Owen mcCoulemie[3]

Teig mcOwen[4] mcCowleoma   ? Shane

Brian[5]   Edmund[5]   Donogh[6]   Shane Oge[7]

Moriertagh mcMorogh of Clarchill: 30 a. in Carchill (*sic*).

Genealogical Table:

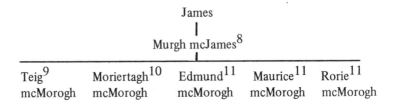

James

Murgh mcJames[8]

Teig[9]   Moriertagh[10]   Edmund[11]   Maurice[11]   Rorie[11]
mcMorogh   mcMorogh   mcMorogh   mcMorogh   mcMorogh

Carroll mcWilliam of Clarechoill, freeholder, was pardoned in 1601[12].

William mcRorie[13]: 22½ a. in Graiguefollagh.

Hugh mcShane: 21 a. in Gragnefollagh.
The shares given in this quarter amount to 2 a. more than its total content.

---

1 *F.E.*, 6523.

2 No patronymic.

3 Owen mcCoulemie of O Donne's Country, 1573 (P.R.O., S.P. 63/51/26, I).

4 S.P. 63/51/26, I; Teig mcOwen of Cappangraigy, 1582 (*F.E.*, 3949); Teig mcOwen mcCowleoma, of Keappanagraigg, 1601 (*F.E.*, 6523). He was allotted 146 a. profitable under the Plantation of Iregan (Add. MS 4756 p. 131), but no grant seems to have been enrolled.

5–5 Brian and Edmond mcTeig mcOwen, of Keappanagraigg, yeomen, 1601 (*F.E.*, 6523).

6 Donogh mcShane mcOwen, of Keappanagraig, 1601 (*F.E.*, 6523).

7 Shane Oge mcShane, of Keappanagraig, yeoman, 1601 (*F.E.*, 6523).

8 Of Clarkhill, husbandman, 1569 (*F.E.*, 1338).

9 Of Clarchill, freeholder, 1601 (*F.E.*, 6523). Were Donogh mcTeig and Shane Boy mcTeig, of Clarchill, yeoman, who occurin the same Fiant, his sons?

10 Murtogh mcMorogh, of Clarchill, freeholder, 1601 (*F.E.*, 6523); 1607.

11–11 Edmond, Maurice and Rorie mcMorgh, of Clarchell, yeomen, 1601 (*F.E.*, 6523).

12 With Donogh mcWilliam of the same yeoman, presumably his brother (*F.E.*, 6523).

13 William Glass mcRory of Graygophully, 1601 (*F.E.*, 6523). Rory mcWilliam of Graygophully, husbandman, whose name precedes his in the Fiant was presumably his father.

GARROUGH (*Gorragh*) QUARTER

Brian O Donne: 20 a. in Beachane, 5 a. in Garrough; 20 a. in Ballydowline (claimed by Patrick mcDavie[1]).
The Beachane and Ballidullen in the quarter of the Garrough are named in the deed from Teig Oge O Doyne to his son Brian recited in the inquisition. In the other deed of July 12, 1593 (App. V), on the other hand, the 80 a. of Brittas and 20 a. of Kylfyan (Killyawn in the east of the modern townland of Brittas) must include the lands in Garrough Quarter as well as those in Lackagh (*q.v.*). The inquisition p.m. on Brian O Donne gives him as dying seised of Brittas, Beaghan

and Ballydowlyn, 80 a., and 5 a. in Garough[2].

Brian O Donne of Garrough: 5 a. in Garrough (claimed by Donogh mcGil-patricke as having been mortgaged by his ancestors).

Donogh mcDonogh of Skarkehowne: 8 a. in Skarhowne, claimed by Teig mcDonell.

Dermott mcRory: 15 a. in Garrough.

William mcTeige: 10 a. in Garrough.

Rory mcMelaghlin[3]: 7 a. in Garrough.

Donogh mcDonogh of Garrough: 7½ a. in Garrough.

Owny neene Donne, in right of her son Derby mcMorough 7½ a. in Garough.

Sheelie neene Doine and her husband, until her marriage goods be paid: 7½ a. in Garrough.

There is 2½ a. (or 7½ a., if the second Brian O Donne be identical with the first) left unaccounted for. Rorie mcMorough and Knoghor Duffe mcHugh of the Skarrowne, who appear as landowners in the Commission, are not in the inquisition.

---

1 Of Brockagh (in Collaboghlan Quarter)?

2 *Repertorium Inquisitionum ... Lageniae*, Queen's County, no. 7 of James I.

3 Of the Skarrowne, Commission.

LACKAGH QUARTER

Brian O Donne: 40 a. in Brittas (of which Rorie Oage O Doine[1] claims 7 a.).
    For these lands see above under Garrough Quarter. Brittas is also named in the deed of conveyance from Teig Oge to Brian recited in the inquisition, and the inquisition *post mortem* on Brian (who died December 23, 1616) found that he died seised of a castle and 80 a. in Brittas, Beaghan and Ballydowllyn[2].

Charles Donne: 5 a. in Lackaghbegge.
    It is not in either of the conveyances to him from his father. That it

was in this quarter (which might otherwise seem doubtful) appears both from the schedule of partition and from Charles's 'Objections' against his brother's regrant.

Patrick mcMorish: 5 a. in Shraghduffe.

Mortagh mcMorgh: 5 a. in Shraghduffe (claimed by Rorie mcShane[2]).

Morish mcDonell: 5 a. in Shraghduffe.

James mcCarroll: 5 a. in Sraghduff.

Patrick mcRory: 5 a. in Shraghduffe.
Of these 15 a. last mentioned William Duffe mcDonnell claimed 10 a. There is 10 a. left unaccounted for, perhaps representing the holdings of Rory mcShane and Donell mcMortaghe, both of Lackaghbegge, named in the Commission but not in the inquisition.

---

1 *Repertorium Inquisitionum ... Lageniae,* Queen's County, no. 7 of James I.

2 Of Lackaghbegge, Commission.

CAPPABROGAN QUARTER

Teige O Donne: 51 a. in Cappabrogan.
72 a. in Cappabrogan were included in the deed of July 12, 1593, from Teige Oge to his son Brian (see App V). This must include part of John mcTirlagh's holding (below).

John O Donne of Kilkevan: 24 a. in Capparogan.

Rorie Oge O Donne of *Glanckrin: 5 a. in Gurtin.
Is he the Rory Oge mcRory mcShayne of the Commission?

COOLAVOGHLAN OR CLONMORCHOW QUARTER

Mortogh O Doine: 50 a. in Coulvoghlan (claimed by Tyrrelagh O Dunne as in mortgage[1], and of which Dermott O Doine claims 20 a. as his inheritance).
For him and his sons see *nn.* 17, 26-8 to Genealogical Table A. His son Shane mcMurtogh O Doyne had a grant under the Plantation of 163 a.

profitable and 150 a. unprofitable in Coolevolan, February 20, 1631/2[2]. He figures in the 1641 Depositions, but his lands are returned by the Book of Survey and Distribution as belonging to Brian Oge O Dunne of Brittas.

Patrick mcDavie: 4½ a. in Brockagh.
Edmond, Connor and Patrick mcDavie of Brockagh, yeomen, had been pardoned in 1601[3].

Edmond mcMurtagh of Killart: 12 a. in Brockagh.

Brian mcDonogh: 4 a. in Brockagh.
There is 9½ a. unaccounted for. Dermott Reaghe mcFinin of Cowlivohalane and David mcDonoghe of the Brockagh[4], named as land-owners in the Commission, do not appear in the inquisition (unless the former is the Dermott O Doine who occurs as a claimant). Nor do Piers mcCarroll, Melaghlin mcRory and Dermott mcCulemie, all of Kilmanvan[5], who also occur in the Commission.

---

1   It is not clear whether in mortgage *to* him or *from* him.

2   See App. VI. He is to be distinguished from John mcMurtagh O Conrahy, a grantee in Ballykenneen (*ibid.*).

3   *F.E.*, 6523.

4   He had been pardoned in 1601 (*F.E.*, 6523).

5   Kilmanman was probably in this quarter (see Records of the Rolls, V, p. 51) but not certainly so. See Ballintegart Quarter.

BALLINTEGART OR CLONMACHOW QUARTER

Brian mcRorie mcDavie: 40 a. in Ballintegart.

Genealogical Table:

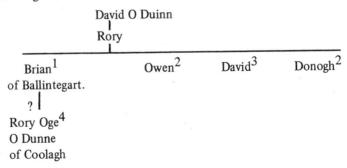

David O Duinn
|
Rory
|

Brian[1]   Owen[2]   David[3]   Donogh[2]
of Ballintegart.
? |
Rory Oge[4]
O Dunne
of Coolagh

Rory mcMelaghlin and Connor mcTeige of Kilmanvan: 10 a. in Shanclone, 5 a. in Aghmonre; 20 a. in Ballinteggart (out of which Mortagh mcOwen has a chief rent, claimed by Owen mcShane[5] and Teige mcEdmond[6] as in mortgage from them. All Rory and Connor's lands were claimed by Patrick O Doogan).

Rory mcMelaghlin might have been the son of Melaghlin mcRory of Kilmanavane, yeoman, pardoned in 1601[7], who appears as a landowner in the Commission (see above, Coolaboghlan Quarter). There is 5 a. of the quarter left unaccounted for in the inquisition; this might have been the freehold of Knogher mcMorish of Shanclowne, who appears in the Commission.

---

1 Brian mcRory O Dunne of Ballientegart, 1601 (*F.E.*,6523). As Brian mcRory he had 183 a. profitable allotted to him in the Plantation (Add. MS 4756 p. 131); there seems to have been no enrolled grant, but this must be the 183 a. which formed the residue of Ballintegart Quarter after the grant to Lord Brittas (App. VI).

2–2 Owen mcRory O Dunne and Donogh mcRory O Dunne of Ballientegart, 1601 (*F.E.*, 6523).

3 David mcRory O Dunne of Ballientegart, 1601 (*F.E.*, 6523), 1607 (Commission).

4 Rory Oge O Dunne of Coolagh, 1641 (Book of Survey and Distribution), holding the lands mentioned in *n.2* above.

5 Of Ballykenneen?

6 Of Clonaghadoo (Roskeen Quarter)?

7 *F.E.*, 6523.

BALLYKENNEEN QUARTER

Morrogh mcCahir and Shane mcEdmond: 23 a. in Ballykenein.

Edmond mcDonogh and Owen mcShane, and Sibell (*or* shilie) neene Edmond: 22 a. in Ballykenin (of which Teige mcMorish claims 4 a. in mortgage).

Owen mcShane, Tirlagh mcOwen and Edmond mcDonogh of Ballykeonyne had been pardoned in 1601[1]. Besides those who occur in the inquisition, the Commission also names David mcEdmond of Balliknine as a landowner.

Kedoghe mcMoriertaghe O Doyne, a minor, *or* Donoughe mcRorie: 35 a. in Ballikenine (of which James Duffe mcCarroll[2] claims 10 a. as in mortgage).

For the dispute over the title to this land see the text of the inquisition and the remarks in the Introduction, above. Kedoghe's father Moriertagh (slain on September 20, 1601) was a natural son of Teige Oge O Doyne (see Genealogical Table A); another son of Teige Oge, Cormock, had been of Ballyknyne in 1582[3]. Keadagh O Doyne had a grant under the Plantation of 120 a. profitable and 153 a. unprofitable in the quarter of Ballykinin (confirmed under the Commission for Defective Titles, 1639; see App. VI), of which the Book of Survey and Distribution still records him as proprietor.

---

1   F.E., 6523. Donogh mcTeig, of Ballykeney, kern, had been pardoned in 1570 (F.E., 1570).

2   Of Shraghduffe (in Lackagh Quarter)?

3   F.E., 3840.

THE SHISSERAGH OF FASAGHELY

Brian mcRorie mcDavie of Ballintegart[1]: 15 a. called Coolebeg.

Joane neene Carroll[2], widow of Cormocke O Donne, for life as her jointure: 10 a. in Garryhider, 12 a. in Killackandrony; 40 a. in Cargin (which 40 a. are claimed by Edmond mcDonogh[3] and his kinsmen). These lands are not in the 1593 conveyance to Cormocke from his father, and they had probably been acquired by the former on his own account. Cormock is styled of Lisnerode (which seems to have been part of the lands listed above) in 1601[4]. Donogh mcCormock, the eldest son of Cormock by Joan, was allotted 150 a. profitable in the Plantation of Iregan[5]; there does not seem to have been an enrolled grant, but the Book of Survey and Distribution shows him as proprietor of 'Ballinehoune and Curraghtober' in this quarter[6].

Owny mcDonogh of Killeine[7]: 8 a. in Killackandrony (claimed by Owen mcCahir O Donne).

Teig Reogh of Lismerood (sic)[8]: 10 a. in Garrihidermore in mortgage (and claimed by Owen mcCahir O Donne).

Owen mcCahir O Doine: 20 a. in Killackandrony; 10 a. in Garryhidermore. There is 5 a. in excess in the holdings given in Fasaghely. Owen mcCahir must have been the heir (grandson?) of Tirrelaugh (mcMoriertagh) O Doine of Garihidert, on whose dispute with the then O Duinn (Teig Oge) the Lord Deputy and Councill made an award in February, 1569/70.

'By the lorde deputie and counsaill.

'At Philipston, the vith of Februarie, 1569.

'Whereas matter of contencion and striffe hath bene moved and dependinge before us betwixt Teige O Donne, Chief of his name, on the one parte and Tirrelaugh O Doine of Garihidert on the other partie concerninge certain rentes, dewties and other services which the said Teig claimethe of the said Tirrelaughe as belonginge to him and his lordeship, which the said Teige affirmethe that he and his ancestors have from tyme to tyme received of the said Tirrelaughe and his auncestors.

'It is therefore ordered, concluded and agreed by the mutuall consent of bothe parties that the said Tirrelaughe shall yelde and pay from henceforthe all such dewties, rentes and services to the said Teige as he and his auncestors have paied or owght of dewtie to have paied. And on the other side of the said Teig hathe undertaken and promised before us to defende the said Tirrelaughe in all his juste and honest quarrells against any that shall oppresse him or offer him wronge or injurie.

'For the trew performance whereof bothe the parties have taken a solempne othe upon the hollie Evangelist before us, and in defaulte or breche of this order thei have entered into bonde to pay the forfeture of thre hunderethe kine, whereof two hunderethe to be paid to the use of our soveraigne ladie the queenes majestie, her heires and successors, and the other hunderethe to the lorde deputie or other governor or governors for the time beinge.

'And for all other contencions that may hereafter chaunce to arise betwixt the said Teige and Tirrelaughe thei have submitted them selves to the arbitrament and order of Dermod O Duggen and Rorie mcDavie[9].

'And if it shall chaunce that the said Dermod and Rorie cannot ende and determine the same, thei have referred themselves to the sainge and orderinge of the freholders of the Country of Oregan, whereunto thei binde themselves to stande and obey.

'It is further ordered that the said Teige shall pay to the Queenes majesties use, by waie of fine for the burnings, murther and other disorders committed by him and his followers upon Tirrelaughe O Doine, one hunderethe kine at or before May daie next ensuinge.

'And for the performance thereof shall enter into good and sufficient bonde of recognizance before his departure, except it shall please the lorde deputie to discharge him thereof.'[10]

Owen mcCahir Doyne had a grant under the Plantation of certain messuages, 80 a. profitable and 82 a. unprofitable in Fasaghely, confirmed under the Commission for Defective Titles in 1639 (App. VI), but the Book of Survey and Distribution gives Walter Hussey as proprietor of these lands.

Genealogical Table:

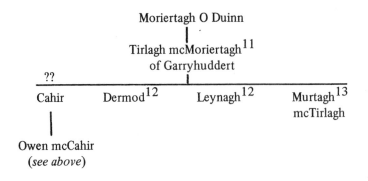

Moriertagh O Duinn

Tirlagh mcMoriertagh[11]
of Garryhuddert

| ?? | | |
| Cahir | Dermod[12] | Leynagh[12] | Murtagh[13] mcTirlagh |

Owen mcCahir
(*see above*)

---

1 See that quarter.

2 See Genealogical Table B, *n*.45.

3 Probably Edmond mcDonogh of Ballykenneen (*q.v.*).

4 *F.E.*, 6523.

5 B.M. Add. MS 4756 p. 131.

6 Note that his brother Art is styled of Ballinahoine in 1638 and 1641 (Genealogical Tables, *n*. 65); was Donogh perhaps abroad?

7 Of Killackandrony, Commission. Wohnie mcDonogh and Shane mcDonogh of Garryhuddert, yeomen, pardoned 1601 (*F.E.*, 6523).

8 Is this Teig Reogh, eldest son of Teig O Donne? It is possible but unlikely.

9 The first of these must be the Dermod O Diggan of Killaghie, chaplain, vicar of Lynally, who died on February 3, 1591/2 (Exchequer Inquisition, King's County (P.R.O.I., R.C. 9/6), no.37 of Elizabeth). Rorie mcDavie is presumably the father of Brian mcRory O Donne of Ballintegart (*q.v.*).

10 'Acts of the Privy County in Ireland, 1556-1571', ed. John T. Gilbert, *Historical MSS Comm., Reports*, XV, App. iii, pp. 244-5.

11 Pardoned 1570 (*F.E.*, 1804).

12–12 Sons of Tirlagh, 1570 (*F.E.*, 1804).

13 Murtagh mcTirlagh O Dunne, of Garryhubert (*sic*), 1601 (*F.E.*, 6523).

THE THREE QUARTERS OF MOINTAGHMILICKE

Teige O Donne: 20 a. in Farrenclankein (claimed by Patrick Malone); 5 a. in Ardarraghmoyle, 6 a. in Garricough, 5 a. in Knockchonecloghaine (claimed by his brother Brian O Doyne by conveyance from their father).

Charles O Doine: 5 a. in Farren Carrollreogh, 24 a. in Garrygallaraide and Ferrenhucristinne, 5 a. in Garruorogh, 5 a. in Garrikenanie.

For these and other place-names see the two deeds of conveyance from Teig Oge O Doyne to Charles (Text).[1]

Brian O Donne: 40 a. in Milicke.

The deed of July 12, 1593, to Brian from his father Teige Oge includes only the chiefry of 'the half quarter of Milick' (App. V), but the other deed of conveyance, recited in the inquisition, conveys 'all that belongeth unto myself in the lande of Milicke'. Brian O Donne was pardoned as of Mylicke in 1601[2]. His inquisition *post mortem* includes not only the 40 a. of *Miluick but also the 5 a. of Garriconough, which had been found for his brother Teige in 1607.[3]

Art mcDonogh [O Doyne[4]] : 40 a. in Gurtin.

See his Bill of Complaint, the Answer of Teige O Doyne, and the order made upon them, in Text. From these it appears that Gurtin was regarded as covered by Teige's Letters Patent, although I cannot find it in the text either in the printed *Calendar* or the Fiant transcribed in the manuscript. Presumably for this reason Art does not appear in the list of native allottees under the Plantation; in 1639, however, his son Donogh Doyne[5] had a confirmation by Letters Patent of the lands of Gurtin (App. VI).

Terrelagh mcOwen, Shane mcOwen, Edmond mcOwen, Murtagh mcOwen and Brian mcOwen: 35 a. in Garrifoolane.

This Shane must be the Shane mcOwen O Dunn of Graige, freeholder, pardoned in 1600[6].

Edmond and Dermott O Melone: 10 a. in Cappaghbegge and Reynn.

Rory O Melane[7]: 7 a. in Cappaghbegge.

Owen O Melane of Newry: 7a. in Rinn.

Morish O Melone[8] of Newry: 4 a. in Rynn.

James O Melone of Newry: 7 a. in Rynn.

Brian O Melone of Newry: 8 a. in Rinne.

Patricke O Melone[9]: 1 a. in Rinn. He also claimed 5 a. more there in mortgage.

Hugh O Melone of Newry: 7 a. in Cappaghbegge and Rinn, claimed by William O Malone.

Connor O Melloyne of Cappaghbeg, carpenter, was pardoned in 1569[10],
Maurice, Patrick, Edmond, Hugh and Hugh Bane O Malone of Graige,
yeomen, and Rorie, Owen and Dermot O Malone of the same, husbandmen, in 1601[11].

Donogh mcWilliam: 4a. in Garricanochie.

---

1 It would seem from these that some of the names in the inquisition have been
corrupted, the last name appearing, for instance, as Garriknaighery and *Garrdha
cnaighin.*

2 *F.E.,* 6523.

3 *Repertorium Inquisitionum ... Lageniae,* Queen's County, no. 7 of James I.

4 Commission. For his descent see Genealogical Table A and *n.*20.

5 See Genealogical Table A, *n.*31.

6. *F.E.,* 6523.

7 Rorie mcConnor O Malone, Commission.

8 Morishe Duffe O Maloyne, Commission.

9 Patrick Duffe O Maloyne, Commission.

10 *F.E.,* 1338.

11 *F.E.,* 6523.

SRAHLEAGH OR CLANRUISH QUARTER

Finola neene Morrogh of Derrin: 5 a. in Dirrin (out of which Teige
mcEdmond[1] and his sept have a chief rent, and which is claimed by
Dermott Oge O Dunne).

Dermott Oge O Doine of Sraghliegh[2]: 10 a. in Garrhowny (claimed by
Morish mcConnor), 5 a. in Dyrren (claimed by Donell mcFarrin, and out
of which Neyle mcDermott[3] claims a chief rent); 50 a. in Straghleigh (of
which Shane mcDavie[4] claims 25 a. as in mortgage, and Patrick mcFirr
claims 4 a. called Larraghbane[5]).

Donell mcNeile: the town and lands of Carehowne.
    This would seem to be identical with the following,

Dermott O Doyne of Sraghleigh[6]: 10 a. in Garhowne *in Dyrry Quarter*[7],
which is the proper inheritance of Donell mcNeyle[8], and out of which
Rossa [mc] Neyle[9] claims a chief rent.

Genealogical Table:

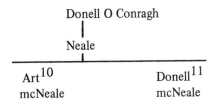

Donell O Conragh

Neale

Art[10]
mcNeale

Donell[11]
mcNeale

1   Of Clonaghadoo (in Roskeen Quarter, *q.v.*).

2   Probably son of the Dermott who was a natural son of Teig Oge O Doyne, and who is certainly the Dermott O Doyne of Sraghleigh named below, but possibly the same man. See Genealogical Table B, *n.*51.

3   Of Clonaghadoo (in Roskeen Quarter), a co-heir with Teige mcEdmond already mentioned as having a chief rent out of the other 5 a. of Dirrin.

4   Of Corbally, *q.v.*

5   See Text and Introduction.

6   See n.2

7   This must be an error.

8   See Text and Introduction.

9   Of Corbally (*q.v.*).

10 Art mcNeale of [   ]llee, gent., 1582 (*F.E.*, 3840); Art mcNeale mcDonell of Shraleigh, 1601 (*F.E.*, 6523).

11 Donell mcNeile of Shraleigh, householder, 1601 (*F.E.*, 6523). As Daniel mcNeile O Conragh he was granted in the Plantation all the messuages or houses in his tenure in the town of Garroone, with 80 a. profitable and 105 a. unprofitable there, 1629; the 1639 confirmation of this grant gives *three* messuages (App. VI). He appears in 1638 as Daniel mcNeile of Garoone, gent., aged near 80 years, and joint agent to Sir Adam Loftus (*Hist. MSS Comm., Reports*, IX, App., p. 308). He is probably the Donnell mcNeale of Clonagh, gent., who occurs in the Depositions (f. 124) with Teige mcDonell of the same, apparently his son.

TINNEEL QUARTER

This was one of the quarters which possessed a *Ceannfine*. It belonged, like Corbally, Clonaheen and Srahleagh, to the O Conrahy family.

Laghlein mcShane: 17 a. in Tenill.
See below, Genealogical Table.

Carroll mcMortagh: 8 a. in Tenill; 2 a. more there mortgaged to Edmond mcOwen. Brian O Donne and William mcLawrence have a chief rent thereout.

Shane mcJames and James mcDavie: 7 a. in Roishinoylish.

Rory mcFyrr and Murtagh mcFyrr of Clonagh: 4 a. in Clony.

Murtagh mcMorishe of Shianbege: 4 a. in Tenill; 1 a. more there in mortgage from William mcLaurence.

William mcLaurence: 30 a. in Tenyll: 1 a. more there mortgaged to Rory Duffe; 1 a. more there mortgaged to More Reaghe; 2½ a. mortgaged to Shane mcJames and James mcDavie. More ny Knawdan claims 4 a., and Melaghlin mcShane and his brother claim their shares of 4 a. there.
    Both William mcLaurence and his father Lauras mcDermott of Tenyll are named in the Commission.

Genealogical Table:

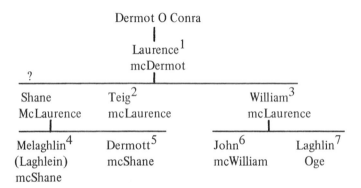

There is 2½ a. left unaccounted for, perhaps representing the holding of Shane Revaghe mcCuratha of Syanbegge, named in the Commission.

1 Laurence mcDiermod O Conra of Tynnyll, 1579 (*F.E.*, 1338); Laurence mcDermot of Tenyeyle, 1601 (*F.E.*, 6523); Lauras mcDermott, 1607 (Commission).

2 Of Tenyle, 1582 (*F.E.*, 3840).

3 Of Tenyeyle, 1601 (*F.E.*, 6523). He was allotted 115 a. profitable and 130 a. unprofitable in the Plantation of Iregan, but there is no enrolled grant.

4 Melaghlin mcShane mcLaurence of Castlebrack, yeoman, 1601 (*F.E.*, 6523). Probably the Laghlein mcShane of Tenyll who held 17 a. there and the Melaghlin mcShane, who with his brother, claimed some lands from William mcLaurence (above).

5 Dermot mcShane mcLaurence of Castlebrack, yeoman, 1601 (*F.E.*, 6523).

6 John mcWilliam of Scappenscarrye, gent., aged 40, 1638 (*Hist. MSS Comm.*, Reports, IX, App., p. 306); of Cappanskery, 1641 (Depositions, f. 19v.; called John mcLaurence of Cappansherye, f. 16, and John mcWilliam *Doyne* of Cappanskerrye f. 10v.).

7 Brother of John mcWilliam, 1641 (Depositions, f. 10).

CORBALLY OR GLANMILL QUARTER

This quarter also possessed a *Ceannfine.*

Rosse mcNeale[1] and Edmond Oge[2]: 12½ a. in Corbolly.

Patrick mcMortagh: 1½ a. in Corbollie.

Brien mcNeile and Mortagh mcBrien[3]: 16 a. in Corbollies.

Patrick O Melone, in right of Lisaghe mcQuinn a child[4]: 1½ a. in Corbollies.

Donogh Moyle: 3½ a. in Corbolly (of which Patrick O Melane claims 1 a. in mortgage).

Shane mcDavie and his brothers[5]: 7½ a. in Corbolly.

Neale mcRory a child[6]: 10 a. in Clonkilly (of which Brian mcRory has a chief rent).

Dermott mcEdmond[7]: 5 a. in Clonkill.

Rory mcTeige: 5 a. in Clonekill (of which Brien mcNeile claims a chief rent).

Shane mcDavid[8] of Cappard: 5 a. in Ballinteggart.

Patrick mcShane[9] of Cappard: 5 a. in Ballinecilly (claimed by Rosse mcNeale and his brother[10]).

Donell mcCormocke O Dunne of Cappard[11]: 7 a. in Ballinekilly.

Melaghlin mcOwen of Cappard: 2 a. in Ballinekilly.

---

1 Of Corbowlie, freeholder, 1601 (*F.E.,* 6523).

2 Edmond Oge mcEdmond Oge mcEdmond, Commission; Edmond Oge mcEdmond of Corbowlie, yeoman, was pardoned in 1601 (*F.E.,* 6523).

3 Brien mcNeale and Morogh (*sic*) mcBrien of Corbowlie, husbandmen, 1601 (*F.E.,* 6523).

4 Was he a son of Conne mcRorie of Corbowlie, yeoman pardoned in 1601 (*F.E.,* 6523)?

5 Shane, William and Tirlagh mcDavie of Corbowlie, yeomen, pardoned in 1601 (*F.E.,* 6523). William mcDavid of the Currally appears in the Commission, as do Owen mcDavid of the Carrawlly and John mcDavid. They were probably sons of the David mcOwen O Conra of Corboyle, gent., pardoned in 1569 (*F.E.,* 1338), perhaps the same as David mcOwen of Iregan, gent., 1550 (*Fiants, Edward VI,*

no. 623) and certainly the *Daui macEoghaine* or Davie mcOwen who witnessed deeds of Teige Oge O Doyne in 1590 and 1593 (Text).

6 Perhaps son of Rory mcDermot of Corbowlie, freeholder, pardoned in 1601 (*F.E.*, 6523).

7 Of Corbowlie, yeoman, 1601 (*F.E.*, 6523).

8 Cf. *n*.5, above.

9 Patrick mcShane of Corbowlie, husbandman, 1601 (*F.E.*, 6523).

10 Is this the David mcNeile of the Carrawlly named in the Commission, but not in the inquisition?

11 Presumably Donell mcCormock who was afterwards of Tinnahinch.

CLONAHEEN QUARTER

Teig mcDermott and Donell mcDermott: 4 a. in Clonheine.

Patrick mcFyrr and William mcFyrr: 36 a. in Clonhein. (Murtagh mcQuin claimed half of all the lands in Clonhein, Hugh mcDermott claimed 20 a. called Ballimoyle and Morogh mcWilliam claimed 4 a.)

Genealogical Table

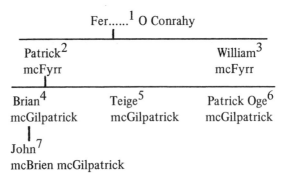

Tirelagh mcMulmory of Ballicowlin[8]: 4 a. in Dirrellemoige.

Brian O Doine of Ballicowlin[9]: 4 a. in Dirrelemoige.

More neene Morogh of Ballicowlin: 4 a. in Dirrlemoige.

Davy mcMurtagh of Ballicowlin[10]: 4 a. in Dirlemoige.

Teig mcWilliam of Ballicowlin[11]: 4 a. in Dirrelemoige.

Melaghlin mcOwen held one stang (¼) of every acre in those holdings in

Dirrelemoige, except that of Davy mcMortagh, where he only *claimed* ¼.

Melaghlin mcOwen: 24 a. in Cappullan and Kinnaghan.

Genealogical Table:

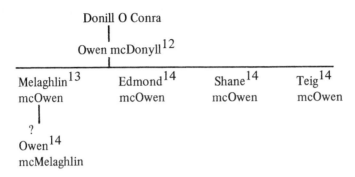

Donill O Conra
|
Owen mcDonyll[12]
|

| Melaghlin[13] | Edmond[14] | Shane[14] | Teig[14] |
| mcOwen | mcOwen | mcOwen | mcOwen |

|
?
|
Owen[14]
mcMelaghlin

Donell mcShane[15], in mortgage: 4 a. in Cappullan and Kinaghan.
This is in excess, and therefore must be part of the 24 a. found for
Melaghlin mcOwen.

1 *macFir* (or *mac an fhir*, mcEnir) can mean either 'son of Fearganainm', son of Feardorcha' or, in this case, perhaps, 'son of Feardubh'.

2 Patrick mcFirr of Clonehehyn, gent., 1582 (*F.E.*, 3840); Patrick mcFyrre, of Clonahine, freeholder, 1601 (*F.E.*, 6523).

3 Of Clonahine, yeoman, 1601 (*F.E.*, 6523). Under the Plantation he was allotted 129 a. profitable and 98 a. unprofitable (Add. 4756 f. 131); no enrolled grant appears, but the acreage shows that these were the lands in Ballymoyle which were regranted to Thomas Piggott (to whom William presumably had sold) in 1639 (App. VI).

4 Bryan mcGilpatrick O Conrahie had a regrant in 1639 of his mansion house in Cloneheene, with 160 a. profitable and 117 a. unprofitable there allotted to him under the Plantation (App. VI; Add. 4756 f.131). As Brian mcGillpatrick of Clownehen he appears frequently in the 1641 Depositions (ff. 10, 19, etc.).

5 'Who sometime had been a sergeant of a company at Knockfergus', brother to Brian mcPatrick (Depositions, ff. 7, 10, 19).

6 Depositions, ff. 10, 19.

7 Son of Brian and nephew of Teige and Patrick Oge (Depositions, ff. 8, 10, 19). Brian had two or three more sons (*ibid.*, f. 75); was Derby mcBrien 'Doyne' of Clonehein, named with John mcBrien 'Doyne' of the same (*ibid.*, f. 10v) one of them?

8 Of Dyrylymeoge, Commission. Tirlagh mcMulmorie of Clonahine, husbandman, and Murtagh mcTirlagh of the same, pardoned 1601 (*F.E.*, 6523).

9 Is this Brian O Doyne of Brittas? These lands are not, however, in his inquisition *p.m.*

10 Of Dyrylymeoge, Commission.

11 Of Dyrylymeoge, Commission. Teige Reogh mcWilliam of Clonehein, yeoman, pardoned 1601 (*F.E.*, 6523).

12 Egidius or Owen mcDonyll O Conra of Capellen, husbandman, 1569 (*F.E.*, 1338).

13 Molaghlen mcOwyn of Capollan, 1582 (*F.E.*, 3840); of Deappaullane, freeholder, 1601 (*F.E.*, 6523). Under the Plantation he was allotted 95 a. profitable and 44 a. unprofitable (Add. 4756 f. 131); which he sold, *c.* 1630, to Sir Adam Loftus (*Hist. MSS Comm., Reports,* IX, App., pp. 308-9).

14–14 All of Keappaullane, yeomen, 1601 (*F.E.*, 6523).

15 Donell, Donogh and Hugh mcShane of Keappaullane, husbandmen, pardoned 1601 (*F.E.*, 6523).

APPENDIX V

Subsidiary documents regarding the controversy between Teige O Doyne and his brothers.

P.R.O.I., R.C. 5/10 (Transcripts of deeds and wills contained in Inquisitions, Chancery series, Queen's County).

SETTLEMENT OF THADEUS O DOYNE AND THADEUS HIS SON AND HEIR TO THE USE OF THE LATTER'S WIFE ELIZE FITZGERALD, 17 APRIL 1591.

(pp. 326-30). Deed (*Sciant presentes,* etc.) by which Thadeus O Doyne, '*capitaneus ac nominis mei principalis*' and Thadeus *alias* Teige his son and heir grant to James FitzGerald of Kilteghan and William FitzGerald of Pollardston, County Kildare, gent., all messuages, lands, tenements, etc., in the towns and fields of Castlebrack, [   ], Parkemore and Aghenvore in the King's[1] County. To hold to the said James and William, their heirs and assigns, to the use of Elize fitzGerald *alias* fitzRedmond for the term of her life and after the death of the said Alize[2] to the use of the said Thadeus the chief or captain and the legitimate heirs male of his body. (Clauses of warranty, etc.) John FitzGerald of Recardeston, King's County, is appointed attorney to give livery of Seisin of the premises to the said James and William. Dated 17 April 1591 and the 33rd year of the reign of Queen Elizabeth. (*Latin*).

'The true meaneinge, Consideration and effect of this former feoffment is and was that the above-named feoffees, theire heires and assignes and the heires and assignes of every of them and of survivor of each of them [*sic*] stand and bee seized of all and singular [the] lands, tenements and hereditaments, with theire appurtenances, afore specified to the use and behoofe of Elize fitz Gerrald *alias* fitzRedmond nowe wife to Tege O Doyne, sonne and heire apparent to O Doyne cheiffe of that name, for and during her life naturall and after her death to the use and behoffe of the Rightfull heires males of the body of the forsaide Teige O Doyne

---

1 *Sic.*

2 *Sic.*

Chiefe of his name for ever, and for the better assurance and true meaninge of this feoffment to be accomplished of our partes according the effect thereof wee the foresaid feoffors doe bynde us and every of us, our heires, Executors, administrators and assignes, jointly and severally, unto the said William and James, theire heires and assignes, in four hundred poundes currant and lawfull money of and in England, to bee extended upon our goods or lands by suite, distresse or any other manner, waye or wayes that those forenamed feoffees or theire heirs shall thinck good or convenient, provided allwayes if that they may quietly take and enjoy the yearly profitts and comodities of those forenamed lands or in default of them twenty pounds Irish yearly issuinge out of O Doynes whole lands, that then this bond to bee voyde or otherwise to stand in full force and effect in lawe.'

Tady O Doyne. Teige O Doine the younger his mark.

(Witnesses to sealing and delivery:) By mee William Wesly presit [   ]. By mee Teige mcOwen O Doyne. By me Donnogh Oge O Conra *alias* Doyne his marke.

(Witnesses to delivery of deed to John FitzGerald to take and deliver livery and seisin:) By me William Wesly present. By me Teige mcOwen O Doyne his marke. By mee Donogh Oge O Conra *alias* Doyne his marke.

(Witnesses to livery of seisin by John fitz Gerrald to James and William fitz Gerrald in the town and fields of Castlebracke in the name of all the lands:) Christ: Hollywood. William Wesly. Lishagh mcBryen O Connor his marke. David mcTeige O Doyne his marke. Teige mcOwen O Doyne his marke.

SETTLEMENT OF THADEUS O DOYNE ON HIS SON
'YOUNG THADY' IN TAIL MALE, 28 APRIL 1593

(pp. 331-7, 392-6 [two copies]). Deed (*Sciant presentes,* etc.) by which Thadeus O Doyne of Tenehensye in the country of Iregan Esqr., Chief of his nation (*mee nacionis principalis*), grants to William fitz Gerrald of Donawne, County Kildare, Hugh McDonnell of Tenekilly, Queen's County, and Callough O Molloy of Shriggan, King's County, gent., all his manors of Castlebrack and Tenehensye in the country or territory of Iregan, and also the quarter of land of Castlebrack, the quarter of Roskyne *alias* Clonshoddowe, the quarter of Clonticarrowle *alias* Kilkevan, the quarter of Monycuddy *alias* Coolenepissy, the quarter of Tynehinsye *alias* Coultiglerchan, the quarter of Bolynumer, the quarter of Ryremore, the quarter of Ryrebegg, the quarter of Boell, the quarter of Dromnebehye *alias*

Dyrrie, the quarter of Clonmullye *alias* Corballye, the quarter of Clony-
hyne, the quarter of Clanragh *alias* Sraleigh, the quarter of Tenniell, the
three quarters of Montagh millick, the quarter of Garrough, the quarter
of Lackagh, the quarter of Clanmurchoe *alias* Coulbohelan, the quarter
of Cappabrogan, the quarter of Ballykinen, the quarter of Clonmachewe
alias Ballinteggart, O Doynes Forest and Fasagh Elye, with all other
castles, messuages, lands, etc., which he has in the aforesaid country, to
hold to them, their heirs and assigns for ever of the chief lords of the
fee. (Clauses of warranty, etc.) Lawrence O Conraha *alias* O Doyne is
appointed attorney to give livery of seisin. 28 April 1593 and the 35th
year of the reign of Queen Elizabeth. (*Latin.*)

'The intent, purpose and true meaninge and consideration of the abovewritten feoffment is and at the perfecting thereof was and nowe is that
the abovenamed feoffees, theire heires and assignes shall forthwith stand
and be seized of all the above mencioned manners, Castles, messuages,
lands, tenements, Rents, revercions and all other the premisses with their
appurtenances to the use of mee the said Thady Doyne for tearme of my
life naturall and after my death to the use of my sonne young Thady O
Doyne and the heires males of his body lawfully begotten and to bee
begotten. And for default of such heires to the use of my second sonne
Cormick O Doyne and the heires males of his boddy lawfully begotten
or to bee begotten. And for default of such heyres to the use of my third
sonne Bryen O Doyne and the heires males of his body lawfully begotten
or to bee begotten. And for defallte of such heires to the use of my fourth
sonne Cahir O Doyne and the heires males of his boddy lawfully begotten
or to bee begotten. And for default of such heires to the use of my
fifth sonne Murtagh O Doyne and the heires males of his boddy lawfully
begotten or to bee begotten. And for defaulte of such heires to the use
of my brother Tyrelagh O Doyne and the heires males of his boddy
lawfully begotten or to bee begotten. And for defaulte of such heires to
the use of my brother Donogh O Doyne and the heires males of his boddy
lawfully begotten or to bee begotten. And for default of such heires to
the use of my said sonne young Thady O Doyne and his heires for ever.
And such is the intent.'

(Witnesses to sealing and delivery by the feoffor, and to livery of seisin
at Tenehensye by the within-named Lawrence O Conraha:) Cornel
Conocher. Edmond Keting (*or* Keating). John Keting (*or* Keating) his
marke. William Coffies marke.

SETTLEMENT IN TAIL MALE BY THADEUS O DOYNE,
21 FEBRUARY 1616/7

(pp. 338-4)³. Deed (*Sciant presentes*, etc.) by which Thady O Doyne of
Tenehensye, Esq., [Sir] James fitzGerald [of Ballysonan, County] Kildare,
[knt.], Hugh mcDonnell of Tenekilly, Queen's County, gent., James
fitzGerald of Osbertston, County Kildare, gent., James Boyce [of Calgagh],
County Meath, gent., Peter Delahoyde of Poyncherston, County Kildare,
gent., and Redmund Reogh fitzGerald of Garvock in the said County,
gent., feoffees to the use of said Thady, grant to Thomas FitzGerald of
Elliceston, County Kildare, gent., Hubert Dillon of Killnenynen, County
Westmeath, gent., and Thady mcOwen mc[   ] of Castlebrack,
yeoman, their heirs and assigns, all the castles messuages, lands, etc., in
Castlebrack, Mony[q]uide, Leawagh, Leacamore, Rosskyne [   ],
Aghanbawne, and all services, etc., out of all the lands, etc., in the quarter
of Castlebrack *alias* Ballyencasey [   ] and Roskyne *alias* Clamoma-
thowe. February 21, 1616. (*Latin.*) The intent (*in English*) of the said
deed being that the said feoffees should hold the said premises to the use
of the said Thady during his life, and after his decease to the use of Ellice
fitzGerald *alias* fitzRedmond his then wife during her life, and after her
decease, to hold the premises for the preferment of Anne and Ellice,
daughters of the said Thady, if they be still unmarried, in such manner
as the said Thady [by his last will and testament?] shall appoint. Remainder
to the use of Edward O Doyne, one of the sons of the said Thady, and the
heirs male of his body. Remainder in default to [John Doyne, another son]
of Thady and the heirs male of his body. Remainder in default to William
Doyne, another son of Thady, and the heirs male of his body. Remainder
in default to Richard Doyne, another son of Thady, and the heirs male of
his body. Remainder in default to [Rory], another son of Thady, and
the heirs male of his body. Remainder in default to Tyrrlagh Doyne,
another son of Thady, and the heirs male of his body. Remainder in
default to Teige Reagh, another son of Thady, and the heirs male of his
body. Remainder in default to Donnell son and heir to Cormock Doyne,
deceased, brother to the said Thady, and the heirs male of his body.
Remainder in default to [Donogh], second brother to the said Donell and
the heirs male of his body. Remainder in default to Owny Doyne, their
[brother] and the heirs male of his body. 'And so to [the] *least of the
brothers of the said Daniel if any more he hath'. Remainder in default to
Bryen [Oge son and heir to Bryen] another of the deceased brothers of

---

3 The transcript of this deed is very mutilated and incomplete, the original apparently having been illegible or damaged. Lord Walter FitzGerald, in his Genealogical
collections (in T.C.D.) gives the remainder list from this deed (with some lacunae),
preceded by an almost identical list apparently from a slightly earlier deed of settlement, made on 29 December 1615, and referred to in the same inquisition (*Repertorium Inquisitionum ... Lagenia*, Queen's Co., no. 27 of Charles I). The names in
square brackets are inserted from these lists.

the said Thady, and the heirs male of the body of the said Bryen Oge. Remainder in default to [Phelim] brother to the said Bryen Oge and the heirs male of his body. Remainder to Donnogh Doyne their brother and the heirs male of his body. 'And so to the least of the said Bryan Oge his brothers if any more he hath'. Remainder in default to [Charles, brother] to the said Thady and the heirs male of his body. Remainder in default to John mcTyrlagh Doyne [of Kilkevan and the heirs male of his body. Remainder in default] to Art mcDonnogh O Doyne of Gurtin and the heirs male of his body. Remainder in default to [   ]^4 and the heirs male of his body. Remainder in default to Murtagh mcOwen Doyne of Mony[quid] and the heirs male of his body. Remainder in default to Dermott mcOwen Doyne of Park and the heirs male of his body. Remainder in default to Cahir [mcLeynagh O Doyne of Park] and the heirs male of his body. Remainder in default to Shane Oge mcShane O Doyne of Park and the heirs male of his body. Remainder in default to Teige mcBryen O Doyne of Park and the heirs male of his body. Remainder in default to Murtagh mcDonnoghe [   ] and the heirs male of his body. 'And in default to such further uses as the said Tady Doyne shall by his last will and testament limit and appoint.

James fitzGerald.
James Boise.
Peter Delahoide
Redmond Reagh fitzGerald his marke
Tady Doyne

(Witnesses to signing and delivery by Tady Doyne and Hugh Donnell:) Phelim Donill. Owen O Doyne his marke. Dermott fitzPatrick. William Doyne.

(Witnesses to signing and delivery by Sir James FitzGerald:) Gerald fitz-Gerald. Anthony Archbold. William Doyne.

(Witnesses to signing and delivery by James Boise:) John Boise. James [   ] his marke. William Pinkeston his marke.

(Witnesses to signing and delivery by Redmond Reagh fitzGerrald:) Gerrald Plunket. Nicholas Helan. Bryan O [   ] his mark. William O Divoy his mark. Edmond Angauran his mark.

(Witnesses to signing and delivery by Peter Delahoid:) By mee Edward Wesly. Terence Coghlan.

---

4   The earlier remainder list given by Lord W. FitzGerald (see n. 3 above) has here a remainder to Rory Oge O Doyne of Glancyn [see App. IV, s.v. Coolbrogan] and his heirs male, followed appear to have had only a single [lost] remainder between Art mcDonnogh and Murtagh mcOwen.

(Witnesses to delivery of sessin by the within-named Donnogh O Molloy to the within-named Teige mcOwen O Conratha in the name of himself and his co-feoffees:) Gerrald Tyrell. Edward Delahoide. [   ] his marke.

(pp. 381-4). Settlement by Charles Dunne of the City of Dublin, a Master in the Court of Chancery, on feoffees 'to such uses as I shall limit and appoint in my last will and testament or by any other instrument deed word or writing', 31 March, 1617[5].

.

WILL OF DR. CHARLES DUNNE, 2 APRIL 1617

(pp. 385-91).

'I Charles Duinne Esqr. one of the Masters of his Majesties [   ] Chancerie of Ireland, being of perfect memorie though not of perfect health thus doe make my last will and testament in the name of the eternall liveinge god the father, the sonne and the Holy goast in whom I hope hereby and believe to bee saved. First [   ] soule unto thy hand, O God, father, sonne and holy gost who hath first made me hath given thy sonne to bee made man and suffer bitter passion for me sinnes O Father for thy sonnes sake have mercy upon mee. O Lord Chirst then saye of god [   ] with thy precious blood have mercy upon mee and bee thow my mercifull mediator unto thy father that I may be saved. O Holy goast god coequall with the father and the sonne have mercy upon mee. Concerninge my body I bequeth [   ] the Earth from whence it came and to be buried where it pleaseth my Executors And I bequeath towards a decency in my funerall which I wishe to bee without Excesse three score pounds sterling. I bequeath to the poore in Iregaine in the Queens County [   ] to bee distributed amongst them according the discreation of my Executors. I leave to Trinitie Colledge nere Dublin ten pounds sterling to buy a silver cupp on which to have my name and arms. I leave allsoe to the said Colledge the Eleaven Bookes [   ] reports and fitzHarbarts grand abridgement which I bought, and wish my name to be written in all. I doe constitute and nominate my worthie wo[r]. friend Lancellott Buckley Archdeacon of Dublin and my nephew Barnabie Duinne my Executors. I bequeath to the RIght Honorable the lord Chancellor of Ireland tenn pounds to bee given by my Executors for a silver Jugg or bowle to his Lordshipp. I bequeathe to my said worthie frend Lancellott Buckley fiftie pounds *vizt.* thirtie pounts sterling of the money that hee receaved for mee as being my Substitute Judge of the

5   The transcript is very mutilated. This deed is calendared in full (from the original) by Mr. (now Sir) John Ainsworth in *Analecta Hibernica,* XXV, 125.

prerogative Court and faculties in Ireland sithence my last goeinge to England and twentie pounds more to bee added [to the] thirtie to make upp the same fiftie pounds. Item [this] I bequeathe to the said Lancellott Buckley for his greate care and intertaynement of mee in my sickness. I bequeath to my worthie frend M^r. Doctor Usher my twoe Gleabes[6]. Item, to Mr. Martyn the greene [   ] that the sister [   ] I leave to my nephew Felym the rent of the Coulaghe untill it make upp twentie pounds. Item, to my nephews Donoughe, Art, Falie and Gerald tenn pounds a peece. To George toward his keepeinge at the Colledge twentie pounds sterling. My neece Margarett fortie pounds and to each of her sisters (*vizt.*) Katherine, Ellis and Elizabeth twentie pounds a peece. Item, to my nephewe Daniell fortie pounds, my best horses and the mortgage that I have on [   ] and on twenty five acres of the lands of Ballykinagher of Callough *mc[7] Arte. Item, to Rorie O Maloyne fortie shillings. To Owen O Maloyne fortie shillings. To Morish duffe[8] fortie shillings. To Patrick Duffe[9] fortie shillings. To [   ]. To my boy Henry twenty shillings and a sute of my apparell. To Thomas McDonnogh twenty shillings besydes twenty shillings more that he oweth mee. Item, to my sister Grany twentie pounds. To Owen mcCahir the nagg that he hath of myne and a [   ] apparell and my best Coloured Cloake. Item, I leave all the rest of my goods, credits and chattles to my said Nephew Barnabie Duynne. And whereas I the said Charles Duynne have made and perfected a deede of feoffment bearinge date the last day of March one thousand six hundred and seaventeene of all my mannors, townes, lands, tenements, tiethes and other hereditaments whatsoever in the territorie of Iregaine in the Queens Countie and else-where within the Realme of Ireland and of all my right, title, interest, Clayme, challenge or demaunde to all and any parte of the manors, lands, tenements, Cheifrie and cheife rents of the said Territorie of Iregaine which my brother Thady Duynne or any other detaynethe from mee, to my wellbeloved in Christe Lancellott Buckley, Archdeacon of Dublin, Robert Leycester of Cloingell in the Kings Countie, Esquire, Henry Lynch of Galway in the County of Gallway, Esquire, and to my nephewe Barnabie Duynne of Brittas in the Queens Countie, gentleman, and to the survivor of them and his and their heires for ever to such uses and limitations as I the said Charles shall will or have Expressed in my last will and testa-ment, or in some other instrument, worde, deede or writeinge. I doe therefore hereby signifye and Expresse that my true pleasure, will and meaneinge was at the perfectinge thereof and now is that my said feoffees and his or their heires and the heires of the survivor of them forever shall stand formerly[10] seized thereof and of all the premisses and appurten-

6   *Gloabes?

7   in, *MS.*

8, 9   O Meloyne. See Appendix IV, *s.v.* Mointaghmilick.

10   *Sic.*

ances thereunto belonginge mencioned or meante to bee mentioned in the said deede of feoffment to the use and beehooffe of mee the said Charles and the heires males of my body lawfully begotten or to bee begotten, and for want of such issue to the use and behooffe of my nephew Barnabie Duynne and the heires males of his boddy lawfully begotten or to bee begotten, exceptinge my mortgages in Farka[ll], which I have left to my Nephewe Daniell Duynne and the heires males of his boddy lawfully begotten. And for want of such issue of the body of the siad Barnabye to the use and behooffe of my said Nephewe Daniell Duynne and the heires males of his boddy lawfully begotten and to bee begotten, Excepting the towne and lands of Culagha mentioned in the said feoffment and the lands of Feartan and Cosbegg which I will to bee to the use of my Nephewe Phelim Duynne for want of the issue of the body of the said Barnabye, And for want of the heyres males of the body of the said Daniell to the use and behooffe of the[11] said Nephewe Felym and the heires males of his body lawfully begotten or to bee begotten, and for want of such issue of the body of the said Felym to the use and behooffe of the younger Brethern of the said Phelym, Donagh, Art, Fely, George and Gerald and the heires males of their bodies lawfullie begotten or to bee begotten according their segnioritie bee Course of lawe. And for want of such issue to my heires Generall. In wittness to all the premises to bee my deede and true will and meaneinge I have hereunto fixed my seale and subscribed my name this second day of Aprill 1617[12].

DECREE OF LORD DEPUTY AND COUNCIL IN FAVOUR OF BARNABY AND DANIELL O DUNNE, 18 MAY 1618

(Reprinted from *Acts of the Privy Council, January 1617 to June 1619*, pp. 480-2, by permission of the Controller of Her Majesty's Stationary Office.)

By the Lord Deputy and Councill.

Whereas upon letters of the lordes of his majesty's honourable Privey Councell in England in the behalf of the plaintiffees bearing date the 15 day of December 1616, the matter in difference betwixt the plaintiffes and defendant hath proceeded to full issue before us, witnesses examined and the cause often and fully hearde, it appeareth unto us by good proofes that the feoffment aledged by the defendant to have ben made and perfected by the late O Dunne to the use of the defendant, after the death of the said O Dunne, of all his landes in the territorie of Iregaine in the Queene's County was indirectly obtained and misreade and misexpounded

---

11 *Read* my?

12 The names of the witnesses are omitted in the transcript.

to the said O Dunne at the tyme of the perfecting thereof, he being then blinde and unlittered, and that upon notice had of the falsety therof by the said O Dunne, he prefered a bill to the late Lord Chancellor of this kingdome in Easter Tearme last, 1593, discovering the practizes used by the defendant in getting that fraudulent feoffment to be perfected. And that the said O Dunne, being afterwardes advised by his learned councell, Sir John Everarde, knight, that that feoffment soe indirectly obtained was voyd or at the least voydable, as in deede it was, hee the said O Dunne the 12 day of July in the yeare 1593 conveyed to the use of his sonne Bryan O Dunne, father to the said Barnabe, one of the plaintiffs, and to his heires, the townes of and landes of Brittas. conteyning fourescore acres arable lande, Cappabrogan, conteyning threescore and twelve acres. Lackamore, conteyning thirtie acres, and Kylfyan, contayning twenty acres, with all and singular their appurtenances whatsoever, together with the chiffree of the quarter of Cloneheyne, the chiffree of Milick, being half a quarter in Moyntagh Milick, and the chifferie of two third partes of the quarter of Garrough. And that likewise the said O Dunne conveyed to the use of his sonne Cormock O Dunne, father to Daniell, the other plaintiffe, the castle, towne and landes of Tenahinsie and Aghamore conteyning fourescore acres, and the castle, towne and landes of Roskyne, and one hundred and thirty acres arrable lande belonging thereunto, in the said Roskyne, Ballynuoume[13], Aghauane and Cluaucaddowe[14], lying all in the quarter of the said Roskyne *alias* Clancowy, with all their appurtenances whatsoever, together with the chiffery of the quarter of Ballintegart. And that it appeareth also unto us by the answere of the said Tadie, the defendant, entred the 20th day of November in the yeare 1593, to the said O Dunn's bill in Chancery, that the said O Dunne had a purpose to convey, and did likewise convey, to the use of each of his sonnes severall parcells of his landes; and that the before recited landes and chiffery were the landes and chiffryes that are proved to be conveyed to the use of the plaintiff's father as aforesaid. And for that, that besides the before recited premisses, there remayneth a reasonable liveing in landes and chiffery to the said Tady answerable to the porcion of land and chiffry that his said father had, haveing respect to all the sonnes he had, being five legittimate sonnes and two bastardes, wee therefore thinke it meete and agreeable to justice and equity and so order that the said Barnabe, one of the plaintiffs, shall have and enjoye to him and his heires for ever and before named townes and landes of Brittas, Cappabrogan, Kyllifan and Lackamore, with all and singular the appurtenances whatsoever, together with the chiffry of the quarter of Cloneheyne, the chifferry two third partes of the quarter of Garrough, and the chiffry of Milick; and that the said Daniell. the other plaintiffe, shall have and enjoye to him and his heires for ever the said castle, towne and landes of Tenahinsie

---

13 *Read* *Ballynuonine.

14 *Read* *Cluancaddowe.

and Aghamore and the said castle, towne and landes of Roskyne with the one hundred and thirty acres belonging thereunto in the before recited places in the quarter of the said Roskyne *alias* Clancowy, together with the chiffry of the foresaid quarter of Ballintegart. And for performance of this our order wee require the sheriffe of the said Queene's County, upon sight hereof, to deliver to the said Barnabe and Daniell, or their attournies respectively, the actual possession of all and singular the premisses; and he, or any other sheriffe of that county for the tyme being, to establish and mayntaine them in quiett possession thereof, according to this our order. Given at his Majesty's Castle of Dublin the 18th day of May, 1618.

This order, beinge grounded upon letters from their lordships, was at the plaintif's request entered into this Register.

APPENDIX VI

Grants made in Iregan under the Plantation
of that territory and the Commission for
Defective Titles, in order of enrolment.

To Giles Rawlins, April 5, 1622.
(*Calendar of the Irish Patent Rolls of James I*, 540, *q.v.*).

To Marmaduke Neilson, April 6, 1622.
(*Ibid., q.v.*).

To Sir Robert Loftus, August 20, 1622.
(*Ibid.*, 552, *q.v.*).

To Thomas Gray, *same date.*
(*Ibid., q.v.*).

To Sir Robert Piggott, September 5, 1622.
(*Ibid., q.v.*).

To Sir Robert Kennedy, April 29, 1622.
(*Ibid., q.v.*).

To Patrick, Lord Dunsany, April 26 1622[1].
(*Ibid.*, 553, *q.v.*).

To Walter Greame, December 31, 1622.
(*Ibid.*, 560, *q.v.*).

To Theobald, Lord Brittas, December 12, 1627. 486 acres arable and
pasture[2] and 440 acres wood and bog in the quarter of Ballintegart and

---

1 He conveyed these lands to Thomas Hussey of Mulhussey, Co. Meath, by deed
of 29 May 1628 (*Repertorium Inquisitionum ... Lagenia*, Queen's County, no. 16
of Charles I; P.R.O.I., R.C.5/10, p. 121).

2 The Lodge abstracts do not give the actual quality of the land in each case, but
merely place it under the two headings as above. That under the first heading may
therefore be *either* arable *or* pasture, or both; that under the second wood *or* bog.

the hamlets and lands of Coolagh, Shyncloane, Dirrisolus, Larga and Bally-ntullagh, parcels of the said quarter, and in the profitable commons of the said quarter, next adjoining to the town or quarter of Coolevolane; 130 a. arable and pasture and 180 acres wood and bog in the quarter of Coolevolane, *alias* Coolebolane, and the villages of Brockagh and Killmanman, next to Ballyntegart Quarter; $\frac{13}{31}$ of the qurater of Rerymore, being 278 a. arable and pasture and 400 a. wood and bog, next to Boghill Quarter; 106 a. arable and pasture, and 106 a. wood and bogg, in the quarter of Montemeelicke and in the hamlets and lands of Farrenclonkeene, Gortyn, Garrefelan, Carrolreagh, Skahan, Garrykeny, Camore (*or* Camoryn), Ryn and Ardaramoyle, parcels of the said quarter, and in the profitable commons of Mountmeelick, next conveniently adjoining to Rerybegge Quarter. (All ancient glebes excepted.) In all 1000 a. arable and pasture and 1126 a. wood and bog, erected in the manor of Ballintegart.

(P.R.O.I., Lodge MSS, Records of the Rolls, v, p. 51).

To Cahir O Doyne, gent., March, 1627/8. 60 a. arable and pasture and 70 a. wood and bog in the quarter of Monyquid and in the lands of Monyquid, Parke, Lawagh, Cowlenepisse and Lackamore, next adjoining to Montemellick Quarter, in the territory of Iregan.

(*Ibid.*, p. 72).

To Daniel O Dunn, gent., December 22, 1629. 112 a. arable and pasture and 115 a. wood and bog in Buolynviner, Tenehinshy and Drumebehy, next to Derry; 50 a. arable and pasture and 9 a. wood and bog in Killegrallagh, Aghamore, Coolemoneighter, Coolemoneoughter, BallymcRory, Ballymcmulrony, Duhart and Ballimartyn, next to Tenehinchy, in the territory of Iregan.

(*Ibid.*, p. 194).

To Daniel mcNeile O Conragh, gent., *same date*. All the messuages or houses in his tenure in the town of Garrone; 80 a. arable and pasture and 105 a. wood and bog in Garroone, Derrynecaske, Conagh, Ould Towne and elsewhere in the quarter of Glarusse, next to the said houses on the northeast side, in the territory of Iregan.

(*Ibid.*).

To William Doyne, gent., *same date*. 72 a. arable and pasture and 85 a. wood and bog in the quarter of Monyquid, in the towns of Monyquid, Parke, Lawagh, Coolenepish and Lackaghmore, and in the profitable commons of the said quarter, next to Castlebracke and Parkmore, in the territory of Iregan.

(*Ibid.*).

To Barnaby Doyne, Esq., December 22, 1629. 419 a. profitable in the towns and lands of Bohill, Clarhill, Cappaghnegraigy, Graigepoll, Ballyntihan, Coulcossan, Shracullin, Ballifarrell and Killart, parcels of the quarter of Bohill, next Cappabrogan and Garrough; 193 a. arable and pasture and 200 a. wood and bog in Derry, Rossemire, Cappaghroe, Collevicknowell and Aghnecrosse, next to the quarter of Mointmellick; 70 a. arable and pasture and 130 a. wood and bog in Brockagh and Coolebrolan, next to Cappabrogan and Bohill; 198 a. arable and pasture and 198 a. wood and bog in Montemeelick, Garryfelon, Garryconnagh, Garrygallridd, Ryn, Cappaghbegg, Nerry, Graige, Camery, Ferranclankyne, Garrykinny, Ardramoyle and Gurtin, parcels of the quarter of Montemeelick, next to the quarter of Derry.

(*Ibid.*, p. 211).

To Keadagh O Doyne, gent., *same date.* 120 a. arable and pasture and 153 a. wood and bog in the town, lands or quarter of Ballykinin, *alias* Ballykynynmore, *alias* Ballykynyndavy, and in the commons thereof, next to Brittas and Ballintegart, in the territory of Iregan.

(*Ibid.*, p. 212).

To Patrick Hussey,[3] October 19, 1629. 400 a. arable and pasture and 270 a. wood and bog in Clonhyne Quarter and the hamlets or towns of Cappullane, Derrlomocke, Ballymoy *alias* Ballymoile *alias* Ballyshane and Ballyfore, next to Glanruish Quarter; 200 a. arable and pasture and 180 a. wood and bog in Gleanruish Quarter and its hamlets of Garroone, Shraley and Derryn, next to Clonhyne Quarter, in the barony of Iregan.

(*Ibid.*, p. 217).

To Peter Hussey, *same date.* 10 a. arable and pasture and 9 a. wood and bog in Nerry *alias* Errye in Moyntaghmeelicke Quarter, next to Cappaghbegge and Mucklone; 194 a. arable and pasture and 147 a. wood and bog in Cosbegge, Fertane and the two Roskeenes, a parcel of common called the Conneyboroughe *alias* the Twenty Acres, and half of another parcel of common called Monynracke in the quarter of Clancovye (except a castle and 60 a., country measure, in Roskeene, granted by Letters Patent to Thady O Doyne of Tenehinche, Esq.).

(*Ibid.*).

To Shane mcMurtagh O Doyne, February 20, 1631/2. 163 a. arable and pasture and 150 a. wood and bog in Coolenolan, next to Killmanne, in the territory of Iregan.

(*Ibid.*, p. 279).

Grant to Peter Hussey, May 30, 1636. The towns and lands of Balligarvan in the quarter of Clancaroll, *alias* Kilkevan; half of the town and lands of

---

3 of Galtrim, Co. Meath. This was no doubt in compensation for his hereditary claim to lands in Ely O'Carroll (T.C.D. MS F.3.15 p. 217).

Ballymonyn; a castle and 60 a., country measure, in Roskeene, in the quarter of Roskeene *alias* Clancowy; the said two quarters of Clancowy *alias* Clancony *alias* Clonecony *alias* Roskeene and Clancarroll *alias* Kilkevan, according to the old reputed mears thereof, and estimated to contain the castles, towns and lands of Coolmerane *alias* Coolevorane, Coolagh, Dirremollen, Clonegah, Aughebaveneneighter *alias* Aughebaven-eighter, Garrimore and the wood of Garrimore, Cooliffernocke, Derry-nehenelly, Direneconer, Oughtmore, Leaneclonegah, Curreaghclonegah, Roskeene, Fertaine, Cosebegg, Monyneracke, a parcel called the Twenty Acres or the Coneybrugh, Lachill, Clonaghedowe, Laght and the commons of the Laght, Pollaghnehaven and the Eskers; the town and lands of Capaloghan, parcel of the quarter of Castlebrack; Nerry and Killane, parcels of the quarter of Monaghmillicke; so much of the river Barrowe as lies near or belongs to the premises. (Excepting the lands of Kilkevan and Killenacriegare, which contain 164 a. arable and pasture and 150 a. bog and wood, the lands of Aughevanenoughter and the other half of Bally-monyn.) He is hold Balligarvan, half of Ballymonyn and 60 a. in Roskeene until he shall be paid £172 by Thady Dunn of Castlebrack, after which he is to have a lease of the said lands from Thady at the annual rent of £12 10s.

   (*Ibid.*, p. 382).

Grant to Daniel Dunne, March 8, 1637/8, of the castle, town, lands and quarter of Tenehinche *alias* Ballynomer; the towns and lands of Aghvolly, Dromnebehie and Ballinderie; 202 a. arable and pasture and 289 a. wood and bog in Koilltegrallagh *alias* Killnegrellagh, Aghamore, Ballemolmore, Ballelugge *alias* Ballenelogge and Cullevonin; 100 a. arable and pasture and 75 a. wood and bog in the quarter of Roskeene *alias* Clonecouie, in the towns and lands of Aghvaneoughter and Ballevonyn.

   (*Idem*, vi, p. 18).

Grant to Thomas Weldon, March 22, 1637/8, of lands granted in the plantation to Walter Greame and Cahir O Doyne[4] (*supra*).

   (*Ibid.*, p. 22).

Grant to Edward Doyne, gent., August 15, 1638. The castle, towns and lands of Castlebracke, Parkemore, Grange, Cappenlug, Mucklane and Gragcore[5]; Aghenegrosse and Cooleveckenavell[6]; Lavagh[7]; Dromin,

---

4 In Easter Term of this year Cahir O Doyne and his wife levied a fine of lands in Coolenepish to Thomas Weldon (P.R.O., Entry Book of Fines 1517-1648, p. 185).

5 In all 447 a., according to the inquisition *p.m.* on his grandfather Teige O Doyne (*Repertorium Inquisitionum ... Lagenia*, Queen's County, no. 27 of Charles I).

6 32 a. arable and 60 a. wood, in the quarter of Derry *alias* Dromevehy (*ibid.*), but see the grant to Barnaby Dun, *infra*.

7 Lawgh, 52 a. arable and 45 a. moor (*ibid.*).

Farrenridderiduffe[8]; Farranclonfyne[9] and Grage[10]; 100 a. profitable in Coolemonyn; a parcell of wood and bog called the Forest[11]; the towns and lands of Grage and Dromin; 100 a. profitable in Coolemonyne, in Kiltegrellagh Quarter; 72 a. arable and pasture and 85 a. wood and bog in Moniquid, Parke, Lavagh, Coolenepissie and Lackamore[12]. (These last-named lands and Parkemore are mortgaged to Barnaby Dunne for £110, and Forrest, Coulevecknowell, Aghenecrossy and Lawagh are mortgaged to Walter FitzGerald for £100.)

(*Ibid.*, p. 136).

Grant to the clergy, June 13, 1639. 'That the old reputed vicarage of Iregan should be dissolved and suppressed, and that within the limits thereof three new vicarages should be instituted, *viz.* those of Rossenallis, Killmananane and Castlebracke, and that 58 a. arable and pasture and 80 a. wood and bog in the town or quarter of Teneele, with its hamlets of Garrory, Shanebegg and Cappa eightragh, and in the profitable commons of Teneele, next to the church of Rossanollis; and 148 a. arable and pasture and 140 a. wood and bog in the town or quarter of Mountmelicke and its hamlets of Farrenclonkeene, Gurtin, Garriselon, Carralreagh, Skahorane, Garrykenny, Camore, Ryn, Gallagaleid, Ardaramoyle, Farrechristen, Knockaraloghan, Cappabègg, Nerry and Graige, and the profitable commons of the said quarter, next to Cappaeightra, shall be reputed part of the said vicarage of Rossenollis for ever.[13]

That 100 a. arable and pasture and 140 a. wood and bog in Coolevolan next Kilmananane, and 100 a. arable and pasture and 124 a. wood and bog in Garrough, Lackagh and Cappabrogane, next Kilmananane, shall be reputed part of the vicarage of Killmananane for ever.

That 67 a. profitable in Castlebrack and 123 a. arable and pasture and 140 a. wood and bog in Coltegrelagh, next to Bohill, shall be reputed part of the said vicarage of Castlebrack for ever.

(*Ibid.*, pp. 78-80).

---

8 Dromen and Farrenridderyduffe, 208 a. arable and 81 a. wood and moor (*ibid.*).

9 88 a. arable and 78 a. moor (*ibid.*).

10 200 a. arable and 200 a. moor (*ibid.*).

11 O Doyne's Forest, 1236 a. (*ibid.*).

12 Formerly granted to Edward's father William O Doyne (*supra*).

13 The wording of Lodge's abstract is confused, but the meaning is made clear at the end of the Patent.

Grant to Barnaby Dun, Esq., April 13, 1639. The towns and lands of Ballyfarrell, Eskarta, Killart and Cappaghnegragy. 48 a. profitable in Gragefolla (*or* Gragepoll) towards the north; 47 a. profitable in Shracullin towards the north; Clarehill, Ballyntyhann, Coolecessan, all lying together on the north side of Bohill Quarter; Derry, Rossenure *or* Rossmire, Cappaghroe, Colevicknowell and Aghinecrosse (except 80 a. profitable and 60 a. unprofitable, assigned to Thady Dun); 70 a. arable and pasture and 130 a. wood and bog in Brockagh and Culevolan, next to Bohill and Cappaghbrogan; 198 a. arable and pasture and 198 a. wood and bog in Mountemeelicke, Garryfelan, Garrycounagh, Garrygalride, Rin, Cappagh-begg, Nerry, Graige, Camery, Ferrenclankmore, Garrykenny, Ardaraghmoile and Gurtine, next to the quarter and lands of Derry; the quarter, towns and lands of Brittas, Garrough, Lackagh, Skarrowne, Keppabrogan and Lackamore (except 106 a. assigned as glebe to Killmanvan Church); the entire rectory of Oregan, called Rossenallis, Ryerymore, Kilmanvan and Castlebracke, with all its glebes, tithes and other profits.

(*Ibid.*, p. 128).

Grant to Terence Doyne, gent., August 15, 1639, of the towns and lands of Kilkevan and Killenacregare.

(*Ibid.*, p. 282).

To Donnogh mcMullmurry Doyne, gent., *same date.* 64 a. arable and pasture and 98 a. wood and bog in Ballynelegg, within the quarter of Killnegrallagh.

(*Ibid.*).

To Bryan mcGilpatrick O Conrahie, *same date.* A mansion house, with 160 a. arable and pasture and 117 a. wood and bog in Cloneheene.

(*Ibid.*).

To Daniel Conrahie, gent., *same date.* Three messuages or houses in Garrone, and 80 a. arable and pasture and 105 a. wood and bog in Garrone, Derrinecaske, Connagh, Ouldtowne and elsewhere in the quarter of Clonrushe, next to the said three houses on the east and north.

(*Ibid.*).

To Shane mcMurtagh Conrahy, gent., *same date.* 71 a. arable and pasture and 95 a. wood and bog in Ballickneeve, Ballykeneenemore, Ballykeeneen-ebegge and Ballykeneenedavey, with one fifth of a house[14] thereon.

(*Ibid.*).

---

14 This does not look correct. Perhaps 'five houses' should be understood, but it is difficult to see how the mistake could have arisen.

To Keadagh Doyne, gent., *same date.* Lands, as previously granted to him, 1629 (*supra*).
    (*Ibid.*).

To Owen mcCahir Doyne, gent., *same date.* Certain messuages, with 80 a. arable and pasture and 100 a. wood and bog in Fasaghelye, Killacken-dronye, Garryhederbegg, Garryhedermore, Ballynehowne and Cargin.
    (*Ibid.*).

To Donogh Doyne, gent., *same date.* 92 a. arable and pasture and 130 a. wood and bog in Gurtin, within the quarter of Mountmelicke.
    (*Ibid.*).

Grant to Thomas Piggott, December 6, 1639. Lands as granted in 1622 to Sir Robert Piggott (*supra*); 139 a. arable and pasture and 98 a. wood and bog in Ballymoyle[15], in the quarter of Clonheene, next to Dirrylumeoge.
    (*Ibid.*, p. 303).

Grant to Richard Reddish, April 10, 1639. The towns and lands of Clarehill, Ballytyan, Bohill and Cullcossane, in the quarter of Bohill; Aghemore, situate in the quarters of Bohill and Killnegrallagh, or one of them; 23 a. profitable in the south part of Graggefolla; 21 a. profitable in the south part of Sracullen; the bog, wood and common of the quarter of Bohill, all lying entire in the south part of the said quarter, as meared and divided and then in his possession.
    (*Ibid.*, p. 306).

Grant to Sir Charles Coote, September 4, 1639. Lands, as granted to Giles Rawlins, 1622, and to Theobald, Lord Brittas, 1627 (*supra*); 60 a. arable and pasture and 80 a. wood and bog in Ballickveere[16] next to Brittas.
    (*Ibid.*, p. 311.

---

15 The acreage shows that this was the Plantation allotment to William mcFirr (O Conrahy) (Add. MS 4756).

16 *Recte* *Ballickneene.

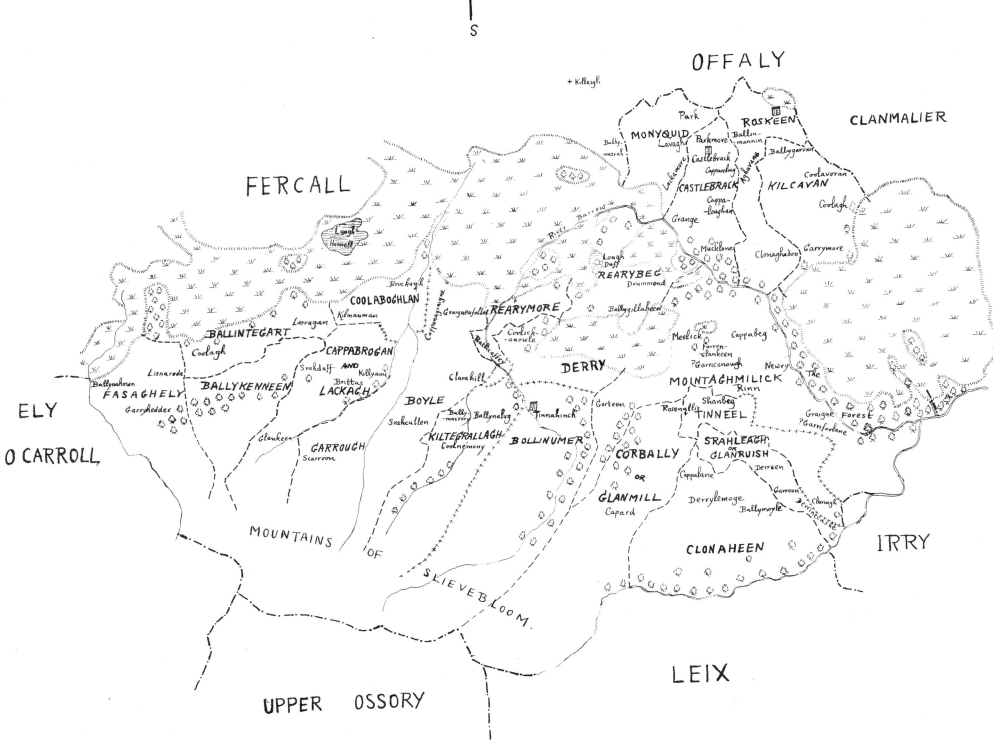

N
W   E
S

OFFALY

FERCALL

CLANMALIER

+ Killeigh

Park

MONYQUID

ROSKEEN

Lavagh

Parkmore

Ballin-
mannin

Bally-
nasrah

Castlebrack

Cappaslig

Ballygarvan

CASTLEBRACK

Coolaveran

KILCAVAN

Cappa-
loughan

Coolagh

Grange

Lough
Hannell

Brackagh

Mucklone

Clonaghadoo

Garrymore

COOLABOGHLAN

Lough
Duff

REARYBEG

Kilmanman

Drummond

Graigueafulla

Larragan

REARYMORE

Ballygillaheen

Cappabeg

BALLINTEGART

Coolick-
anowle

Meelick

Farren-
clankeen

Coolagh

CAPPABROGAN

Rathcolley

?Garriconough

Newry

Lisnarode

AND

Sraduff

Killyaun

DERRY

The

Ballynahown

Brittas

LACKAGH

Clarahill

MOUNTAGHMILICK

Garryhedder

BALLYKENNEEN

Rinn

Graigue Forest

FASAGHELY

Gorteen

Rosenallis

Shanbeg

Glenkeen

BOYLE

Srahculen

Ballynalug

Tinnahinch

TINNEEL

?Garrisootane

Ballymacrory

SRAHLEAGH
OR
GLANRUISH

GARROUGH

Scarroon

KILTEGRALLAGH

BOLLINUMER

CORBALLY

Derreen

Coolnemony

OR

Cappalane

Garroon

Clonagh

GLANMILL

Capard

Derrylemoge

Ballymoyle

ELY

O CARROLL

MOUNTAINS

OF

CLONAHEEN

IRRY

SLIEVE BLOOM

LEIX

UPPER   OSSORY

The territory of IREGAN (Oregan, *Uí Riagáin)* or
O Doyne's Country (the modern barony of Tinnahinch, County Laois) at the beginning of the 17th
century. Based on the Ordnance Survey Maps by
permission of the Government (Permit no. 4117).

Names of 'quarters' and
of adjacent territories   **REARYBEG**

Other placenames   Gorteen

Boundaries of 'quarters'   — — — — — —

Approximate or doubtful
boundaries of quarters'   + + + + + +

Lowland bogs

The extent of woodland was certainly much
greater than has been indicated by the present
map, as woodland has only been marked where
there is definite contemporary evidence of its
presence *and precise location,* or where the 1st
edition of the 6" O.S. Map shows the presence of
old relict woodland. The boundaries of the lowland bogs, as indicated, can only be taken as
approximate; mountain bogs, which certainly
covered a large area on the Slieve Bloom, have
not been indicated.

transcript by O'Curry, Royal Irish Academy, MS 23 P. 1.

MQ. Merchants' Quay (now Franciscan Library, Dún Muire, Killiney) Gaelic MS XXXI, O Duinn genealogies and memoranda, printed by Rev. Cuthbert Magrath, O.F.M., in *Collectanea Hibernica,* II, pp. 13-7.

N.L.I. National Library of Ireland, Dublin.

P.R.O.I. Public Record Office of Ireland, Dublin.

Records of the Rolls. Extracts of grants of lands, etc., from Patent Rolls, by John Lodge, in Lodge MSS, P.R.O.I.

R.S.A.I. Royal Society of Antiquaries of Ireland.

T.C.D. Trinity College Dublin.

ABBREVIATIONS

A. Clon. Annals of Clonmacnois, ed. D. Murphy, Dublin, R.S.A.I., 1896.

A.F.M. Annals of Ireland, by the Four Masters, ed. John O'Donovan, Dublin, 2nd ed., 1856.

C. 626. Lambeth Palace Library, (Carew) MS 626.

C. 635. Lambeth Palace Library, (Carew) MS 635.

Calendar of Christ Church Deeds (in *Reports of the Deputy Keeper of the Public Records in Ireland,* XX, XXIII-IV, Appendices).

Commission. Commission for taking inquisition on Iregan (Text, pp.   ).

C.P. P.R.O.I., Salved Chancery Pleadings.

C.P.L. *Calendar of Papal Registers: Letters.*

. Depositions. Depositions, Queen's County, T.C.D. MS F.2.8.

F.E. Fiants, Elizabeth, in *Reports of the Deputy Keeper of the Public Records in Ireland,* XI-XVIII, Appendices.

Fiants, Edward VI, in *Reports of the Deputy Keeper of the Public Records in Ireland,* VIII, Appendix IX.

Fiants, Henry VIII, in *Reports of the Deputy Keeper of the Public Records in Ireland,* VII, Appendix X.

Fiants, Philip and Mary, in *Reports of the Deputy Keeper of the Public Recrods in Ireland,* IX, Appendix IV.

Funeral Entries, in Genealogical Office, Dublin.

Kild. Arch. Journal. Journal of the County Kildare Archaeological Society.

MacFirbisigh, Book of Genealogies, in University College, Dublin; facsimile

INDEXES

Prepared by Mary Lyons

Reference numbers are to pages

INDEX OF PERSONS

Talbott, William, clerk in Chancery (Ireland), 102

Terrell, *alias* Tyrrell, James of Castleloste, arbitrator between Charles and Tadhg O'Duinn, 9, 11, 12, 93, 97, 102, 132; the arbitration, 28-9; witness to settlement between Tadhg and his brothers following the death of Tadhg Og, 28

Tyrell, Gerald, witness to a delivery associated with 1616 enfeoffment to use, 170

Tyrell, Gerrot, son of James Tyrell of Castlelost, married to Elinor, daughter of Tadhg O'Duinn, 132

Usher, William, his schedule of the division of the lands and chiefries of Iregan, drawn up in May 1608, 40-6

Ussar, possibly an additional judge at Court of Common Pleas (Ireland) – no actual record of his appointment survives. His opinion on the November 1612 petition of Art O'Duinn, 108-9

Ussher, Dr. James, Provost of Trinity College, Dublin, later archbiship of Armagh, mathematician and bibliophile, legacy of two globes under 1617 will of Charles O'Duinn, 171

Vere, Henry de, eighteenth earl of Oxford, Lord Chamberlain, signatory to letter from Privy Council in favour of Tadhg O'Duinn, 19

Waghan, William, acquired jointly with Greffyth ap David, 21 year lease of tithes of Oregan in 1552, 137

Walshe, Sir Nicholas, Chief Justice of the Common Bench, (Ireland), 47

Weldon, Thomas, grant of land to, following plantation of Iregan, 134, 178

Wesly, Edward, witness to a delivery associated with the 1616 enfeoffment to use, 169

Wesley, William, priest, witnessed in various capacities the enfeoffment to use of Elizabeth fitz Gerald in 1591, 166

Whitney, Robarte, of Shaen, juror involved in compilation of 1607 inquisition, 2

Winche, Sir Humfrey, Chief Justice of the King's Bench (Ireland). His opinion sought by the Lord Deputy on the O'Duinn case, January 1612, 105, 106

Wingfield, Sir Richard, Escheator of Ireland, Marshal of the Army and Kingdom of Ireland, 29

Wotton, Edward, first baron Wotton of Marley, signatory to letter from Privy Council in favour of Tadhg O'Duinn, June 1608, 91

Y Alaguin, *see* O'Halagan

INDEX OF PLACES

Achanahaha, field name in Castlebrack, barony of Tinnahinch, County Laois, 44

Achatry Caoynain, Achachaynaine, field name in Castlebrack, barony of Tinnahinch, Co. Laois, 40

Achmore, i.e., Aghamore or Ashbrook, barony of Tinnahinch, parish of Kilmanman,Co. Laois, 3, 38, 146, 153, 173, 174, 176, 178, 181

Achne Cross, Aghanecrosse, now obsolete, in Derry, barony of Tinnahinch, Co. Laois, 3, 29, 42, 75, 80, 146, 177, 178, 179, 180

Achuane, Achauayne, Aghvane, Achvoan, see Aghanbawne

Aculagha, see Naculagha

Aghanbawne, i.e., Aughans, parish of Castlebrack, barony of Tinnahinch, Co. Laois, 3, 19, 25, 38, 43, 44, 75, 80, 142, 168, 173, 178

Aghvolly, i.e., Afoley, barony of Tinnahinch, parish of Kilmanman, 178

Aghene, Agheny, i.e., *Acha an Fheich*, now obsolete, Moneyquid quarter, barony of Tinnahinch, parish of Rosenallis, Co. Laois, 74, 145

Allone, i.e., Allen, Co. Kildare, 9, 12

Ardarraghmoyle, *alias* Ardaragh Meyly in Mountmellick quarter, parish of Rosenallis, Co. Laois, 3, 45, 75, 80, 156, 176, 177, 180

Ardea, *alias* Ardia, parish in the barony of Portnahinch, Co. Laois, 138, 140

Arklow, barony and parish of Co. Wicklow, labour services on the earl of Ormond's lands, xiv

Arra, in barony of Owney and Arra, Co. Tipperary, xiii

Aughebaveneneighter, *see* Aghanbawne

Aughevanenoughter, *see* Aghanbawne

Aughrim, battle of, 133

Baile Mic Cuaighin, *see* Garrikenanie

Ballemolmore, now obsolete, but lying within the quarter of Tinnahinch, 23, 178

Balliboy, i.e., Ballyboy, barony of Ballyboy, Co. Offaly, 52, 96, 181

Ballickemoyler, i.e., Ballickmoyler, barony of Slievemargy, parish of Killaban, Co. Laois, 2, 23, 147

Ballickiny, see Ballykenneen

Ballickneen, see Ballykenneen

Ballickveere, see Ballykenneen

Ballicowlin, Ballycowline, unidentifiable, but perhaps in Derrylemoge (q.v.), Co. Laois, 19, 39, 162

Balliduffe, i.e., Ballyduff, barony of Stradbally, parishes of Curraclone and Moyanna, Co. Laois, 2

Ballidullen, see Ballydowline

Ballifarrell, now obsolete, but lying within the quarter of Boyle, 177, 180

Balliglas, now obsolete, but in the vicinity of Gorteen barony of Tinnahinch, parish of Rosenallis, Co. Laois, 128

Ballikeneine, Ballikeneinn, *see* Ballykenneen

Ballikell Kein Roe, i.e., Ballygillaheen, barony of Tinnahinch, parish of Rearymore, Co. Laois, 13, 145

Ballimartyn, now obsolete, but close to Tinnahinch, 176

Ballimickmullore, *see* Ballemolmore

Ballimoyle, i.e., Ballymoyle, barony of Tinnahinch, parish of Rosenallis, Co. Laois, 24, 162, 177, 178, 181

Ballimoyn, *see* Ballimoyle

Ballinderie, now obsolete, but lying within the quarter of Tinnahinch, 178

Ballinecilly, Ballinekilly, i.e., Ballynakill, barony of Tinnahinch, parish of Kilmanman, Co. Laois, 22, 161

Ballinloigge, i.e., Ballynalug, barony of Tinnahinch, parish of Rearymore, Co. Laois, 16, 144, 147, 178, 180

Ballimunnin, Ballimonine, in the quarter of Roskeen (q.v), Co. Laois, 3, 42, 40, 55, 139, 142, 178

Ballinnovin, *see* Ballimunnin

Ballinraly, i.e., Ballinrally, barony of Upperwoods, parish of Offerlane, Co. Laois, 2

Ballintegart, i.e., Castlecuffe, barony of Tinnahinch, parish of Kilmanman, Co. Laois, 14, 16, 19, 31, 41, 52, 77, 82, 83, 110, 152, 153, 161, 173, 174; exactions in kind, heriots etc., 5, 175, 176, 177

Ballinteian, Ballyntihan, now obsolete, but lying within Boyle, barony of Tinna-

.